FRESH EVERY DAY

MORE GREAT RECIPES FROM FOSTER'S MARKET

FRESH EVERY DAY

MORE GREAT RECIPES FROM FOSTER'S MARKET

BY SARA FOSTER

WITH CAROLYNN CARREÑO

PHOTOGRAPHS BY QUENTIN BACON

For Mitch: enjoy!
Sara Foster
2005

CLARKSON POTTER/PUBLISHERS
NEW YORK

Published by Clarkson Potter/Publishers, imprint of the Crown Publishing Group,
a division of Random House, Inc., New York.
www.clarksonpotter.com

CLARKSON N. POTTER is a trademark and POTTER and colophon are registered trademarks of
Random House, Inc.

Foster's Market is a registered trademark.

Printed in the United States of America

Design by Blue Cup Creative, Inc./Wayne Wolf

Library of Congress Cataloging-in-Publication Data is available upon request.

ISBN 1-4000-5285-8

10 9 8 7 6 5 4 3 2 1

First Edition

For my mom, my teacher and my friend.

Introduction

When I finished writing my first book, *The Foster's Market Cookbook*, I had so many more recipes to share with my readers, I knew I had other books to write. But I didn't know what the next book would be. It was my customers, friends and family, and readers who pointed the way.

As the owner of two prepared-food markets in Durham and Chapel Hill, North Carolina, I feed some two thousand customers a day. Some customers who come back twice, even three times in a day, call Foster's Market their "kitchen" and have become like family. Kids who were in strollers when we opened now want summer jobs at the market. We know each other's lives and habits.

These customers are surprised to learn that I rarely take anything—beyond some bread or cheese or a slice of pound cake—home from the store myself. Why would I? For me, the half hour I spend putting together dinner after work is therapeutic. It's like a ritual, it's my wind-down time. Besides, as I try to tell them, it's just so easy.

When I began giving cooking demonstrations, classes, and book signings to promote *The Foster's Market Cookbook*, I couldn't believe how difficult and time-consuming many people think it is to make the kinds of seasonally inspired soups, salads, and entrees we serve at Foster's Market. I found that these customers—students, housewives, recent college grads, newlywed couples, businessmen and women—lacked some basic information and techniques that would make the process of preparing a meal so much easier. All it takes is a little organization, a few basic skills, and flavorful, fresh ingredients. Of course, you also need easy-to-follow recipes for the kinds of food you want to eat, tailored for the home cook, which is what I've tried to give you in this book.

In the first book, I gave readers the recipes most requested by customers at the Market. In this book, I give you recipes for the way I adapt these ideas to cook at home, and I tell all the tips, tricks, and shortcuts I've learned from mentors, co-workers at the market, my aunts, and, of course, my mother. I divided the main dishes into three chapters: "Quick and Tasty Meat Main Dishes" and "Fast and Fresh Fish, Pasta, and Risotto Meals" include recipes for those things that cook while you're standing in front of the stove, so that just by stopping at the market to pick up a few fillets of fish or a piece of beef after work, you can have a dinner of Pan-Seared Red Snapper with Fresh Butter Beans, Tomatoes, and Corn or Tequila Lime Skirt Steak within a half hour of getting home. The other entree chapter, "Meals That Cook Themselves," has my favorite recipes for cooking while I'm home doing other things: Chipotle Maple Barbecue Beef Brisket, Red Wine–Braised Chicken with Onions and Thyme, and Port-Braised Lamb Shanks with Rosemary. From scrambled eggs for dinner, to salad meals born of leftovers, to ice cream sandwiches assembled from a combination of homemade and some store-bought ingredients, this is the kind of fast and easy cooking anyone can realistically do at home.

It's also the kind of food we want to eat at home: vibrant, comforting foods like Cornbread Panzanella with Avocado or Crispy Pan-Roasted Chicken with Spaghetti Squash and Balsamic-Roasted Tomatoes. Mom's Pot Roast (my mother is an integral player in my life as a cook and at Foster's Market) and Peter's All-World Burgers (Peter is my husband, the burger maker in the family, and a Sunday morning employee at Foster's Market) are foods we grew up eating and those that we will always have a soft spot for. As for desserts, you won't find any elaborately iced layer cakes in this book. Instead, you'll find simple, homey desserts, such as Summer Blueberry Pie and Blackberries and Cherries in Red Wine, which rely on the natural juicy sweetness of seasonal fruits; classics like pound cakes, gingerbread, shortcakes, and shortbreads that we all love, and exalted, grown-up versions of childhood favorites like the Dark Chocolate Soufflé Cake.

More than just giving you recipes, though, I've tried to encourage you to develop and use your instincts. So much of cooking is about the way food feels, smells, even sounds while it's cooking. To help you develop those instincts, I've tried to describe in these recipes what oil sounds like when it's ready for frying, what a fruit crisp looks like, or what a sweet potato feels like when it's done.

I want you to feel free to cook using these recipes as guidelines and inspiration, not strict rules. In "Tricks of My Trade," I tell you what I know about preparation, planning, and organization to make the cooking process easier. The "Basics" boxes provide fundamental cooking instruction for those who might not know, for instance, how to roast a bell pepper. "For All Seasons" and "Think Outside the Recipe" notes suggest ways to adjust recipes based on what you like, what you have on hand, or what seasonal ingredients you find at the market. I also give "What to Serve When" notes to help you plan the meal. And "Reinvention" notes show you some of my favorite ways to turn leftovers into an entirely different fresh-tasting meal.

With so much practical information, it is my hope that you will eventually learn to think and cook for yourself. So take these recipes, take this information, take everything you know and feel about food, about what you like and don't, and have fun cooking.

one
breakfast for anytime

Foster's Homemade Granola ○ One-Eye Jacks ○ Creamy Scrambled Eggs ○ Foster's Market's Famous Breakfast Tortillas ○ Eggs Benedict on Grilled Toast with Bacon, Roasted Tomatoes, and Foolproof Blender Hollandaise ○ Country Ham Hash with Chipotle Mustard Sauce ○ *Creamy Cheesy Corn Grits for All Seasons—Winter:* Ham and Parmesan with Balsamic-Roasted Tomatoes; *Spring:* Shrimp, Tasso, Asparagus, and Leeks; *Summer:* Summer Vegetables and Basil; *Fall:* Sweet Potato, Bacon, Blue Cheese, and Rosemary ○ Savory Breakfast Bread and Sausage Pudding ○ Sweet Fruit-Full Breakfast Bread Pudding ○ Blue Heaven Smoothie ○ Caramel Apple Smoothie ○ Very Berry Smoothie ○ Sunshine Smoothie ○ Angel Biscuits with Flavored Butters ○ Sweet Potato Buttermilk Biscuits ○ Banana Nut Muffins ○ Corn Blackberry Muffins ○ Lemon Poppy Seed Muffins ○ Pumpkin Muffins ○ Orange Chocolate Muffins

I named this chapter as I did because my hope is that you'll feel free to make these recipes any time of day. Few people really have the time or inclination to sit down to a big breakfast first thing in the morning. If you're like me, you're on the run with a cup of coffee. As much as I like the idea of breakfast, the only time I eat it is on the occasional weekend, day off, vacation—or when I serve "breakfast" for lunch or dinner.

One of the great things about breakfast foods is that they tend to be quick and easy to make. There are no marinades, few sauces, and no long baking times involved. Breakfast meats like sausage, bacon, and ham are so full of flavor that all you have to do is fry them. Eggs are the most convenient food I can think of to make. Savory Breakfast Bread and Sausage Pudding—a sort of egg, bread, and sausage casserole—is easy to make in advance to feed a crowd or a house full of guests. Creamy Scrambled Eggs can be customized with endless variations. And One-Eye Jacks make a comforting, light late-night supper.

Foster's Homemade Granola

When I opened the Market, I had many customers request that I offer granola. I tasted a bunch of different brands, but I didn't like any of them; they didn't taste fresh. I'd never made granola before, but I figured it couldn't be that hard. I started playing with different fruits, nuts, and seasonings and eventually, after lots of testing and tasting, came up with this. It's one of our most popular breakfast items, served over vanilla yogurt with seasonal fruit. The same customers who eat it for breakfast often leave with a bag to take home.

MAKES ABOUT 6 CUPS

2 cups old-fashioned rolled oats
1 cup shredded sweetened coconut
1 cup sliced almonds
1 teaspoon kosher or sea salt
¼ cup canola or safflower oil, plus more for greasing the pan
¾ cup maple syrup
¼ cup honey
½ cup dried cherries or cranberries
½ cup dried apricots, chopped

1. Preheat the oven to 275°F.

2. Spread the oats, coconut, and almonds on a large baking sheet with sides. Sprinkle with salt and bake for 12 to 15 minutes, stirring occasionally, until the ingredients are lightly toasted but not yet golden. Transfer the ingredients to a large bowl.

3. Increase the oven temperature to 350°F. Lightly grease the baking sheet with oil or spray with vegetable oil spray.

4. Stir the maple syrup, oil, and honey together in a small bowl, pour over the oats, nuts, and coconut, and toss to coat evenly. Spread the granola onto the prepared baking sheet and bake for 25 to 30 minutes, until the granola is just crispy and golden brown, stirring several times while baking. Let the granola cool completely on the baking sheet, breaking up any large clumps while it is still warm.

5. When the granola has cooled completely, add the cherries and dried apricots and toss to mix. In an airtight container, this will keep at room temperature for up to 2 weeks.

One-Eye Jacks

My friend Katie always makes these when she comes to visit from New York City. They're made one at a time and served hot out of the pan to each guest; just multiply as needed. Fry the cutout circles in the skillet with butter to dip in the egg yolk, or toast and serve with butter and jam. WHAT TO SERVE WHEN If you want to dress these up a bit, serve them with Balsamic-Roasted Tomatoes (page 135) or top with a fresh salsa (page 196).

SERVES 1

1 slice bread (such as brioche, challah, whole-wheat, or whole-grain)
1 teaspoon unsalted butter, or more as needed
1 teaspoon olive oil
1 large egg
  Sea salt and freshly ground black pepper to taste
1 teaspoon finely chopped fresh flat-leaf parsley, chives, or basil

1. Use a cookie or biscuit cutter (or the rim of a glass) to cut a 2- to 2½-inch round from the center of the bread slice.

2. Melt the butter and olive oil together in a medium skillet over medium heat. Place the bread in the skillet and turn it over to coat each side. Cook the bread for about 1 minute on one side, until it is light golden brown. Crack the egg so that it falls into the hole in the center. Fry the egg in the bread for 1 minute longer. Flip the egg and bread and fry the other side for 1 minute or longer, depending on how done you want the egg. Season with salt and pepper, sprinkle with the fresh herbs, and serve immediately.

Note: *If the pan is dry when you flip the bread and egg, add a little more butter (about 1 teaspoon) to the pan.*

Creamy Scrambled Eggs

Scrambled eggs can be so good if they're made right, but there are a few tricks to getting them just perfect. First is not to overcook them; they should look a little wet when you take them out of the pan. By the time you get them from the plate to the table, they're going to be cooked just enough and firm up. It's also necessary to cook scrambled eggs in a pan they won't stick to, whether it's nonstick or just a good, seasoned pan. Even if you've broken up the eggs already, to ensure light and fluffy scrambled eggs, give the eggs a quick whisk right before you pour them into the pan. And make sure the pan is good and hot before you pour the eggs in.

SERVES 4

1 tablespoon unsalted butter
1 tablespoon olive oil
8 large eggs
½ teaspoon sea salt, plus more to taste
¼ teaspoon freshly ground pepper, plus more to taste

1. Melt the butter and olive oil together in a large nonstick skillet over medium heat until the butter begins to foam.

2. Whisk the eggs with the salt and pepper until the whites and yolks are completely combined. Pour the eggs into the skillet to cook, undisturbed, until the eggs begin to set. When the eggs are slightly firm and set around the edges, stir them gently with a heatproof rubber spatula or wooden spoon and continue to cook, stirring constantly, for 2 to 3 minutes, until the eggs are no longer runny. You want them to be slightly moist, as they will continue to cook after you remove them from the heat. Taste for salt and pepper and add more if desired. Serve immediately.

VARIATIONS

One or 2 tablespoons of leftover cooked vegetables or cheese is just enough to dress up plain scrambled eggs. Here are my standby combinations:

Cream Cheese and Wilted Spinach
Take the eggs off the heat and stir in several tablespoons of cream cheese and 1 cup Wilted Spinach (page 191) or Garlicky Greens (page 112).

Roasted Tomatoes and Crumbled Goat Cheese
Take the eggs off the heat and stir in several tablespoons of crumbled goat cheese. Top with Balsamic-Roasted Tomatoes (page 135) or any Fresh salsa (page 196).

Sautéed Mushrooms and Crispy Bacon
Take the eggs off the heat and top the cooked eggs with ½ cup sautéed mushrooms and several slices of crispy bacon, crumbled.

Smoked Salmon and Scallions
Take the eggs off the heat and stir in 2 to 3 thin slices smoked salmon and a tablespoon of minced scallions.

Chorizo, Cheddar, and Salsa
Take the eggs off the heat and stir in ½ cup crumbled or chopped cooked chorizo (spicy Spanish or Mexican sausage) with ½ cup shredded Cheddar cheese. Top with fresh salsa, such as Roasted Green Tomato and Apple Salsa (page 199), Black Bean Salsa (page 196), or Roasted Sweet Potato Salsa (page 198).

Fresh Herbs and Goat Cheese
My personal favorite. Take the eggs off the heat and stir in 1 tablespoon chopped fresh herbs (such as basil, parsley, thyme, oregano, chives, or a combination) with ½ cup grated or crumbled goat cheese.

Foster's Market's Famous Breakfast Tortillas

We're known for our breakfast tortillas at the Market. They vary from day to day; we make them using seasonal ingredients and the meats and cheeses we have on hand in whatever combinations the cooks are inspired to put together that day. The thing that makes them "breakfasty" and the thing they all have in common, is that they all contain an egg, either scrambled or fried. The term "tortillas" is vague, in that it refers to anything we make with tortillas. We use both flour and corn and we prepare them differently: we roll corn tortillas into enchiladas; we roll flour tortillas into burritos; we toast, grill, and sauté corn tortillas for tostadas; and we fold both corn and flour tortillas into a loose definition of a taco. I give you some ideas for tortillas below, but I encourage you to invent your own, using ingredients you have on hand. It's a great use of leftovers. Another nice thing about these tortillas is that they're easy to make for one person.

Country Ham Hash with a Fried Egg and Chipotle Mustard Sauce Wrapped in a Warm Flour Tortilla

Heat a flour tortilla in a dry skillet for about 1 minute per side, until it is warm and lightly toasted. Fry an egg to your liking and place it on top of the warm flour tortilla. Top the egg with about ½ cup of Country Ham Hash (page 20). Drizzle with the Chipotle Mustard Sauce (page 21) or leftover chipotle peppers pureed in a blender, roll up the tortilla like a burrito, and serve warm.

Quesadilla with Scrambled Eggs, Crispy Bacon, and Heirloom Tomato Salsa

Fry 1 to 2 pieces of bacon until crispy and drain on a paper towel. Scramble 1 or 2 eggs and place the scrambled egg(s) and bacon on one half of a flour tortilla. Sprinkle with grated or thinly sliced cheese (such as Cheddar, Monterey or pepper Jack, or goat cheese) and fold the tortilla in half. Heat a teaspoon of olive oil in the same skillet you fried the egg in and put the quesadilla in the skillet to toast until slightly crisp, about 1 to 2 minutes per side. Serve warm, with Heirloom Tomato Salsa (page 199) or any fresh salsa.

Grilled Corn Tostada with Melted Cheddar, Fried Egg, and Fresh Salsa

Grill a small corn tortilla over an open flame or heat in a dry skillet until it is warm and lightly toasted, but still soft. While the tortilla is still warm, top it with about 2 tablespoons of shredded Cheddar cheese. Fry the egg to your liking and place on top of the cheese. Top the fried egg with a spoonful or a dollop of fresh salsa and serve open-face, like a tostada.

Chopped Pork Burrito with Sweet Potato Salsa and a Fried Egg

Warm a flour tortilla over the open flame of a stovetop burner or in a dry skillet until warm but still soft. Fry an egg to your liking and place the egg on the warm tortilla. Top with chopped or shredded pork or beef (Slow-Roasted Pork Shoulder, page 212; Chipotle Maple Barbeque Beef Brisket, page 216; Hoisin-Marinated Grilled Pork Tenderloin, page 169), Roasted Sweet Potato Salsa (page 198), Black Bean Salsa (page 196), or any fresh salsa. Roll the tortilla like a burrito and serve warm.

Barbecue Egg and Cheese Enchilada

Sauté a corn tortilla in oil until it is soft and barely golden but not crisp. Scramble one egg and spoon it in a line down the center of the tortilla. Top the egg with grated cheese and drizzle it with barbecue sauce. Roll up the tortilla and place in a 350°F oven to bake until the cheese is melted and the enchilada is warmed through. You can make one enchilada this way, or a whole baking dish full.

Eggs Benedict on Grilled Toast with Bacon, Roasted Tomatoes, and Foolproof Blender Hollandaise

Eggs Benedict is easy enough to make—it's like making a sandwich!—so there's no reason it should be reserved for special occasions. If you can get your hands on farm-fresh eggs, this is the place to use them. Poaching allows you to really taste the egg. Eggs are best hot, straight from the pan, so have the rest of your components ready and partially assembled before cooking the eggs. One egg is enough for most people, but it's not unusual to serve two per person. (See photo on page 10.)

SERVES 4 TO 8

For the tomatoes

4 plum tomatoes, halved lengthwise
2 tablespoons olive oil
  Leaves from 3 or 4 fresh thyme sprigs (about 1 tablespoon)
  Sea salt and freshly ground black pepper to taste

For the poached eggs

8 large eggs
1 teaspoon sea salt, plus more to taste
2 teaspoons white vinegar
  Freshly ground black pepper to taste

8 thick slices country white bread, lightly toasted
1/2 pound fresh mozzarella, cut into 8 slices
1/4 pound thinly sliced peppered bacon or pancetta, fried to crispy and drained on a paper towel
  Foolproof Blender Hollandaise (recipe follows)

1. Preheat the oven to 400°F.

2. Place the tomato halves on a baking sheet with sides, drizzle with the olive oil, sprinkle with half of the thyme, and the salt and pepper, and toss to coat. Spread the tomatoes in a single layer on the baking sheet and roast for about 30 minutes, until they are slightly shriveled.

3. To poach the eggs, fill a large skillet with 3 inches of water. Bring the water to a boil over high heat. Add the salt and vinegar and reduce the heat to low so there are only a few bubbles simmering on the surface.

4. Break one egg into a small bowl or measuring cup, taking care not to break the yolk. Turn the egg out of the bowl into the skillet with a quick motion so the egg keeps its shape when it hits the water. Repeat with the remaining eggs.

5. Cook the eggs for 2 to 3 minutes, until the whites set and a thin translucent film has formed over the yolk. For a firmer yolk, cook 1 to 2 minutes longer.

6. While the eggs are poaching, place 1 or 2 pieces of toast on each plate. Lay a slice of mozzarella on each piece of toast.

7. Use a slotted spoon to gently lift the eggs out of the water and place them on a paper towel to drain. Season with salt and pepper and place one egg on top of each mozzarella slice. Top with the bacon and a tomato half. Drizzle with the hollandaise and serve immediately.

> *Baking bacon is so much easier than frying it. Just put it on a baking sheet in a 350°F oven and after 15 minutes, without fussing with it or having oil splatter, it's done.*

Foolproof Blender Hollandaise

When my sister Judy comes to visit, she spends most of her time in the Foster's Market kitchen. It was during one of those visits that she taught me to make this foolproof hollandaise. Conventional hollandaise can be tricky: getting the sauce to emulsify to a creamy consistency without separating when the lemon juice is added takes care. Unlike conventional hollandaise, you can make this a few hours in advance. Leave it at room temperature until you're ready to serve it; it cannot be reheated.

MAKES ABOUT 1 CUP

2 large egg yolks, at room temperature
1 teaspoon sea salt
1/4 teaspoon cayenne pepper
8 tablespoons (1 stick) unsalted butter, melted and
   cooled to room temperature
   Juice of 1 lemon
   Freshly ground black pepper to taste

Place the egg yolks in the jar of a blender. Sprinkle with the salt and cayenne pepper, and blend until smooth. With the blender running, add the melted butter and the lemon juice slowly through the feed tube, alternating between the two, until all is incorporated. Season with black pepper to taste and additional salt if desired. Serve immediately or store at room temperature in an airtight container for up to 2 hours. This sauce cannot be refrigerated or heated.

VARIATIONS

I make a different Eggs Benedict every time, depending on what I have on hand and what's in season. Some of my favorite combinations are:

Smoked Salmon and Roasted Asparagus
Top grilled toast with smoked salmon slices, a poached or fried egg, and Foolproof Blender Hollandaise (left). Surround with Lemon Roasted Asparagus (page 115) or Wilted Spinach (page 191).

Country Ham with Toasted Cornbread
Slice cornbread (see Skillet Cornbread, page 76), slice, toast and top with a slice of fried country ham, a poached or fried egg, and sliced or roasted tomatoes.

Grilled Sweet Potato and Prosciutto
Grill sweet potato slices and top with slices of prosciutto, a poached or fried egg, and Pesto Your Way (page 138).

Biscuits with Canadian Bacon and Green Tomatoes
Top Sweet Potato Buttermilk Biscuits (page 31) with Canadian Bacon, a poached or fried egg, and Roasted Green Tomato and Apple Salsa (page 199).

Note: *Eggs Benedict has many make-ahead steps, so if you're having company you can prep ahead, then making breakfast will be nothing more than an assembly job. If you want to make the eggs several hours in advance, poach them as described above, pulling them out of the water when they're slightly underdone so they don't overcook when you reheat them. Keep the cooked eggs refrigerated in an airtight container. Reheat the poached eggs in a skillet of gently simmering water just before serving.*

Country Ham Hash with Chipotle Mustard Sauce

This is a very popular brunch dish that we serve on week-ends at the Market. The eggs baked on top of the hash give it a festive look. You could also make the hash without the eggs or with fried or scrambled eggs on the side. WHAT TO SERVE WHEN I like to serve this hash in unexpected ways: with vegetables, like Garlicky Greens (page 112 and slices of toasted country-style bread, or with warm corn tortillas and a fresh salsa.

SERVES 4

1¼ pounds Yukon Gold potatoes (4 to 6 medium potatoes), peeled and diced
1 teaspoon salt, plus more to taste
2 tablespoons unsalted butter
2 tablespoons olive oil, plus more for cooking the eggs
1 yellow onion, diced
4 ounces country ham, diced
1 red bell pepper, cored, seeded, and diced
1 jalapeño pepper, cored, seeded, and diced
  Freshly ground black pepper to taste
2 garlic cloves, minced
4 large eggs
2 tablespoons chopped fresh chives or scallions
2 tablespoons chopped fresh flat-leaf parsley
¼ cup **Chipotle Mustard Sauce** (recipe follows)

1. Place the diced potatoes and salt in a medium saucepan. Add enough water to cover by 1 to 2 inches and bring to a boil over high heat. Reduce the heat and simmer the potatoes for 3 to 4 minutes, until they are almost tender but still holding their shape. Drain and set aside.

2. Heat the butter and olive oil together in a large skillet over medium-high heat until the butter melts. Add the potatoes and onion and cook, stirring occasionally, for 7 to 10 minutes, until the potatoes are tender and golden brown. Reduce the heat if the potatoes are browning too quickly.

3. Add the ham, red pepper, and jalapeño. Season with salt and pepper and cook the hash for 5 to 6 minutes, stirring occasionally, until the ham browns and the peppers soften. Add the garlic and sauté 1 minute, stirring constantly.

4. With a spoon, push the hash aside to create four 3-inch openings in the hash. Pour a drop of olive oil into each hole and let it warm for about 1 minute. Break one egg into each hole. Reduce the heat to low, cover the pan, and cook until eggs are set to the desired doneness, 3 to 4 minutes for slightly runny eggs, 1 to 2 minutes longer if you like your eggs firmer. Sprinkle the chives and parsley over the hash and the eggs, season with additional salt and pepper if desired, and serve immediately. Use a large spoon or spatula to scoop out the hash so each person gets one egg with hash around it. Drizzle each serving with Chipotle Mustard Sauce to taste.

REINVENTION

To turn leftovers of this hash into a warm breakfast tortilla, lightly toast a flour tortilla in a dry skillet for about 1 minute per side. Fry an egg to your liking and place it on top of the tortilla. Top the egg with about ½ cup of Country Ham Hash. Drizzle with the Chipotle Mustard Sauce (or leftover chipotle peppers pureed in a blender), roll up like a burrito, and serve warm.

Think Outside the Recipe
IF YOU CAN'T FIND OR DON'T CARE FOR COUNTRY HAM, SUBSTITUTE ANY HAM YOU LIKE, SUCH AS PROSCIUTTO, FRIED PANCETTA, BACON, OR SMOKED TURKEY.

> *I prefer flat-leaf parsley to curly parsley. I like the texture better. I don't think they taste drastically different, and curly parsley can certainly be substituted for flat-leaf without a problem.*

Chipotle Mustard Sauce

I always have some of this sauce in a squeeze bottle at home. It's such an easy way to give a kick to anything from eggs to tostadas, grilled chicken breasts, or steaks.

MAKES ABOUT 1½ CUPS

- 2 chipotle peppers in adobo, or more to taste
- 3 tablespoons Dijon mustard
- 1 tablespoon Colman's dry mustard
  Grated zest and juice of 1 orange
- 2 tablespoons honey
- 2 tablespoons white vinegar
- ¼ cup olive oil
- ½ teaspoon ground cumin
- 1 teaspoon sea salt, plus more to taste
- ½ teaspoon freshly ground black pepper, plus more to taste

Combine the peppers, mustards, orange zest and juice, honey, vinegar, olive oil, cumin, salt, and pepper in the jar of a blender or the bowl of a food processor fitted with a metal blade. Blend for about 1 minute, stopping once or twice to scrape down the sides, until you have a smooth sauce. Taste for seasoning and add more salt, pepper, or another chipotle if desired. Use immediately or refrigerate in an airtight container for up to 2 weeks.

Note: *This sauce will thicken after it's been refrigerated; thin it with a bit of orange juice or vinegar if needed.*

about . . .
CHIPOTLE PEPPERS

Chipotle peppers are smoked jalapeño peppers; they have an inimitable deep, smoky flavor. You can buy them dried or canned, but I prefer the canned. If you're making a recipe that calls for just a few chipotle chiles, either transfer the leftover peppers (including the liquid) to an airtight container and refrigerate, or, better yet, pour the peppers and the liquid into the jar of a blender and puree until smooth. This makes a table salsa that is smoky, earthy, spicy—and instant. Eat it with eggs, steak, grilled chicken, or tacos and tostadas.

Creamy Cheesy Corn Grits for All Seasons

In the South, we don't traditionally put fancy toppings on our grits; we often eat them with nothing but a little Texas Pete's Hot Sauce. If we're getting really fancy, we add Cheddar cheese or shrimp. That said, I like to treat grits as a creamy, cheesy vehicle for all kinds of different flavors. Below is a recipe for grits dressed up with fresh corn, Parmesan, and black pepper, along with seasonal variations.

SERVES 4

- 2 teaspoons sea salt, plus more to taste
- 1 cup stone-ground yellow grits
- 1 cup milk
- 1 cup fresh or frozen corn kernels (kernels from about 2 ears)
- 3 tablespoons unsalted butter
- 1 cup grated Parmesan cheese (about 3 ounces)
- 1 teaspoon freshly ground black pepper, plus more to taste

1. Bring 3 cups of water to a boil in a large saucepan over high heat. Stir in the salt. Add the grits in a slow, steady stream, whisking constantly as you add them. Reduce the heat to medium-low and cook the grits, stirring frequently, for 40 to 45 minutes, until they are thick-soupy and the grains are tender to the bite. Stir in the milk and corn kernels and cook for about 2 minutes longer to warm the corn through.

2. Remove the grits from the heat; stir in the butter, grated Parmesan, and pepper, and continue to stir until butter and Parmesan are melted. Taste for salt and pepper and season with more if desired. If the grits are stiff rather than loose and creamy, stir in more milk to loosen them. Serve immediately or cover the saucepan to keep the grits warm until you're ready to serve. To serve later, warm the grits over medium heat, stirring often and adding more milk to thin them if they have thickened as they cooled.

> **The only secret to making grits is that you add the grits to the boiling water slowly. If you add them too quickly, they will be lumpy.**

WINTER: *Ham and Parmesan with Balsamic-Roasted Tomatoes*
To Creamy Cheesy Corn Grits, add 1 cup diced country or baked ham, sautéed to golden brown, when you add the Parmesan. Top each serving of grits with one or two halves of Balsamic-Roasted Tomatoes (page 135).

SPRING: *Shrimp, Tasso, Asparagus, and Leeks*
Substitute Cheddar for the Parmesan in the Creamy Cheesy Corn Grits. Cook ¼ cup diced tasso (cured pork; a spicy Cajun specialty) or chorizo with ¼ cup minced leek (or onion) in a large skillet with 1 tablespoon olive oil and 1 tablespoon butter until the tasso and leek are tender. Add ¼ pound garlic-sautéed peeled shrimp and 12 to 15 asparagus spears, and sauté about 2 minutes longer, until the shrimp turn pale orange and the asparagus are bright green and barely tender. Spoon over the warm Creamy Cheesy Corn Grits.

SUMMER: *Summer Vegetables and Basil*
Substitute pepper Jack cheese for the Parmesan in the Creamy Cheesy Corn Grits. Chop or dice 1 small summer squash or zucchini and 1 red bell pepper and sauté in 1 tablespoon butter and 1 tablespoon olive oil until the vegetables are tender. Pour the vegetables over the warm Creamy Cheesy Corn Grits and top with thinly sliced basil leaves.

FALL: *Sweet Potato, Bacon, Blue Cheese, and Rosemary*
Peel and chop a medium sweet potato. Toss with 1 tablespoon olive oil, 1 tablespoon melted butter, and 1 tablespoon chopped fresh rosemary, and spread on a baking sheet. Roast in a 400°F oven for 30 to 40 minutes, until the potatoes are golden brown and soft. Serve the sweet potatoes over the warm Creamy Cheesy Corn Grits and top with crumbled crispy bacon and crumbled blue cheese.

about . . .
GRITS

Grits, also called hominy grits, get their name from the term "hominy grist," meaning fresh-ground whole corn grist. To a Southerner, it's almost impossible to believe that many people in other parts of the country have never heard of or tasted them. It's just something we grew up with. At the Market, we use Anson Mills grits, which are whole-grain grits that are made from heirloom grains. You can find Anson Mills (and other artisinally produced stone-ground grits) at specialty markets or online (www.ansonmills.com).

Savory Breakfast Bread and Sausage Pudding

During the summer, friends from all over the country come and pile into our house at Lake Placid. I often make this before they arrive. The recipe calls for the bread pudding to sit in the refrigerator for an hour before it's baked, giving the bread a chance to absorb the liquid; but it's even better when it sits overnight. The next morning, all I have to do is bake it, and breakfast for eight is on the table. WHAT TO SERVE WHEN This dish is so rich that I like to serve it with a mixed green salad, whether it's for brunch or a light dinner.

SERVES 8 TO 10

- 2 tablespoons unsalted butter, plus more for buttering the baking dish
- 1 large yellow onion, diced
- 1/2 pound breakfast or Italian sausage, removed from the casing
- 4 cups spinach leaves, washed and drained (about 6 ounces or 1 large bunch)
- 2 1/2 cups milk
- 8 large eggs, lightly beaten
- 2 tablespoons Dijon mustard
- 1/2 teaspoon sea salt
- 1/2 teaspoon freshly ground black pepper
- 6 cups 1 1/2-inch cubes day-old country Italian or French bread
- 1 1/2 cups shredded Swiss cheese (about 6 ounces)
- 1 cup grated Parmesan cheese (about 3 ounces)
- 2 tablespoons chopped fresh thyme leaves
- 1 tablespoon chopped fresh rosemary

1. Butter a 9 × 13-inch glass baking dish. Melt but don't brown the 2 tablespoons of butter in a large skillet over medium heat. Add the onion and cook for 3 to 5 minutes, until it is soft and translucent. Add the sausage and cook about 4 minutes, breaking the sausage into pieces as it cooks, until it is cooked through. Stir in the spinach and sauté just until it is wilted, about 2 minutes. Remove the skillet from the heat. Drain off the liquid.

2. Whisk the milk, eggs, mustard, salt, and pepper together in a large bowl. Add the bread and stir to coat. Stir in the sausage, cheeses, thyme, and rosemary and pour into the prepared baking dish. Cover and refrigerate for at least 1 hour or overnight.

3. Preheat the oven to 350°F.

4. Twenty minutes before you're ready to bake the bread pudding, remove it from the refrigerator and bring to room temperature. Bake the bread pudding for 45 to 50 minutes, until it is puffy and light golden brown. Remove the bread pudding from the oven and let it sit for about 5 minutes before serving. Serve warm.

about . . .
SPINACH

Spinach sold in bunches with the stems and roots attached seems the freshest to me. Even though it's a little extra work to wash the spinach and remove the stems (compared with pre-washed bagged spinach), if I see good, fresh spinach, I buy it. If you prefer the convenience of pre-washed bagged spinach, look for baby spinach, which has tender leaves and almost no stems. I don't use frozen spinach, but I have to admit that when I'm served frozen spinach, I'm always surprised at how good it tastes, so if frozen spinach is what works for you, use it. Just make sure to thaw the spinach in a colander and press out the excess water before adding it to a recipe.

Sweet Fruit-Full Breakfast Bread Pudding

Laura Cyr, who's known as the "Casserole Queen" at Foster's Market, created this. She gave me this recipe, but admits she never sticks to it. Depending on what she finds when she arrives at the Market in the morning, she might use day-old bread, or pound cake, scones, or biscuits.

SERVES 10 TO 12

Butter for greasing the baking dish

2 cups well-shaken buttermilk

2 cups half-and-half

6 large eggs, lightly beaten

2 tablespoons pure vanilla extract

6 cups 1 1/2-inch cubes day-old country Italian or French bread (or any day-old bread, biscuits, or cake)

2 cups fresh or frozen fruit (such as blueberries, blackberries, strawberries, raspberries, pitted cherries, sliced peaches, nectarines, or plums)

Buttery Glaze

4 tablespoons unsalted butter, melted

2 tablespoons heavy cream

1/2 cup confectioners' sugar, sifted

1. Preheat the oven to 350°F. Grease a 9 × 13-inch baking dish with butter or spray with vegetable oil spray.

2. Stir the buttermilk, half-and-half, eggs, and vanilla together in a large bowl. Add the bread cubes and let them sit in the liquid for 10 to 15 minutes, until the bread is soft and has absorbed almost all the liquid. Add the fruit and stir gently to combine. Pour the bread into the buttered baking dish, making sure to get all the liquid out of the bowl.

3. Cut a sheet of aluminum foil large enough to cover the baking dish, grease the foil with butter, and place it, buttered side down, over the baking dish. Bake the bread pudding for 1 hour. Uncover and bake for 15 to 20 minutes more, until the top is golden brown and crispy.

4. While the bread pudding is baking, whisk the butter and cream together in a small bowl. Slowly add the sifted confectioners' sugar, whisking until the glaze is smooth. Drizzle the glaze over the still-warm pudding. Serve warm.

Think Outside the Recipe

IF YOU'RE LIKE ME AND THINK THAT CHOCOLATE IS THE PERFECT WAY TO START THE DAY, SUBSTITUTE 12 OUNCES GOOD-QUALITY CHOCOLATE, CUT INTO CHUNKS, FOR THE FRUIT.

SMOOTHIES

Often when I don't have time for breakfast but feel I need to eat something, I make a smoothie. Smoothies are satisfying enough to tide you over until lunch, and you can whip one up in less than five minutes with whatever fruit you have on hand. Below are some of my favorites.

MAKES TWO 8-OUNCE SMOOTHES

Blue Heaven Smoothie

Juice of 1 orange
Juice of 1 lemon
1/2 cup chopped fresh pineapple
1/2 cup chopped peeled peaches
1/2 cup fresh blueberries, plus more for garnish
1 tablespoon honey
1 1/2 cups crushed ice or ice cubes
Pinch of cinnamon

Place the orange juice, lemon juice, pineapple, peaches, blueberries, honey, ice, and cinnamon in a blender and blend on high speed until smooth. Pour into two tall glasses, top each smoothie with a few fresh blueberries, and serve immediately.

Caramel Apple Smoothie

1/2 cup apple cider or unfiltered apple juice
2 tablespoons caramel syrup or caramel sauce
3/4 cup vanilla yogurt
1 1/2 cups crushed ice or ice cubes
1/2 apple, cored and cut into 4 wedges, for garnish

Place the apple cider, caramel syrup, yogurt, and ice in the jar of a blender and blend on high speed until the smoothie is smooth. Pour into two tall glasses and garnish with the apple wedges.

Very Berry Smoothie

1/2 cup fresh blueberries, stems removed
1/2 cup fresh strawberries, stems removed
1/3 cup fresh raspberries
Juice of 1 orange
1 tablespoon honey
1 1/2 cups crushed ice or ice cubes

Reserve a few of each type of berry for garnishing the smoothies. Place the orange juice, the remaining blueberries, strawberries, raspberries, the honey, and ice in the jar of a blender and blend on high speed until smooth. Pour into two tall glasses, garnish with the reserved berries, and serve immediately.

Sunshine Smoothie

Juice of 2 oranges
2/3 cup fresh chopped pineapple, plus more for garnish
1 banana, peeled and sliced
1 1/2 cups crushed ice or ice cubes
1 tablespoon honey

Place the orange juice, pineapple, banana (reserving a few slices for garnish), ice, and honey in the jar of a blender and blend on high speed until it is smooth. Pour into two tall glasses, garnish with the remaining banana slices and pineapple, and serve immediately.

Think Outside the Recipe WHEN YOU BUY SMOOTHIES IN MEXICO, YOU HAVE THE OPTION OF HAVING GRANOLA BLENDED INTO IT. THE RESULT IS DELICIOUS—LIKE A YOGURT-COVERED GRANOLA BAR IN A GLASS. IF YOU WANT TO TRY IT, ADD A HANDFUL OF FOSTER'S HOMEMADE GRANOLA (PAGE 14) OR STORE-BOUGHT GRANOLA AND BLEND UNTIL THE GRANOLA IS FINELY GROUND.

Angel Biscuits

Angel biscuits are a North Carolina specialty. I'd never made them until I moved here and one of the cooks at the Market introduced me to them. They're perfect for the Market because, where buttermilk biscuits are good only fresh from the oven, the combination of yeast, baking soda, and self-rising flour gives these a shelf-life of two or three days. WHAT TO SERVE WHEN You can serve these flaky biscuits at any meal, morning or night. Or use them to make hors d' oeuvre–size sandwiches with Chicken Salad with Apples, Grapes, and Spicy Pecans (page 97) or thin slices of New York Strip Steak (page 159).

MAKES TWELVE TO FIFTEEN 2½-INCH BISCUITS

- 1 ¼-ounce package active dry yeast
- 1 teaspoon sugar
- 3 cups self-rising flour, or 3 cups all-purpose flour mixed with 2 teaspoons baking powder, plus more for dusting
- 1 teaspoon baking soda
- ½ teaspoon salt
- ¼ cup vegetable shortening
- 8 tablespoons (1 stick) cold unsalted butter, cut into ¼-inch pieces, plus more for buttering the baking sheet
- 1 cup well-shaken buttermilk
- 3 tablespoons unsalted butter, melted and cooled to room temperature

1. Preheat the oven to 425°F. Lightly butter a baking sheet, spray it with vegetable oil spray, or line it with parchment paper.

2. Stir the yeast and sugar together in a small bowl. Stir in ¼ cup of warm water. Set the bowl in a warm place for about 5 minutes, until the mixture bubbles and doubles in volume.

3. Meanwhile, stir the flour, baking soda, and salt together in a large mixing bowl. Add the shortening and the cold butter pieces and cut them into the flour with a pastry blender or two knives until the mixture resembles coarse cornmeal.

4. Add the buttermilk to the yeast and stir to combine. Pour the buttermilk-yeast mixture into the flour-butter mixture and stir with a wooden spoon until the dough just starts to stick together. Turn out the dough onto a lightly floured surface and knead until it forms a ball.

Do not add more flour than is needed to keep the dough from sticking and do not mix or work the dough any more than is necessary to bring it together. Barely working the dough ensures light and flaky biscuits.

5. Roll the dough about ¾ inch thick and cut with a 2½-inch biscuit cutter, leaving as little space between each cut as possible. If the dough sticks to the cutter, dip the cutter into flour.

6. Place the biscuits on the buttered baking sheet. If you want the sides of the biscuits to be soft, arrange the biscuits with their sides touching. If you want the sides of the biscuits to be crispy, leave 1 inch between the biscuits. Brush the tops and sides (if they're not touching) of the biscuits lightly with the melted butter and bake for 18 to 20 minutes, or until the tops are golden brown. Serve warm or at room temperature.

Note: *You can re-roll biscuit dough once, but no more or the dough will get tough, resulting in heavy, doughy biscuits.*

Think Outside the Recipe
TO MAKE SAVORY HERB ANGEL BISCUITS, ADD FINELY CHOPPED WATER-CRESS OR PARSLEY WITH THE FLOUR MIXTURE BEFORE ADDING THE BUTTERMILK.

about . . .
SELF-RISING FLOUR

I grew up in a house where the only kind of flour we had was self-rising flour. Self-rising flour has baking powder and salt added. It makes baked goods lighter and fluffier. You don't have to worry about getting the right proportions of salt or baking powder to flour; it just always works. Every Southerner has a brand that he or she swears by. My mom uses Martha White; I like White Lily. If you don't have self-rising flour, add 2 teaspoons baking powder to every 3 cups all-purpose flour. If the recipe does not include salt, add ½ teaspoon salt to the flour.

Sweetened Butter

When I worked as a caterer for Martha Stewart in the 1980s, quick bread and strawberry butter was the "in" thing to serve for brunch. Over the years, I've played with the butter idea and made every kind of sweetened butter imaginable. It's a special treat spread on toast, muffins, scones, and biscuits. When I make them at home or at our Lake Placid house, I always make two or four times the recipe. I find it's actually easier to whip the butter when there's more in the bowl. And I like to wrap the little logs in parchment paper to give to friends and neighbors who stop by. People appreciate homemade things—and who doesn't like butter?

Some flavor combinations I like are:
- Maple syrup and minced toasted pecans, walnuts, or hazelnuts
- Brown sugar and cinnamon
- Plum jam
- Strawberry jam and black pepper

8 tablespoons (1 stick) unsalted butter, softened
2 tablespoons sweeteners, such as honey, maple syrup, brown sugar, strawberry jam (or any fruit jam), pumpkin butter, apple butter, or cranberry relish
  Optional: 2 tablespoons roasted minced pecans, walnuts, or hazelnuts; 1 teaspoon cinnamon; freshly ground black pepper; minced rosemary; or thyme

Cream the butter in a medium bowl with the paddle attachment of an electric mixer or by hand using a wooden spoon until it is smooth and fluffy. Stir in the additions of your choice and continue to stir vigorously to combine. Spoon the butter into a small dish and serve soft, or roll the butter into a log, wrap tightly in plastic, refrigerate, and slice to serve.

> **“** *Sift baking soda through a strainer as you add it to flour to break up large clumps.* **”**

Herb Butter

Herb butter is so easy to make, and so nice to have around to use on many things: steak, chicken, fish, baked potatoes, corn on the cob (see Corn on the Cob Your Way, page 111), biscuits, or to make toasted bread.

Some flavor combinations I like:
- Chili powder and lime
- Roasted garlic and thyme
- Horseradish with mixed herbs
- Honey and rosemary

8 tablespoons (1 stick) unsalted butter, softened
2 tablespoons chopped fresh herbs, such as thyme, rosemary, or flat-leaf parsley
1/2 teaspoon lemon or lime juice
1/2 teaspoon sea salt
1/2 teaspoon freshly ground black pepper
  Optional: chili powder, cayenne pepper, roasted garlic cloves, freshly grated horseradish

Cream the butter in a medium bowl with an electric mixer (using the paddle attachment if yours has one) or by hand with a wooden spoon until smooth and fluffy. Stir in the herbs, lemon juice, salt, and pepper. Serve immediately or roll into a log, wrap tightly in plastic, refrigerate, and slice as needed.

Sweet Potato Buttermilk Biscuits

I give the method for baking a sweet potato in this recipe, but the truth is that leftover sweet potatoes, like Orange-Maple Roasted Sweet Potatoes (page 110) are invariably what inspires me to make these. In a perfect world, I eat them warm topped with maple Sweetened Butter (page 29).

MAKES TWELVE 2½-INCH BISCUITS

- 1 medium sweet potato (or 1 cup cooked mashed or canned sweet potato)
- 3½ cups all-purpose flour, plus more for dusting
- 2 teaspoons baking powder
- 1 teaspoon baking soda
- ¼ teaspoon salt
- 1 tablespoon sugar
- 12 tablespoons (1 stick plus 4 tablespoons) cold, unsalted butter, cut into ¼-inch cubes
- Grated zest and juice of 1 orange
- 2 tablespoons unsalted butter
- 1¼ cups (or more) well-shaken buttermilk

1. Preheat the oven to 400°F. Lightly grease a baking sheet, spray it with vegetable oil spray, or line it with parchment paper.

2. Wrap the sweet potato in foil and place it in the oven to bake for 40 minutes to 1 hour, depending on the size, until it is soft to the squeeze and tender when pierced with a knife. Allow it to cool slightly before unwrapping it. Peel off the skin, place the potato in a bowl, and mash it with a fork. Measure 1 cup for this recipe.

3. Increase the oven temperature to 425°F.

4. Stir the flour, baking powder, baking soda, salt, and sugar together in a large bowl. Add the cubed butter and cut it into the flour using a pastry cutter or two knives until the mixture resembles coarse cornmeal.

5. Place the orange juice in a small saucepan and bring it to a boil. Reduce the heat and simmer until it has reduced by half. Add the remaining 2 tablespoons of butter and stir until the butter melts.

6. Stir the orange zest, buttermilk, and sweet potato together in a small bowl. Add to the flour-butter mixture and stir until the dough just begins to stick together; do not over-mix. Add more buttermilk, 1 tablespoon at a time, if the dough is still crumbly and not sticking together.

7. Turn the dough out onto a lightly floured surface and knead just until it comes together, adding only as much flour as you need to keep the dough from sticking to the work surface or your hands. Form the dough into a flat round. Sprinkle more flour on the work surface and pat or roll the dough on the floured surface to a ¾-inch thickness.

8. Cut the dough with a floured 2½-inch biscuit or cookie cutter, leaving as little space as possible between each cut. Place the rounds on the prepared pan, leaving ½ inch between the biscuits. Brush with the melted butter–orange juice and bake the biscuits for 15 to 17 minutes, until they are golden brown. Serve fresh from the oven.

> **"** *I pour my baking soda down the drain every few months and buy a new box. That way I know it's always good. After a few months, baking soda loses its effectiveness, and since it freshens the drain, I don't feel like I'm being wasteful.* **"**

Banana Nut Muffins

I spent every weekend with my Granny Foster when I was a child, and without fail she made either a date cake or a batch of these muffins every visit. I still love them just as she served them to me: warm, with butter and a drizzle of honey. To make them more decadent, I often add 1 cup chopped good-quality dark chocolate. For the best flavor, use overripe or at least very ripe bananas.

MAKES 12 LARGE MUFFINS

　 2　cups all-purpose flour
　 2　teaspoons baking powder
$1/2$　teaspoon baking soda
$1/2$　teaspoon freshly grated or ground nutmeg
$1/2$　teaspoon salt
　 8　tablespoons (1 stick) unsalted butter, softened
　 1　cup sugar
　 2　large eggs
　 3　overripe bananas, mashed (about $1/2$ cups)
$1/4$　cup sour cream, or plain yogurt or well-shaken buttermilk
　 1　teaspoon pure vanilla extract
　 1　cup chopped walnuts or pecans

1. Preheat the oven to 375°F. Line a muffin tin with 12 paper liners and spray the top of the tin with vegetable oil spray or grease lightly.

2. Stir the flour, baking powder, baking soda, nutmeg, and salt together in a large bowl.

3. In a separate medium bowl, beat the butter and sugar together with an electric mixer on high speed until light and creamy. Beat in the eggs, bananas, sour cream, and vanilla and stir to mix well.

4. Add the flour mixture to the butter-sugar mixture and stir just until the flour is moist and no longer visible. Do not mix more than necessary. Gently stir in the walnuts or pecans.

5. Scoop the batter with a $1/3$-cup measure or ice cream scoop to fill the muffin tins to just below the top of the liner. Bake the muffins on a center rack for 25 to 30 minutes, until the tops spring back when pressed lightly and a toothpick inserted in the center of a muffin comes out clean. Let the muffins rest for about 5 minutes before turning them out. Serve immediately or cool on a wire rack.

Corn Blackberry Muffins

At the Market, we make these only in the summertime, when blackberries are in season, but at home, I freeze bagsful of blackberries so I can make these muffins all year long. You can use blueberries, raspberries, or a combination in place of the blackberries. But I think cornmeal and blackberries just go together.

MAKES 12 LARGE MUFFINS

$1^1/2$　cups all-purpose flour
$1^1/2$　cups yellow cornmeal
$3/4$　cup sugar
　 2　teaspoons baking powder
　 1　teaspoon baking soda
$1/2$　teaspoon salt
　 2　large eggs, lightly beaten
$3/4$　cup well-shaken buttermilk
$3/4$　cup canola oil
　 1　teaspoon pure vanilla extract
$1^1/2$　cups fresh or frozen blackberries

1. Preheat the oven to 375°F. Line 12 large muffin cups with liners and spray the top of the pan lightly with vegetable oil spray or grease lightly.

2. Stir the flour, cornmeal, sugar, baking powder, baking soda, and salt together in a large bowl.

3. In a separate large bowl, stir the eggs, buttermilk, oil, and vanilla together. Gradually add the flour-cornmeal mixture, stirring just until the dry ingredients are moist and no flour is visible. Do not mix more than necessary. Gently fold in the blackberries.

4. Scoop the batter with a $1/3$-cup measure or ice cream scoop to fill the muffin tins to just below the top of the liner. Bake the muffins for 25 to 30 minutes, until the tops spring back when pressed lightly and a toothpick inserted into the center of a muffin comes out clean. Allow the muffins to cool in the pan for 5 minutes before turning them out. These are best served fresh from the oven.

> **❝** *Muffin batter can be a bit lumpy. Don't worry; the lumps will disappear after baking.* **❞**

1. Preheat the oven to 375°F. Line 12 large muffin cups with liners and spray the top of the pan with vegetable oil spray or grease lightly.

2. Stir the flour, poppy seeds, baking soda, baking powder, and salt together in a large bowl.

3. In a separate large bowl, beat the butter and sugar together with an electric mixer on high speed until light and fluffy. Add the eggs, one at a time, scraping down the bowl and mixing well after each addition.

4. Combine the buttermilk, lemon zest and juice, and vanilla in a small bowl or large glass measuring cup. Add to the egg mixture alternating with the flour mixture and stir just until no flour is visible. Do not overmix.

5. Scoop the batter with a 1/3-cup measure or ice cream scoop to fill the muffin cups to just below the top of the liner. Bake the muffins on a center rack for 20 to 25 minutes, until the tops spring back when touched lightly and a toothpick inserted in the center of a muffin comes out clean. Allow the muffins to cool slightly in the tin before turning them out. Serve warm or cool on a wire rack. If you are making cupcakes, allow them to cool to room temperature before icing.

Lemon Cream Cheese Frosting

2 1/2 cups confectioners' sugar, sifted
  3 ounces cream cheese, softened
  1 teaspoon pure vanilla extract
    Grated zest of 1 lemon
  1 tablespoon fresh lemon juice, or to taste

Cream the sugar and cream cheese together with an electric mixer on high speed until fluffy. Beat in the vanilla, lemon zest, and enough juice to make the frosting a spreadable consistency.

Think Outside the Recipe
TRY USING ORANGE OR
TANGERINE IN PLACE OF
OR IN COMBINATION WITH
THE LEMON.

Lemon Poppy Seed Muffins

These are as moist and lemony as any lemon muffins I've ever tasted. Topped with cream cheese frosting, they're outed as the little cakes they really are.

MAKES 12 LARGE MUFFINS

2 1/2 cups all-purpose flour
 1/4 cup poppy seeds
  1 teaspoon baking soda
  1 teaspoon baking powder
 1/2 teaspoon salt
  8 tablespoons (1 stick) unsalted butter, softened
 3/4 cup sugar
  2 large eggs
 1/2 cup well-shaken buttermilk
    Grated zest and juice of 2 lemons
  1 teaspoon pure vanilla extract

Pumpkin Muffins

Late September our regular customers start requesting these muffins; there's just something about those first cool days of fall that makes people crave pumpkin.

MAKES 12 LARGE MUFFINS

3 cups all-purpose flour
2 teaspoons baking powder
1 teaspoon baking soda
2 teaspoons ground cinnamon
1 teaspoon freshly grated or ground nutmeg
1/2 teaspoon salt
1 cup sugar
6 tablespoons unsalted butter, melted and cooled to room temperature
2 large eggs
1 15-ounce can pumpkin puree (1 1/2 cups)
1 cup milk
1 1/2 cups golden raisins

1. Preheat the oven to 375°F. Line 12 large muffin cups with liners and spray the top of the pan with vegetable oil spray or grease lightly.

2. Stir the flour, baking powder, baking soda, cinnamon, nutmeg, and salt together in a large bowl.

3. In a separate large bowl, stir the sugar, butter, and eggs together. Stir in the pumpkin puree, milk, and raisins and pour into the bowl with the flour mixture. Stir until the dry ingredients are just moistened; do not mix any more than necessary.

4. Using a 1/3-cup measure or ice cream scoop, scoop the batter into the muffin tins, filling each to just below the top of the paper liner. Bake the muffins on a center rack for 25 to 30 minutes, until the tops of the muffins spring back when touched lightly and a toothpick inserted in the center of a muffin comes out clean. Allow the muffins to cool for a few minutes in the tin before turning them out. Serve immediately or cool on a wire rack.

Think Outside the Recipe
- ADD DRIED FRUITS LIKE CURRANTS, RAISINS, DRIED CHERRIES, DRIED CRANBERRIES, OR CHOPPED DRIED APRICOTS.
- MAKE TINY MUFFINS TO SERVE AS HORS D'OEUVRE WITH HERB-GRILLED TURKEY BREAST WITH CHIPOTLE MUSTARD SAUCE.

Orange Chocolate Muffins

I love chocolate and orange together, and I just think there's something wonderful about having chocolate for breakfast. These are best served warm, fresh from the oven.

MAKES 12 LARGE MUFFINS

1/2 cup bran flakes or All Bran cereal
1 teaspoon baking powder
2 cups all-purpose flour
1 teaspoon baking soda
1/4 teaspoon salt
1 teaspoon ground cinnamon
6 tablespoons unsalted butter, softened
3/4 cup packed light brown sugar
1 large egg
1/2 cup sour cream
Grated zest of 2 oranges and 1/2 cup of their juice
1 teaspoon pure vanilla extract
1/3 cup semisweet chocolate chips

1. Preheat the oven to 375°F. Line 12 large muffin cups with liners and spray the top of the pan with vegetable oil spray or grease lightly.

2. Stir the bran flakes, flour, baking powder, baking soda, salt, and cinnamon together in a large bowl.

3. In a separate large bowl, cream the butter and sugar together with an electric mixer on high speed until fluffy, scraping down the sides of the bowl occasionally. Add the egg and mix to combine. Add the sour cream, orange zest and juice, and vanilla and mix until incorporated.

4. Add the bran-flour mixture to the butter-sugar mixture, stirring with a wooden spoon or the paddle attachment of an electric mixer until the dry ingredients are just moistened. Stir in the chocolate chips to combine. Do not mix any more than necessary.

5. Use a 1/3-cup measure or ice cream scoop to scoop the batter into the prepared muffin cups, filling them to just below the rim of the cup. Bake the muffins for 20 to 25 minutes, until a wooden skewer comes out clean when inserted in the center of a muffin and the muffins spring back when touched. Let the muffins rest for about 5 minutes before turning them out. Serve immediately or cool on a wire rack.

two

simple soups

Chipotle-Squash Soup with Fresh Rosemary and Toasted Pumpkin Seeds ○ Potato, Leek, and Blue Cheese Soup ○ Roasted Red Bell Pepper and Carrot Soup with Tarragon ○ Creamy Tomato Dill Soup ○ Sweet Pea Soup with Fresh Mint Pesto ○ Roasted Sweet Potato and Tomato Soup with Herbs ○ Summer White Corn Soup ○ Roasted Asparagus Soup ○ Chilled Avocado Soup ○ Golden Gazpacho ○ Wild Mushroom Soup with Sherry and Thyme ○ Puree of Watercress Soup ○ Beef and Bean Chili ○ Green Chili with Crispy Corn Tortilla Strips ○ Chunky Chicken Vegetable Minestrone ○ Navy Bean Soup with Rosemary and Smoky Ham Hocks ○ Soup Toppers

I like the process of making soup—how imprecise it is and how you end up with a big pot of something satisfying and delicious. I especially like that when I make soup, I have some to serve now, some for later, and some to share with friends.

When I make soup at our house in Lake Placid, I make an extra-big pot and give some to the guys who work on our house and in our garden. They're single guys and they don't cook much, and they just love the soup.

The recipes in this chapter are for really simple soups, things like Green Chili or Navy Bean Soup with Rosemary and Smoky Ham Hocks, where the finished dish isn't compromised by the use of canned beans or tomatoes. There are also a lot of recipes for pureed soups using vegetables that cook really quickly or not at all as is the case with like watercress, spinach, or avocado. All of these pureed soups take less than an hour from start to finish, and the result is a vibrantly colored, rich and creamy meal.

But the best thing about these soups is not the convenience of making them but how good they taste. Soup makes a warm, healthy, satisfying lunch to take to work or to heat up when you don't have time to cook. With a grilled cheese sandwich, quesadilla, or a salad on the side, it's a light, comforting late-night supper. Hearty soups, like the Beef and Bean Chili or Chunky Chicken Vegetable Minestrone, are the perfect choice for a crowd, not just because they are easy cooking but because you can make them a day in advance—they taste even better the next day.

Chipotle-Squash Soup with Fresh Rosemary and Toasted Pumpkin Seeds

Chipotle chiles give this soup a pleasant heat and smokiness without making it too spicy. I often dress up it up with a dollop of Crème Fraîche (page 277) or sour cream mixed with fresh lime juice. (See photo on page 36.)

SERVES 8 TO 10 (MAKES ABOUT 2½ QUARTS)

- 1 small winter squash such as pumpkin, butternut, or acorn (2 to 2½ pounds), halved and seeds removed
- 3 tablespoons olive oil
- 2 tablespoons unsalted butter
- 1 large yellow onion, chopped
- 2 large carrots, chopped
- 1 red bell pepper, cored, seeded, and chopped
- 2 garlic cloves, chopped
- 6 cups chicken or vegetable broth
- 2 chipotle chiles in adobo, seeded and chopped
- 2 teaspoons sea salt, plus more to taste
- ½ teaspoon freshly ground black pepper, plus more to taste
- 2 tablespoons chopped fresh rosemary
- ½ cup pumpkin seeds, toasted and salted, for garnish (see page 82)

1. Preheat the oven to 400°F.

2. Place the squash, cut side down, on a baking sheet with sides. Add 1 cup water and 1 tablespoon of the olive oil to the pan and roast the squash until it is soft to the touch, 40 to 45 minutes.

3. Meanwhile, melt the butter and the remaining 2 tablespoons olive oil together in a large saucepan over medium heat. Add the onion, reduce the heat to low, and cook, stirring occasionally, for 10 to 15 minutes, until the onion is very soft and light brown. Add the carrots and bell pepper and continue to cook and stir until the carrots are soft, about 10 minutes. Add the garlic and cook, stirring constantly, for 1 to 2 minutes, until it is fragrant but not brown.

4. Add the broth, chipotle chiles, 2 teaspoons salt, and ½ teaspoon pepper and bring the soup to a low boil over medium-high heat. While the soup is coming to a boil, scoop out the squash flesh with a large spoon.

Discard the skin and add the flesh to the soup. Reduce the heat to low and simmer, uncovered, for 25 to 30 minutes.

5. Remove the soup from the heat and stir in the rosemary. Allow the soup to cool slightly before pureeing. Working in batches if necessary, pour the soup into the bowl of a food processor fitted with a metal blade and puree until it is smooth, or puree the soup directly in the pot using an immersion blender. Reheat if necessary and serve warm, garnished with toasted, salted pumpkin seeds.

Note: *I use good-quality sea salt when toasting nuts or seeds like the pumpkin seeds for this. I think it makes them taste so much better. Using cranberry salt on these pumpkin seeds gives them a tangy, unusual kick.*

about . . .
WINTER SQUASH

I use winter squash in many different ways: pureed into soups, roasted and tossed into salads, mashed as a side dish, and baked into muffins and pies. Squash is such a convenient thing to have in the house—its hard skin protects it, so it lasts a long time, and it doesn't require refrigeration. There are many different kinds of winter squash; if you go to the farmers market in the fall and winter months, you'll see them in all their odd shapes, colors, and sizes. They taste subtly different, so I urge you to try different varieties. You can use them interchangeably in recipes. Some varieties to look for are pumpkin (look for the light-skinned varieties known as cheese pumpkins or pie pumpkins), acorn, butternut, golden hubbard, blue hubbard, Turk's turban, and red kuri.

TRICKS OF MY TRADE

Making soup is not an exact science. Experiment with these recipes depending on the season and what you have on hand; soup is almost impossible to mess up. Soup is a great way to clean out your refrigerator. If I have extra steamed clams, I'll make clam chowder. I might make vegetable minestrone with leftover roast vegetables or a lot of vegetables that need to be cooked right away. If I've roasted a chicken, I always use what's left after dinner to make some kind of chicken soup.

○ **Double a recipe.** Freeze some for later or bring some to a friend who just had a baby, a busy colleague, or neighbor. Make bean soups and chili when you're inspired, not when you're hungry. You'll be happy to have them in the refrigerator or freezer for a quick, healthy meal.

○ **Select a recipe by season.** Especially with pureed soups, which are all about the concentration of flavors, the natural flavor of the fresh ingredients you start with will make all the difference.

○ **Top the soup with a garnish or accent** to provide contrasting flavor and texture. I think it makes the soup more satisfying—and elegant. Some soup additions I like are:

Grilled cheese sandwich cut into small cubes and floated like croutons

A dollop of Crème Fraîche (page 277) topped with minced herbs or citrus zest

A swirl of good-quality extra-virgin olive oil

Crab Cake (page 174) with soup poured around it

Slices of salted avocado

Pan-seared scallop or shrimp with soup poured around it

A sprinkling of crab or lobster meat

Crispy Corn Tortilla Strips, Oven-Baked Tortilla Chips, or Spicy Pita Chips (page 59)

Crispy Fried Shallots (page 59)

Toasted pumpkin seeds (page 82)

○ **Make a quick broth out of vegetable trimmings.** Place the vegetable trimmings in a saucepan while you prep the vegetables for the soup. Add just enough cold water to cover the trimmings, salt and pepper, and a bay leaf or two and simmer for 25 to 30 minutes. You will have a delicious flavored broth to add to your soup.

○ **Stir or swirl buttermilk or yogurt into chilled soups** to add an extra tangy flavor.

○ **Add flour tortillas,** cut into strips to make small dumplings, to make a heartier soup.

○ **Vegetable pureed soups make a nice sauce** for grilled fish or chicken.

○ **To give added flavor to risotto or polenta,** stir in a few spoonfuls of vegetable soups like Potato Leek and Blue Cheese or Roasted Sweet Potato and Tomato with Herbs.

> *Salt soup while it's cooking, not after it's done; this way the flavor of the salt is in the soup. After the soup is cooked, taste it to see if it needs more.*

Potato, Leek, and Blue Cheese Soup

It's important to use quality cheese in this soup because the soup is all about the cheese. Ask the counterperson at your local cheese shop or gourmet market to point out a good blue, Gorgonzola, or Roquefort (a pungent French blue cheese). Stay away from packaged, already-crumbled blue cheese as it tends to be very salty and of lesser quality.

SERVES 6 TO 8 (MAKES ABOUT 2 QUARTS)

- 4 leeks (about 2 pounds), trimmed, split lengthwise, and cut into 1/4-inch rounds
- 2 tablespoons unsalted butter
- 2 tablespoons olive oil
- 3 celery stalks, chopped
- 1 pear, peeled, cored, and chopped
- 4 garlic cloves, minced
- 1 1/2 pounds russet or Yukon Gold potatoes, peeled and chopped
- 6 cups chicken or vegetable broth
- 1 teaspoon sea salt, plus more to taste
- 1/2 teaspoon freshly ground black pepper, plus more to taste
- 1 tablespoon chopped fresh rosemary or sage leaves
- 1 cup (4 ounces) crumbled blue cheese, plus more for garnish

1. Place the leeks in a large bowl or sink full of cold water and let them soak for 10 to 15 minutes to remove all the sand and dirt. Carefully skim out the leeks, leaving the grit behind; drain well.

2. Melt the butter and olive oil together in a large saucepan over medium heat. Add the leeks and cook, stirring often, until very tender, about 10 minutes. Reduce the heat if the leeks begin to brown. Add the celery and cook, stirring occasionally, to soften, about 5 minutes. Add the pear and garlic and sauté for 2 minutes longer, being careful not to brown the garlic.

3. Add the potatoes, broth, 1 teaspoon salt, and 1/2 teaspoon pepper and bring the soup to a low boil over medium heat. Reduce the heat to low and simmer, uncovered, stirring occasionally, until the potatoes are tender, 20 to 25 minutes.

4. Cool the soup slightly before pureeing. Ladle half of the soup into the bowl of a food processor or the jar of a blender fitted with a metal blade and puree until smooth. (Or puree the soup with an immersion blender directly in the pot, making sure to leave some of the vegetables chunky to give the soup texture.) Return the pureed soup back to the pot with the chunky soup and stir to mix. Reheat the soup if necessary.

5. Remove the soup from the heat and stir in the rosemary and blue cheese. Serve warm, topped with additional crumbled cheese.

Think Outside the Recipe
FOR AN EVEN HEARTIER WINTER SOUP, STIR IN A HANDFUL OF ROUGHLY CHOPPED FRESH SPINACH OR SORREL LEAVES AND COOK JUST TO WILT.

about . . .
HANDHELD IMMERSION BLENDERS

The handheld immersion blender is a simple, elegant little tool you immerse directly into what you're working with. I use mine to emulsify vinaigrette or to make whipped cream, but I especially like it for making pureed soups. With an immersion blender, you don't have to wait for soup to cool before pureeing it as you do (to avoid burns) when you use a food processor. But more important, it means no spillage on the counter and no food processor to clean.

Roasted Red Bell Pepper and Carrot Soup with Tarragon

The roasted bell peppers give this soup an intense, smoky flavor—and also make it sweet. It's just delicious served warm or chilled.

SERVES 6 TO 8 (MAKES ABOUT 2 QUARTS)

 4 tablespoons olive oil
 2 tablespoons unsalted butter
 2 red bell peppers, cored, seeded, and chopped
 4 medium carrots, chopped
 1 large yellow onion, chopped
 4 shallots, chopped
 1 pear, peeled, cored, and chopped
 3 garlic cloves, chopped
 6 cups chicken or vegetable broth
 4 red bell peppers, roasted, peeled, cored, seeded, and chopped (see "Peppers," page 54)
 $1/2$ teaspoon crushed red pepper flakes, or more to taste
 $1/8$ teaspoon cayenne pepper
 2 teaspoons sea salt, plus more to taste
 1 teaspoon freshly ground black pepper, plus more to taste
 2 tablespoons chopped fresh tarragon or 2 teaspoons dried

1. Melt the olive oil and butter together in a large saucepan over medium heat. Add the raw bell peppers, carrots, onion, shallots, and pear. Reduce the heat to low and cook the vegetables for 12 to 15 minutes, stirring often, until very soft. Add the garlic and cook for several minutes longer, being careful not to let the garlic burn.

2. Add the broth, roasted peppers, crushed red pepper, cayenne pepper, 2 teaspoons salt, and 1 teaspoon pepper to the saucepan and stir to mix. Bring the broth to a low boil over high heat. Reduce the heat to low and simmer the soup for about 30 minutes. Cool slightly.

3. Working in batches if necessary, pour the soup into the bowl of a food processor or the jar of a blender fitted with a metal blade and puree until smooth. (Or puree the soup directly in the pot using an immersion blender.) Pour the soup back into the pot you cooked it in. Stir in the tarragon, season with additional salt and pepper if desired, and serve hot or chilled. This soup will keep, refrigerated in an airtight container, for several days. It also freezes well.

Creamy Tomato Dill Soup

When I lived in a sorority house at Ole Miss, I always looked forward to the lunch of grilled cheese sandwiches and creamy tomato soup. The soup came from a can, I'm sure, but I loved it. This is my homemade version. It's probably our most requested soup at the Market. You can serve it warm or chilled. WHAT TO SERVE WHEN Make grilled Cheddar cheese sandwiches and cut them into small cubes to float on the soup. Use this soup as a sauce over Grilled Salmon (page 195) or Pan-Seared Sea Scallops (page 176).

SERVES 8 TO 10 (MAKES ABOUT 2½ QUARTS)

 2 tablespoons olive oil
 2 tablespoons unsalted butter
 1 large yellow onion, diced
 2 carrots, diced
 2 celery stalks, diced
 1 28-ounce can chopped tomatoes
 1 28-ounce can crushed tomatoes
 6 cups chicken or vegetable broth
 2 teaspoons sea salt, plus more to taste
 1 teaspoon freshly ground black pepper, plus more to taste
 1 teaspoon crushed red pepper flakes
 2 tablespoons chopped fresh dill
 2 tablespoons chopped fresh flat-leaf parsley leaves
 1 cup heavy cream

1. Heat the olive oil and butter in a large saucepan over medium-low heat. Add the onion and cook, stirring often, for 10 to 12 minutes, until the onion is light brown. Add the carrots and celery and cook another 10 minutes, until the vegetables are soft.

2. Add the chopped and crushed tomatoes, broth, 2 teaspoons salt, 1 teaspoon black pepper, and the red pepper flakes, and stir to combine. Bring to a low boil; reduce the heat and simmer, uncovered, for about 45 minutes, stirring occasionally.

3. Remove the soup from the heat and stir in the dill, parsley, and cream. Season with additional salt and pepper to taste. Serve immediately or refrigerate in an airtight container for up to 3 days. Serve hot or chilled.

Note: *If you make this soup in advance, add the fresh herbs and the cream when you serve it, stirring them into the soup while it's warming over low heat.*

Sweet Pea Soup with Fresh Mint Pesto

The first time I ever had sweet pea soup was when Martha Stewart made it for lunch for her staff of four people. She used shelled fresh English peas and butter lettuce from the garden of her Connecticut home where we worked. I remember at the time thinking it was the best thing I'd ever tasted. And it was so simple. I added the mint pesto because I love the combination of peas and mint. If you use frozen peas, buy petite green peas; they're sweeter than the others.

SERVES 6 TO 8 (MAKES ABOUT 2 QUARTS)

 2 tablespoons unsalted butter
 2 tablespoons olive oil
 1 large yellow onion, chopped
1 1/2 pounds Yukon Gold potatoes (3 to 4 medium), peeled and chopped
 3 celery stalks, chopped
 5 cups chicken or vegetable broth
 2 cups shelled fresh or frozen green peas (1 16-ounce bag)
 1 head butter (Bibb) lettuce (about 4 cups loosely packed)
 3 tablespoons chopped fresh mint leaves
 2 teaspoons sea salt, plus more to taste
 1 teaspoon freshly ground black pepper, plus more to taste
   Fresh Mint Pesto (recipe follows)

1. Melt the butter and olive oil together in a large saucepan over medium heat. Add the onion, reduce the heat to medium-low, and cook, stirring often, until soft and translucent, about 10 minutes. Add the potatoes and celery and cook for about 5 minutes longer.

2. Add the broth and peas and bring to a low boil over high heat. Reduce the heat and simmer until the potatoes are tender when pierced with a knife, about 15 minutes. Add the lettuce and simmer until it is tender, about 2 minutes more. Stir in the mint, 2 teaspoons salt, and 1 teaspoon pepper, and remove from the heat. Cool slightly.

3. Working in batches if necessary, pour the soup into the bowl of a food processor or the jar of a blender fitted with a metal blade and puree until smooth. (Or puree the soup directly in the pot using an immersion blender.)

Season with additional salt and pepper to taste. Serve warm or chilled, with a teaspoon of Fresh Mint Pesto spooned onto each serving. This soup will keep, refrigerated in an airtight container, for up to 3 days.

Fresh Mint Pesto

Years ago, I planted mint in our yard in Durham. Mint grows like crazy. I hate to see it go to waste, so I use it to make big batches of this pesto, which I freeze or give to friends. I toss the pesto with pasta and goat cheese, drizzle it over Rosemary-Mint Lamb Chops (page 166), and dollop it on soups.

MAKES ABOUT 1 CUP

 1 cup fresh mint leaves, washed and dried well
 1 cup fresh flat-leaf parsley leaves, washed and dried well
 4 garlic cloves
1/2 cup extra-virgin olive oil
1/4 cup blanched slivered almonds
 3 ounces Asiago or Parmesan cheese, grated (about 1 cup)
 1 teaspoon sea salt
1/2 teaspoon freshly ground black pepper

1. Place the mint, parsley, and garlic in the bowl of a food processor fitted with a metal blade. Add the garlic and pulse several times to roughly chop the garlic and herbs.

2. With the motor running, pour the olive oil in a slow, steady stream through the feed tube of the machine. Stop to scrape down the sides of the bowl several times while adding the oil.

3. Add the almonds, cheese, salt, and pepper and puree until the mixture is smooth, about 1 minute more. Use immediately, refrigerate in an airtight container for up to 1 week, or freeze for up to 3 months.

Note: *If you're making this pesto to use later, add a vitamin C tablet while you're pureeing the pesto to keep it bright green. If you are freezing the pesto, you may want to add the cheese when you are using the pesto; the freshly grated cheese will liven up the flavor.*

Roasted Sweet Potato and Tomato Soup with Herbs

The sweet potatoes give this soup a rich creaminess, even though it contains no cream or milk. Chilled, it can be served as a starter on a warm Indian summer night.

SERVES 8 TO 10 (MAKES ABOUT 3 QUARTS)

- 3 pounds sweet potatoes (5 to 6 medium)
- 1/4 cup olive oil, plus more for rubbing on the sweet potatoes (about 2 tablespoons)
- 6 plum tomatoes (about 1 1/2 pounds), cored and halved
- 4 garlic cloves
- 1 tablespoon balsamic vinegar
- 4 tablespoons unsalted butter
- 1 red onion, chopped
- 2 carrots, chopped
- 2 celery stalks, chopped
- 6 cups chicken or vegetable broth
- 2 teaspoons sea salt, plus more to taste
- 1 teaspoon freshly ground black pepper, plus more to taste
  Leaves from 8 to 10 fresh thyme sprigs (about 3 tablespoons) or 2 teaspoons dried, crumbled, plus more for garnish
- 2 tablespoons chopped fresh chives
- 1 tablespoon chopped fresh sage leaves or 1 teaspoon dried, crumbled, plus more for garnish
  Juice of 2 oranges

1. Preheat the oven to 450°F.

2. Rub the sweet potatoes with a small amount of olive oil, place them on a baking sheet with sides, and roast for 40 to 45 minutes, until they are soft to the squeeze and tender when pierced with a knife. When they are cool enough to handle, remove and discard their skins.

3. While the sweet potatoes roast, toss the tomatoes and garlic with 2 tablespoons of the olive oil and the balsamic vinegar on a baking sheet with sides. Roast (along with the sweet potatoes) until the tomatoes are squishy and the skins slightly shriveled, 30 to 35 minutes. When they are cool enough to handle, tear the tomatoes into small pieces over a small bowl.

4. Melt the butter and the remaining 2 tablespoons of olive oil in a large saucepan over medium heat. Add the onion and cook, stirring often, until it is soft and translucent, about 10 minutes. Add the carrots and celery and cook, stirring often, until the vegetables are soft, about 10 minutes longer. Add the broth, 2 teaspoons salt, and 1 teaspoon pepper, reduce the heat to low, and simmer, uncovered, for about 20 minutes. Add the sweet potato flesh and dried herbs, if using, to the soup and simmer about 20 minutes longer, stirring occasionally. Remove from the heat, stir in the fresh thyme, chives, and sage, and allow the soup to cool slightly.

5. Working in batches if necessary, pour the soup into the bowl of a food processor or the jar of a blender fitted with a metal blade (or puree it directly in the pot with an immersion blender) until it is smooth. Return the pureed soup to the pot, add the tomatoes and their liquid and the orange juice, and stir to combine. Season with additional salt and pepper to taste. Serve warm or chilled, topped with fresh sage and thyme.

Think Outside the Recipe

- FOR ADDED RICHNESS, SWIRL A LITTLE HEAVY CREAM AT THE END, OR TOP EACH SERVING WITH SOUR CREAM MIXED WITH MINCED JALAPEÑO PEPPERS AND FRESH LIME JUICE.
- FLOAT A CROSTINI TOPPED WITH LUMP CRABMEAT ON EACH SERVING.
- TO TURN THE SOUP INTO A MEAL IN A BOWL, ADD CRUMBLED COOKED SAUSAGE OR A FEW PUMPKIN RAVIOLI TO EACH SERVING.

Summer White Corn Soup

I make this soup only at the height of summer, when sweet, just-picked corn is piled high at farmers markets. Of course, you can make it with yellow corn, but I especially like the color and flavor of white corn. The corn broth, if you take the time to make it, gives the soup an intense corn flavor; it's well worth the effort. WHAT TO SERVE WHEN To make this soup into a meal, top it with sautéed shrimp or steamed lobster. Turn the soup into a light summer meal by using it as a sauce poured around the Pan-Seared Sea Scallops (page 176) or Crab Cakes (page 174).

SERVES 6 TO 8 (MAKES ABOUT 2 QUARTS)

   5 ears sweet white corn, shucked
 1/2 cup (or more as needed) milk
   1 tablespoon unsalted butter
   1 tablespoon olive oil
   1 large yellow onion, chopped, trimmings reserved
   2 celery stalks, chopped, trimmings reserved
   2 garlic cloves, minced
   1 large Yukon Gold potato, peeled and chopped
   4 to 5 cups **Corn Broth** (see box right) or chicken or vegetable broth
   1 teaspoon sea salt, plus more to taste
 1/2 teaspoon freshly ground black pepper, plus more to taste
  16 fresh basil leaves, cut into thin strips, stems reserved

1. Cut the corn kernels off the cob with a large knife and place in a medium saucepan, reserving the cobs to make Corn Broth. Add the milk and bring to a low boil over medium heat. Reduce the heat and simmer for 5 minutes.

2. In a separate, large saucepan, melt the butter and olive oil together over medium heat. Add the onion, reduce the heat to low, and cook, stirring often, until the onion is very soft and translucent, about 10 minutes. Add the celery and cook, stirring often, for 4 to 5 minutes longer, to soften. Stir in the garlic and sauté for 1 minute, stirring constantly, being careful not to let the garlic brown.

3. Add the potato, 4 cups of the broth, 1 teaspoon salt, and 1/2 teaspoon pepper and bring to a low boil over medium-high heat. Reduce the heat and simmer for 15 to 20 minutes, until the potatoes are soft. Stir in the corn-milk mixture and half of the basil. Cool slightly.

4. Ladle half the soup into the bowl of a food processor or the jar of a blender fitted with a metal blade and process until smooth or use an immersion blender making sure to stop blending before the soup is pureed. You want some of the vegetables to remain slightly chunky. Add the pureed soup back to the pot and stir to mix. If the soup seems too thick, thin it with broth or milk. Season with additional salt and pepper to taste and serve warm or chilled, garnished with the remaining basil.

CORN BROTH

Stripped corncobs make a sweet, corn-flavored broth to use in corn soup or Risotto with Summer Corn and Tomatoes (page 203). Place the stripped corncobs in a large saucepan with 1 bay leaf, the trimmings from the onion (or 1 additional onion) and celery, and the stems from the basil. Cover with 4 quarts cool water and bring to a low boil over medium-high heat. Reduce the heat to low and simmer for 45 minutes to 1 hour. Strain the broth into a large bowl and discard the solids. Refrigerate in an airtight container for up to 3 days or freeze for up to 3 months.

Roasted Asparagus Soup

I'm always so excited to see asparagus when it first appears at the farmers market in Durham. In the following weeks, it seems like I eat it every day. I try to prepare it in ways that don't mask its flavor. This soup is one of those; it is pure asparagus. WHAT TO SERVE WHEN Dress this soup up with a dollop of Crème Fraîche (page 277) and a sprinkling of chive or garlic chive blossoms.

SERVES 8 TO 10 (MAKES ABOUT 2½ QUARTS)

  6 tablespoons unsalted butter
  3 shallots, diced
  2 parsnips, peeled and chopped
  1 cup dry white wine
  6 cups chicken or vegetable broth
  1 tart apple (such as Granny Smith or Pippin), peeled, cored, and chopped
  2 tablespoons chopped fresh tarragon (or 2 teaspoons dried)
  1 teaspoon sea salt, plus more to taste
½ teaspoon freshly ground black pepper, plus more to taste
   Juice of 2 lemons
1½ pounds asparagus, trimmed of tough ends
  1 cup heavy cream
  2 tablespoons chopped fresh flat-leaf parsley leaves or chives

1. Preheat the oven to 400°F.

2. Melt 4 tablespoons of the butter in a large saucepan over medium heat, being careful not to let it brown. Add the shallots, reduce the heat to low, and cook, stirring occasionally, for about 10 minutes to soften. Add the parsnips and cook until the parsnips soften, about 10 minutes.

3. Add the wine, increase the heat, and simmer until the wine reduces by half, 3 to 4 minutes. Add the broth, apple, tarragon, 1 teaspoon salt, and ½ teaspoon pepper and bring a low boil. Reduce the heat to low and simmer the soup for 20 minutes.

4. Meanwhile, melt the remaining 2 tablespoons butter in a small saucepan over low heat. Turn off the heat and stir in the lemon juice.

5. Cut the asparagus into 2-inch pieces and set the tips aside. Spread the remaining asparagus pieces in an even layer on one half of a baking sheet with sides. Place the tips at the other end of the baking sheet. Pour the lemon-butter over the asparagus pieces, toss to coat, and roast for 5 to 7 minutes, just until the asparagus turns bright green.

6. Add the asparagus stems to the soup and remove the soup from the heat to cool slightly.

7. Working in batches if necessary, pour the soup into the bowl of a food processor or the jar of a blender fitted with a metal blade and puree until smooth. (Or use an immersion blender to puree the soup directly in the pot.) If your asparagus is large, the soup may have fibers floating in it; if so, pass it through a strainer.

8. Return the pureed soup to the pot you cooked it in. Stir in the cream and reheat over low heat. Taste for salt and pepper and add more if necessary. Stir in half of the asparagus tips. Serve warm, garnished with the remaining tips and the parsley or chives and serve immediately.

BASICS: *Trimming Asparagus*

To rid asparagus spears of their tough ends, I usually start by snapping one spear. Asparagus will automatically break at the point where it becomes tough and fibrous. Then, rather than snap each one individually, I line up the remaining spears and use a knife to chop them all at the same point. It's faster, but if you prefer snapping, snap away.

Chilled Avocado Soup

Years ago at the Market, I found myself in the desperate situation of having an entire case of avocados so ripe they needed to be used right away. It was summer, when our customers request chilled soup. This soup was the brainchild of that desperation. Since none of the ingredients are cooked, you can whip it up in a few minutes. WHAT TO SERVE WHEN To dress up this soup, top it with Crispy Corn Tortilla Strips (page 55) and chopped tomatoes.

SERVES 6 TO 8 (MAKES ABOUT 2 QUARTS)

 3 ripe Hass avocados, peeled, pitted, and roughly chopped
 1 medium cucumber, peeled, seeded, and roughly chopped
 5 scallions, roughly chopped (white and green parts)
 2 garlic cloves, roughly chopped
 4 cups chicken or vegetable broth
 1 cup well-shaken buttermilk
   Grated zest and juice of 2 limes
 1 cup spinach leaves, stems removed, washed, and drained
 1/4 cup fresh cilantro leaves, plus more for garnish
 2 teaspoons sea salt, plus more to taste
 1/2 teaspoon freshly ground black pepper, plus more to taste

1. Put the avocado, cucumber, scallions, garlic, 1 cup of the chicken broth, buttermilk, lime zest and juice, spinach, cilantro, 2 teaspoons salt, and 1/2 teaspoon pepper in the bowl of a food processor fitted with a metal blade or in the jar of a blender and process until smooth. (Depending on the size of your food processor, you may need to work in batches.)

2. Pour the soup into a large plastic container. Gradually stir in the remaining broth until the soup reaches a smooth, soupy consistency. Season with additional salt and pepper to taste. Cover and chill for about 1 hour. This soup is best served the day it's made.

> *Anytime you find Key limes, also called Mexican limes, use them. They are tangier, sweeter, juicier—just more limelike than conventional limes.*

Golden Gazpacho

I think of this soup as the soup version of a tomato salad, which means I make it only when tomatoes are in season, and I make it with the very best, fruity green olive oil I have. I use yellow tomatoes, but of course red would work just fine. WHAT TO SERVE WHEN On a hot summer afternoon, there's no sweeter lunch than a bowl of gazpacho. To make it into a meal, sprinkle cooked crab or lobster meat over the soup.

SERVES 6 TO 8 (MAKES ABOUT 2 QUARTS)

 2 pounds yellow heirloom tomatoes, cored and chopped
 1 yellow bell pepper, roasted, cored, seeded, and diced (see "Peppers," page 54)
 1 banana pepper, cored, seeded, and diced
 2 celery stalks, diced
 1 cucumber, peeled, halved, seeded, and diced
 2 small yellow summer squash, chopped
 1 tart apple (such as Granny Smith or Pippin), peeled, cored, and diced
 1 large sweet yellow onion, such as Vidalia or Walla Walls, diced
 2 garlic cloves, minced
 4 cups chicken or vegetable broth
 2 tablespoons extra-virgin olive oil, plus more for drizzling on the soup
 8 fresh basil leaves, cut into thin strips, plus more for garnish
 2 tablespoons chopped fresh chives
 1 tablespoon chopped fresh mint leaves
 2 teaspoons hot sauce (Tabasco or Texas Pete)
 1 teaspoon sea salt, plus more to taste
 1/2 teaspoon freshly ground black pepper, plus more to taste

Combine the tomatoes, yellow pepper, banana pepper, celery, cucumber, squash, apple, onion, garlic, broth, olive oil, basil, chives, mint, Tabasco, salt, and pepper in a large airtight container and stir to mix. Cover and refrigerate for several hours to allow the flavors to meld. Serve chilled, topped with a drizzle of extra-virgin olive oil and a sprinkling of basil strips.

Wild Mushroom Soup with Sherry and Thyme

We made this soup one year for our Thanksgiving take-out menu at the Market. Our customers loved it so much, we now serve it at the store all through the fall. If you don't mind the extra step, make a quick broth from the mushroom trimmings (I give an easy recipe below) to intensify the mushroom flavor of the soup.

SERVES 8 TO 10 (MAKES ABOUT 2½ QUARTS)

2½ pounds assorted wild mushrooms such as chanterelle, oyster, portobello, cremini, shiitake, or dried porcini
4 tablespoons unsalted butter
4 tablespoons olive oil
1 large yellow onion, diced, trimmings reserved
4 shallots, minced, trimmings reserved
2 celery stalks, diced, trimmings reserved
1 tart apple (such as Granny Smith or Pippin), peeled, cored, and diced
2 garlic cloves, minced
1 cup dry sherry
Leaves from 3 fresh thyme sprigs (about 1 tablespoon)
6 cups **Mushroom Broth** (recipe follows), or chicken or vegetable broth
2 teaspoons sea salt, plus more to taste
1 teaspoon freshly ground black pepper, plus more to taste
2 tablespoons chopped fresh flat-leaf parsley leaves

1. Wipe the mushrooms clean with a damp cloth or paper towel. Cut the tough stems off the mushrooms and coarsely shop. (Reserve the stems to make the Mushroom Broth.) If you are using dried mushrooms, soak them in warm water for 30 minutes, rinse, and roughly chop.

2. Melt 2 tablespoons of the butter and 2 tablespoons of the olive oil together in a large saucepan over medium heat. Add the onion and shallots, reduce the heat to low, and cook about 10 minutes, stirring occasionally, until the onion is soft and translucent. Add the celery and apple and cook about 5 minutes longer. Add the remaining 2 tablespoons butter, 2 tablespoons oil, and the mushrooms to the pan. Increase the heat to high and cook until the mushrooms are golden brown and have reduced in size, 10 to 15 minutes. Add the garlic and cook and stir for 1 minute longer, being careful not to brown the garlic.

3. Stir in the sherry and cook to reduce for about 1 minute. Add the thyme, broth, salt, and pepper and bring it to a low boil. Reduce the heat and simmer the mushrooms for about 30 minutes so the flavors can meld. Cool slightly.

4. Ladle out 2 cups of the soup and place it in the bowl of a food processor or the jar of a blender fitted with a metal blade. Puree until smooth and add the pureed soup back to the pot with the chunky soup or use an immersion blender to puree the soup directly in the pot, making sure to leave it slightly chunky. Stir in the parsley and serve warm.

Mushroom Broth

The discarded stems of mushrooms make a rich, flavorful broth that will enhance the mushroom flavor of Wild Mushroom Soup or the Wild Mushroom and Spinach Risotto (page 202). Place the cleaned mushroom stems in a large saucepan with the vegetable trimmings from the soup, 3 bay leaves, 1 halved large onion, 1 roughly chopped carrot, roughly chopped celery stalk, 1 tablespoon salt, and 1 teaspoon freshly ground black pepper. Cover with 2 to 3 quarts of water and bring to a low boil over high heat. Reduce the heat and simmer for 45 minutes to 1 hour. Strain the broth through a strainer or colander. In an airtight container, this broth will keep, refrigerated, for up to 3 days or in the freezer for up to 3 months.

about . . .
WILD MUSHROOMS

When a recipe calls for wild mushrooms, use whatever variety you like, or what you find at the market. There are so many unusual varieties, each with a distinct flavor. Some varieties, like chanterelle, carry a heavy price tag, but mushrooms are so light and you need only a few to add great flavor to a dish, so they're not as expensive as you might think—and they are always worth it. I urge you to experiment with mushrooms you haven't tasted before. Some to consider are oyster, blue foot, lobster, dried porcini, shiitake, chanterelle, portobello, cremini, pig ear, yellow foot, queen bolete, butter bolete, hedgehog, black trumpet, coral, and wood blewit.

Puree of Watercress Soup

The secret to keeping this soup a beautiful bright green is cooking the watercress and parsley just enough to be tender. You could also make this soup with spinach or sorrel in place of the watercress.

SERVES 4 TO 6 (MAKES ABOUT 1½ QUARTS)

- 2 tablespoons unsalted butter
- 2 tablespoons olive oil
- 1 large sweet yellow onion, such as Vidalia or Walla Walla, chopped
- 1½ pounds russet potatoes (about 2 medium), peeled and chopped
- 4 celery stalks, chopped
- 2 teaspoons sea salt, plus more to taste
- 4 cups chicken or vegetable broth, or more as needed
- 1 cup milk, or more as needed
- 4 cups watercress, washed and trimmed of tough stems
- ¼ cup chopped fresh flat-leaf parsley leaves
- 1 teaspoon freshly ground black pepper, plus more to taste

1. Melt the butter and olive oil in a large saucepan over medium heat. Add the onion, reduce the heat to medium-low, and cook, stirring constantly, until tender and translucent, about 10 minutes. Add the potatoes, celery, and salt and continue to cook and stir for 5 minutes to soften the vegetables. Add the broth and milk and bring to a low boil over medium-high heat. Reduce the heat and simmer for 25 to 30 minutes, until the potatoes are tender.

2. Remove the soup from the heat and stir in the watercress, parsley, and 1 teaspoon pepper and allow the soup to cool slightly.

3. Working in batches if necessary, pour the soup into the bowl of a food processor or the jar of a blender fitted with a metal blade and puree until very smooth. (Or puree the soup directly in the pot with an immersion blender.) Pour the soup back in the pot you cooked it in and warm it over medium heat. Season with additional salt and pepper to taste. If the soup is too thick, thin it with milk or broth while it's warming. Serve warm.

BASICS: Broth and Stock

Broth and stock are both made from vegetables and/or meat cooked in water. The difference between the two is that, traditionally, stock is made with bones that were browned first, giving it a richer flavor. Not many people take the time to make either broth or stock anymore. That's a shame because it is so easy to do, and no matter how simple a broth you make, it tastes much better than anything you'll get out of a can or carton. When I give cooking demonstrations, while I'm prepping vegetables for the dish I'm making, I put the vegetable trimmings—carrot and potato peels, celery leaves, onion ends, herb stems—in a pot of water. I let the vegetables simmer while I'm doing other things, and 30 minutes to an hour later, I give everyone a cupful of the broth to taste. They're always amazed at how much flavor it has after cooking for such a short time, and with almost no effort. We make many types of broth at the Market. We make one with corncobs that we use in corn soup and chowder. In the summer, when we make chilled soups, we make a fruit stock with leftover apple peels, pineapple peels and cores, and peach pits. And we always make chicken and beef broth. At home, I try to keep at least one kind of broth in the refrigerator or freezer. Occasionally, though, I have to resort to canned broth. I buy fat-free and low-sodium varieties or those sold at health food stores in cartons. Standard canned broths tend to contain more salt than I like.

Just stand the pepper upright on a cutting surface, then use a large knife to cut straight down from top to bottom. Do this four times to cut off all four sides of the pepper. You'll be left holding the core with all the seeds still attached so you can toss it away without getting seeds all over your work surface. (I use this method with anything that has a core, such as apples, pears, and pineapples.)

Roasting peppers changes their nature entirely. They go from a crunchy vegetable to a sweet, smoky, tender, almost meaty delight. And since you remove the seeds from roasted peppers, you lose a lot of the peppers' heat. I roast all kinds of peppers, including bell peppers, jalapeño peppers, and poblano peppers. Roasted peppers have so many uses. You can toss them in salads or pasta, serve them with sliced steak or chicken, layer them in sandwiches, or turn them into a delicious condiment, like the Roasted Red Bell Pepper Salsa (page 198). You can roast peppers in the oven or over an open flame.

To roast peppers in the oven: Preheat the oven to 400°F. Rub the peppers with olive oil, place them on a baking sheet with sides, and roast, turning occasionally, until charred on all sides, 30 to 35 minutes. Immediately place the charred peppers in a plastic bag, paper bag, or a bowl covered with plastic wrap to steam for 5 to 10 minutes; this loosens the charred skin from the flesh. Peel the skin off the peppers and discard; try to resist the temptation to hold the peppers under running water—you will wash away some of the smoky flavor. Tear out the core and seeds and discard.

To roast peppers over an open flame: Set the un-oiled peppers directly over a gas flame or on a hot outdoor grill until they char on all sides, 8 to 10 minutes. Turn several times with tongs. Remove the peppers from the flame and proceed as above.

Roasted peppers will keep, refrigerated in an airtight container, for 1 week.

Beef and Bean Chili

My mom taught me to make this chili when I was in junior high school; it's the first thing I remember knowing how to cook.

SERVES 6 TO 8 (MAKES ABOUT 2½ QUARTS)

- 2 tablespoons olive oil
- 2 large yellow onions, diced
- 1 red bell pepper, cored, seeded, and diced
- 4 small jalapeño peppers, cored, seeded, and minced
- 4 garlic cloves, minced
- 1½ pounds ground beef chuck
- ¼ cup chili powder
- 2 teaspoons dried basil
- 1 tablespoon ground cumin
- ¼ cup Worcestershire sauce
- 1 28-ounce can chopped tomatoes
- 2 tablespoons tomato paste
- 6 cups chicken or beef broth
- 1 15-ounce can black beans, rinsed and drained
- 1 15-ounce can kidney beans, rinsed and drained
- 3 bay leaves
- 1 tablespoon sea salt, plus more to taste
- 1 teaspoon freshly ground black pepper, plus more to taste
- 1 teaspoon crushed red pepper flakes

1. Heat the olive oil in a large saucepan over medium heat. Add the onions, reduce the heat to low, and cook, stirring occasionally, until they are softened and light brown, about 15 minutes. Add the bell pepper and jalapeño peppers and cook, stirring occasionally, to soften, about 5 minutes longer. Add the garlic and cook, stirring constantly, for about 1 minute, being careful not to let it brown.

2. Increase the heat to medium-high; add the ground chuck, chili powder, basil, and cumin and cook until the beef is brown all over, 5 to 7 minutes, using a wooden spoon or spatula to break the beef into small pieces as it cooks. Drain off excess fat. Stir in the Worcestershire, tomatoes and their juices, tomato paste, broth, beans, bay leaves, salt, pepper, and crushed red pepper and bring to a low boil. Reduce the heat to low and simmer for 45 minutes to 1 hour so the flavors meld and the liquid reduces and thickens. Serve warm. The chili will keep, refrigerated in an airtight container, for up to 3 days. It also freezes well.

Green Chili with Crispy Corn Tortilla Strips

This is one of my favorite ways to use leftover Thanksgiving turkey; the spicy, south-of-the-border flavor is a welcome change from the season's ubiquitous candied sweet potatoes and cranberry sauce.

SERVES 8 TO 10 (MAKES ABOUT 3 QUARTS)

- 2 pounds fresh tomatillos, husks removed, or 1 28-ounce can tomatillos
- 2 tablespoons olive oil
- 2 large yellow onions, chopped
- 2 celery stalks, diced
- 1 green bell pepper, cored, seeded, and diced
- 2 jalapeño peppers, seeded and minced
- 4 garlic cloves, minced
- 1 tablespoon ground cumin
- 2 teaspoons dried marjoram, basil, or Mexican oregano
- 1 4$\frac{1}{2}$-ounce can chopped green chiles
- 6 cups chicken or vegetable broth
- 4 cups cooked shredded turkey, chicken, or pork
- 2 bay leaves
- 1 15-ounce can chickpeas (garbanzo beans), rinsed and drained
- 1 15-ounce can navy beans or great northern beans, rinsed and drained
- 2 teaspoons sea salt, plus more to taste
- 1 teaspoon freshly ground black pepper, plus more to taste
  Crispy Corn Tortilla Strips (page 59) or Oven-Baked Tortilla Chips (page 59) or good-quality tortilla chips, crumbled
- 2 limes, cut into wedges

1. If you are using fresh tomatillos, preheat the broiler.

2. Spread the tomatillos on a baking sheet with sides and place them under the broiler until they are blistered in several spots. Turn and place under the broiler again until the other side blisters and the tomatillos are squishy to the touch. Let them cool on the baking sheet.

3. Place the roasted or canned tomatillos in a medium bowl and mash with a potato masher or fork.

4. Heat the olive oil in a large saucepan over medium heat. Add the onions, reduce the heat to low, and cook, stirring often, for about 15 minutes or until the onions are soft and light brown. Add the celery, bell pepper, and jalapeño peppers and cook and stir for about 5 minutes more, until the vegetables soften. Add the garlic and cook, stirring constantly, for 1 minute longer, being careful not to let it brown. Stir in the cumin and marjoram and cook the vegetables with the seasonings, stirring constantly, for 2 to 3 minutes.

5. Add the canned green chiles, mashed tomatillos, broth, turkey, bay leaves, chickpeas, navy beans, the 2 teaspoons salt, and 1 teaspoon pepper to the soup pot and stir to combine. Bring to a low boil over medium-high heat. Reduce the heat to low and simmer for about 1 hour, uncovered, stirring occasionally. Taste for seasoning and add more salt or pepper if desired. Serve warm, topped with a small handful of the tortilla strips or chips and with lime wedges alongside to squeeze into the chili. The chili will keep, refrigerated in an airtight container, for up to 3 days. It also freezes well.

Chunky Chicken Vegetable Minestrone

I love having soup for dinner, especially on a winter night. With garlic bread and a glass of red wine, you won't need anything else (except maybe a little something sweet!). I usually use leftover chicken or a store-bought rotisserie chicken to make this soup. If you want to start from scratch, poach a 3^1/$_2$- to 4-pound chicken, reserving the poaching water as the broth for the soup.

SERVES 8 TO 10 (MAKES ABOUT 3 QUARTS)

2 tablespoons olive oil
1 large yellow onion, diced
2 carrots, diced
1 red bell pepper, cored, seeded, and diced
3 plum tomatoes (about ^{3}/$_4$ pound), cored and chopped
1 medium zucchini or yellow squash, diced
4 garlic cloves, minced
8 cups chicken broth
1 15-ounce can chickpeas (garbanzo beans), rinsed and drained
3 cups shredded cooked chicken (1 3^1/$_2$- to 4-pound roasted or poached chicken)
2 teaspoons sea salt, plus more to taste
^{1}/$_2$ teaspoon freshly ground pepper, plus more to taste
^{1}/$_2$ cup small pasta, such as elbow macaroni or bow ties
^{1}/$_2$ pound green beans, trimmed and cut into 2-inch pieces
1 cup chopped green cabbage (about ^{1}/$_4$ medium head)
2 cups fresh spinach, stems removed, washed, and drained (about 3 ounces)
8 basil leaves, cut into thin strips
3 tablespoons chopped fresh oregano or marjoram leaves
^{1}/$_2$ cup grated Parmesan cheese (about 1^1/$_2$ ounces)

1. Heat the olive oil in a large saucepan over medium heat. Add the onion and cook, stirring often, until the onion is translucent and has a little bit of color on it, about 15 minutes. Add the carrots, bell pepper, tomatoes, and zucchini and cook about 5 minutes longer, stirring occasionally, until the vegetables are soft and lightly browned. Add the garlic and cook 1 minute longer, being careful not to brown the garlic.

2. Add the broth, chickpeas, chicken, 2 teaspoons salt, and ^{1}/$_2$ teaspoon pepper and bring to a low boil over medium heat. Reduce the heat to low and simmer, uncovered, for about 1 hour.

3. Add the pasta, green beans, and cabbage; bring the soup back to a low boil over medium heat. Reduce the heat and simmer for 10 to 15 minutes, stirring occasionally, until the pasta is al dente. Stir in the spinach, basil, and oregano. Remove the soup from the heat and season with additional salt and pepper to taste. Serve immediately, topped with freshly grated Parmesan.

Think Outside the Recipe
- USE CANNELLINI, KIDNEY, PINTO, OR LIMA BEANS IN PLACE OF THE GARBANZO BEANS.
- MAKE THE SOUP WITH LEFTOVER COOKED TURKEY INSTEAD OF CHICKEN OR ELIMINATE MEAT ENTIRELY.

Toasted Garlic Bread

Garlic bread is so simple to make and such an indulgence served with soup or alongside any pasta dish, like the Linguine with Clams (page 205).

^{1}/$_4$ cup extra-virgin olive oil
2 garlic cloves
6 slices rustic country or whole-grain bread, cut in half

1. Preheat the oven to 400°F.

2. Combine the olive oil and garlic in a small bowl. Smash the garlic with the back of a wooden spoon to release its juices into the oil.

3. Brush both sides of each slice of bread with the garlic oil and gently rub the garlic clove directly over one side of the bread. Place the bread on a baking sheet and toast until golden brown on both sides, 5 to 7 minutes. Serve warm.

Navy Bean Soup with Rosemary and Smoky Ham Hocks

My mom often requests this soup when she comes to visit. She claims to love it, but always adds so much extra hot sauce I wonder how she can taste it! She usually makes cornbread (see Skillet Cornbread, page 76) to go with it, and that's our dinner.

SERVES 6 TO 8 (MAKES ABOUT 2 QUARTS)

- 3 tablespoons olive oil
- 2 medium yellow onions, diced
- 4 celery stalks, diced
- 4 garlic cloves, chopped
- 1½ cups dried navy or great northern beans, rinsed and picked through; soaked overnight or quick-cooked (see "Quick-Cooking Dried Beans," left)
- 8 cups chicken broth
- 1 smoked ham hock
- 2 bay leaves
- 1 teaspoon sea salt, plus more to taste
- 1 teaspoon freshly ground black pepper, plus more to taste
- 1 teaspoon dried rosemary
- 1 tablespoon chopped fresh rosemary

1. Heat the olive oil in a large soup pot over medium heat. Add the onions, reduce the heat to low, and cook and stir until soft and light brown, about 15 minutes. Add the celery and cook and stir for 8 to 10 minutes longer, until it is soft. Add the garlic and cook, stirring constantly, about 1 minute more, being careful not to let it brown.

2. Add the drained beans, chicken broth, ham hock, bay leaves, 1 teaspoon salt, 1 teaspoon pepper, and dried rosemary to the pot and bring to a boil. Reduce the heat to low and simmer, uncovered, for about 1 hour 30 minutes, until the beans are tender.

3. Remove the bay leaves from the soup and discard. Remove the ham hock and place it on a plate to cool. When the ham hock is cool enough to handle, pull the meat from the bone and return it to the soup. Stir in the fresh rosemary and more salt and pepper to taste. This soup is even better the day after it's made. It will keep, refrigerated in an airtight container, for up to 4 days. It also freezes well.

SOUP TOPPERS

Crispy Corn Tortilla Strips

Tortilla strips like these are traditionally floated in many Mexican soups, like classic tortilla soup. It's a great idea, like a corn crouton. They soften when in the warm soup so they're partly chewy, partly crispy. They're delicious sprinkled on almost any soup, including Chilled Avocado Soup (page 50), Chipotle-Squash Soup (page 40), and Summer White Corn Soup (page 48).

- 4 6-inch corn tortillas
  Olive oil for frying
  Sea salt to taste

Cut the tortillas in half and cut each half into strips about ½ inch wide. Pour in enough olive oil to fill a small skillet ¼ inch deep and heat the oil over medium-high heat until it is sizzling hot. Add the tortilla strips, a few at a time, and fry until crisp and golden brown, 30 to 45 seconds. Use a slotted spoon or spatula to transfer the strips to a paper towel to drain. Sprinkle with sea salt and repeat with the remaining tortillas. Serve while the strips are still warm or cool to room temperature. Let the strips cool to room temperature before placing them in a sealable bag to store. They'll keep for at least a week.

Oven-Baked Tortilla Chips

These make a nice crouton for any soup, or with fresh salsa (page 196).

- 4 6-inch corn tortillas
  Olive oil for brushing the tortillas (about 2 tablespoons)
  Sea salt to taste

1. Preheat the oven to 350°F.

2. Cut the tortillas in half and cut each half into four pie-shaped wedges. Spread the wedges in one layer on a baking sheet with sides, brush lightly with oil, and sprinkle with salt. Bake until crisp and lightly browned, 8 to 10 minutes. Season with additional salt to taste. Serve while the strips are still warm or cool to room temperature. Let the strips cool to room temperature before placing them in a sealable bag to store. They'll keep for at least a week.

Spicy Pita Chips

I like to make these chips with pita bread because they toast up really crisp. Pita is also convenient—easy to slice, and it freezes well so you can always have some on hand. They're wonderful floated atop any soup. I also serve them topped with Egg Salad (page 99), Tuna Salad (page 96), or any of the fresh salsas on pages 196 to 199.

- ¼ cup olive oil
- 2 tablespoons unsalted butter, melted
- 2 tablespoons chopped fresh flat-leaf parsley leaves
- 1 garlic clove, minced
- 1 teaspoon chili powder
- 1 teaspoon crushed red pepper flakes
- 1 teaspoon freshly ground black pepper
- 4 plain or whole-wheat pita breads, each separated into 2 rounds and cut into 8 wedges
- 1 teaspoon sea salt

1. Preheat the oven to 400°F.

2. Combine the oil, butter, parsley, garlic, chili powder, red pepper flakes, and black pepper in a small bowl and stir to mix.

3. Spread the pita wedges in a single layer on a baking sheet with sides. Brush the tops of the pita wedges with the olive oil–melted butter mixture and sprinkle with the salt.

4. Toast the wedges until light golden brown around the edges, 10 to 12 minutes. Serve immediately or cool completely before storing. These will keep in an airtight container for up to 1 week.

Think Outside the Recipe
- YOU CAN USE THIS RECIPE TO MAKE CRISPS OUT OF ALMOST ANY TYPE OF BREAD: SOURDOUGH, ITALIAN COUNTRY BREAD, BAGUETTE SLICES, THINLY SLICED BAGELS, OR SYRIAN FLATBREAD.
- THE BREAD CAN BE COOKED OVER A CHARCOAL FIRE, OR IN A STOVETOP GRILL PAN INSTEAD OF IN THE OVEN.

three

seasonal salads and salad meals

Fresh Mozzarella Salad with Avocado, Roasted Corn, and Grape Tomatoes ○ Jonathan's Grilled Eggplant and Portobello Mushroom Salad with Fresh Mozzarella ○ Fried Green Tomato and Ripe Red Tomato Salad with Goat Cheese and Sweet Basil Vinaigrette ○ Roasted Beet Salad with Oranges, Fennel, and Mint ○ Roasted Acorn Squash Salad with Warm Goat Cheese Rounds ○ Arugula and Endive with Shaved Parmesan ○ Roasted Tomato, Corn, and Potato Salad with Wilted Spinach ○ Corn and Sugar Snap Pea Salad with Blue Cheese Vinaigrette ○ Apple and Avocado Salad with Fresh Mint and Lime ○ Cornbread Panzanella with Avocado ○ White Bean Salad with Tarragon Vinaigrette ○ Black-Eyed Pea Salad with Roasted Butternut Squash and Goat Cheese ○ Chicken Salad with Crunchy Vegetables and Sesame Ginger Vinaigrette ○ Zucchini Slaw Two Ways ○ Spicy Pad Thai Salad ○ Classic California Cobb Salad ○ All-American Chef Salad ○ Italian Chef Salad with Tangy Italian Dressing ○ Grilled Ahi Tuna Niçoise Salad with Black Olive Vinaigrette ○ Tuscan Tuna and White Bean Salad with Sun-Dried Tomatoes ○ Tuna Salad with Apple, Sunflower Seeds, and Avocado ○ Southern-Style Tuna Salad with Pickles and Eggs ○ Tuna Salad with Cilantro and Pickled Jalapeño Peppers ○ Chicken Salad with Apples, Grapes, and Spicy Pecans ○ Egg Salad with Fresh Dill and Green Olives ○ Deviled Eggs on Sliced Heirloom Tomatoes

The recipes in this chapter truly reflect the way we cook and eat today. There are no in-depth preparations involved— just the layering and combining of flavors to make healthy, fresh-tasting dishes.

"Salad" can mean many things. In addition to the green salads that you'd most likely serve as a first course, a salad like Roasted Acorn Squash with Warm Goat Cheese Rounds puts so many distinct flavors and textures on one plate that it's satisfying enough to the palate to be a light meal in itself. And the Roasted Tomato, Corn, and Potato Salad with Wilted Spinach or the Chicken Salad with Apples, Grapes, and Spicy Pecans make a delicious snack to take to the beach or on an airplane.

Throughout this chapter, I give ideas for variations depending on what you have on hand, what you like, and what's in season. I know it's a cliché to say you should cook with the seasons, but it's a cliché because it's true: if the raw ingredients don't taste good, the finished dish won't taste good, either. Nowhere is this truer than in recipes like these, which depend on the juxtaposition of flavors and textures rather than fancy (or indeed any) cooking techniques.

Fresh Mozzarella Salad with Avocado, Roasted Corn, and Grape Tomatoes

I tasted fresh mozzarella for the first time when I moved to New York City in the '80s. Growing up in Tennessee, I'd had only the mozzarella you find in grocery stores; that was considered "gourmet cheese" in our house. As with the first time I tasted fresh herbs, roasted peppers, or asparagus that didn't come from a can, tasting fresh, creamy mozzarella was literally a life-changing experience for me. This was one of many experiences that made me want to become a cook. WHAT TO SERVE WHEN This salad is so summery it goes with just about anything off the grill, like the Tequila Lime Skirt Steak (page 162) or Herb-Marinated Grilled Chicken Breast (page 136). With warm flour tortillas, you can serve them all together like fajitas. (See photo on page 60.)

SERVES 4 TO 6

 4 ears sweet corn, in the husk
 1/2 pound fresh mozzarella, cut into 1/4-inch cubes, or bocconcini
 2 ripe avocados, halved, peeled, and cut into 1/4-inch cubes
 1/2 pint grape or other small tomato varieties, halved
 8 to 10 fresh basil leaves, cut into thin strips
   Sea salt and freshly ground black pepper to taste
 1/2 cup **Summer Herb Vinaigrette** (recipe follows)
   Several handfuls of young arugula or baby greens

1. Preheat the oven to 400°F.

2. Soak the corn in the sink or a bowl filled with cold water for 10 to 15 minutes. Place on a baking sheet with sides and roast for 20 to 25 minutes, until the kernels are tender. Cool to room temperature, then pull off and discard the husks and silks. Cut the kernels off the cob into a large bowl.

3. Add the mozzarella, avocados, tomatoes, basil, salt, and pepper to the bowl with the corn. Drizzle 1/2 cup of the vinaigrette over the salad and toss gently. Be careful not to over-mix or mash the avocado. Season with more salt, pepper, or vinaigrette to taste. Serve on a bed of the arugula or baby greens.

Summer Herb Vinaigrette

MAKES ABOUT 1¼ CUPS

 1/3 cup red wine vinegar
 2 teaspoons Dijon mustard
   Grated zest and juice of 1 lemon
 2 or 3 fresh basil leaves, cut into thin strips
 2 tablespoons chopped fresh oregano leaves
 2 tablespoons chopped fresh flat-leaf parsley leaves
 3/4 cup extra-virgin olive oil
   Sea salt and freshly ground black pepper to taste

Combine the vinegar, mustard, lemon zest and juice, basil, oregano, and parsley in a small bowl and stir to mix. Whisk in the olive oil in a slow, steady stream until all of the oil is incorporated. Season with salt and pepper. Use immediately or store refrigerated in an airtight container for up to 3 days.

about . . .
AVOCADOS

I prefer Hass avocados to other varieties for their rich, buttery flavor. To get as much of the avocado flesh out of the skin as possible, first halve the avocado and remove the pit. Then run your thumb around the rim where the flesh meets the skin. I recently discovered a great new gadget: an avocado slicer. It looks like an egg slicer; it slices and peels the avocado in one quick movement—and it gives you perfect slices.

Jonathan's Grilled Eggplant and Portobello Mushroom Salad with Fresh Mozzarella

My friend Jonathan Waxman, whom I worked for in the 1980s when he had his legendary restaurant JAMS, made this salad at our house in Durham. He has a knack for putting unexpected twists on the obvious. For instance, grilling vegetables was nothing new to me, but I never would have thought to chop them after they were grilled, as he did, and toss them together as they are in this salad. WHAT TO SERVE WHEN This salad is delicious served alongside a T-Bone for Two (page 160) or any grilled fish or chicken.

SERVES 4 TO 6

$1/4$ cup olive oil
  2 tablespoons balsamic vinegar
  1 garlic clove, minced
 15 basil leaves, cut into thin strips
  1 medium eggplant (about $1^1/4$ pounds), sliced into $1/2$-inch-thick rounds
  3 portobello mushrooms (about $3/4$ pound), stems removed and caps wiped clean
    Sea salt and freshly ground black pepper to taste
$1/2$ pound fresh mozzarella cheese, cut into $1/4$-inch cubes

1. Prepare a red-hot fire in a charcoal or gas grill or heat a grill pan over medium-high heat.

2. Stir the olive oil, vinegar, garlic, and half of the basil together in a small bowl.

3. Place the eggplant and mushrooms on a baking sheet with sides and brush both sides lightly with the vinaigrette. Season with salt and pepper.

4. Grill the eggplant for 3 to 4 minutes per side, depending on the heat of the fire or your pan, until it is tender and light golden brown. Remove from the heat and set aside to cool to room temperature.

5. Grill the mushrooms for 2 to 3 minutes per side, until they have shrunk and wilted slightly but are still firm.

6. Chop the eggplant and mushrooms into $1/2$-inch pieces and place them in a large bowl. Add the mozzarella and the remaining basil, season with additional salt and pepper if desired, and toss gently just to mix. Serve at room temperature.

TRICKS OF MY TRADE

○ **Toss salads only once.** Put your ingredients in the bowl you're going to toss them in as you prep them. Just before serving the salad, drizzle it with vinaigrette and give it a gentle toss. If you're adding something that mashes easily, like soft cheese or avocado, add it halfway through the tossing. You may have to add more salt or pepper after you toss the salad, in which case you'd want to toss it again lightly; try to be gentle.

○ **Prep ahead, especially if you're entertaining.** Do what we do at the market—think about what tasks you can do now that wouldn't compromise the flavor or texture of the finished dish: roasting vegetables, cooking dried beans or peas, baking potatoes, making vinaigrette. You can even layer ingredients up to a day in advance in a bowl or a large plastic container. Cover and refrigerate. Let the salad come to room temperature before proceeding with your recipe and serving.

Think Outside the Recipe
USE SMOKED MOZZARELLA OR BOCCONCINI, BITE-SIZE MOZZARELLA BALLS, IN PLACE OF THE FRESH MOZZARELLA CUBES OR OMIT THE MOZZARELLA AND CRUMBLE GOAT CHEESE OVER THE SALAD.

Fried Green Tomato and Ripe Red Tomato Salad with Goat Cheese and Sweet Basil Vinaigrette

I grew up eating fried green tomatoes—and loving them. I created this salad to take advantage of the unique, tart flavor and wonderful cornmeal crunch of fried green tomatoes but lightened it up with juicy, ripe tomatoes. It looks especially pretty when you use different colors and shapes of heirloom tomatoes. WHAT TO SERVE WHEN I always serve this with summertime picnicky foods, like Fall-off-the-Bone Baby Back Ribs (page 211) or a steak grilled outdoors.

SERVES 6 TO 8

  2 large ripe beefsteak or heirloom tomatoes (about 1 pound), cored and sliced ½ inch thick
  1 teaspoon sea salt, plus more to taste
 ½ teaspoon freshly ground black pepper, plus more to taste
 ½ cup all-purpose flour
 ½ cup yellow cornmeal
  2 tablespoons sugar
  1 large egg
 ½ cup well-shaken buttermilk
     Canola oil for frying (about ½ cup)
  4 large green tomatoes, cored and sliced ½ inch thick
 ½ pint grape or small heirloom tomatoes (such as Sungolds or Sweet 100's), halved lengthwise
  4 ounces goat cheese, crumbled (about 1 cup)
     Sweet Basil Vinaigrette (recipe follows)
  8 fresh basil leaves, cut into thin strips

1. Preheat the oven to 200°F. Line a baking sheet with paper towels.

2. Arrange the ripe tomato slices in one layer on a large platter or on individual plates. Season with salt and pepper to taste.

3. Stir the flour, cornmeal, sugar, 1 teaspoon salt, and ½ teaspoon pepper in a small bowl.

4. Whisk the egg and buttermilk together in a separate small bowl.

5. Pour enough oil in a large skillet to fill to ¼ inch deep and heat over medium-high heat to about 375°F, or until the oil sizzles when you drop a small amount of flour into the skillet.

6. Dip a green tomato slice in the egg-buttermilk mixture to coat both sides, dredge it in the flour mixture to coat both sides, and place it in the hot oil. Repeat with enough tomato slices to fill the skillet without crowding and fry until the under sides are golden brown, about 2 minutes. Turn and fry the other side to golden brown. Use tongs or a slotted spatula to transfer the fried tomato slices to the prepared baking sheet to drain; place the sheet in the oven while you fry the remaining green tomatoes.

7. Arrange the fried tomato slices on top of the fresh tomato slices. Scatter the small tomatoes over the slices and sprinkle with the crumbled goat cheese. Drizzle with ½ cup of the vinaigrette and top with the basil strips. Season with additional salt and pepper and add more vinaigrette to taste. Serve immediately.

Note: *It's best if you let the green tomatoes get nice and crispy before you turn them and that you turn them only once. If you flip them any more, the coating will fall off.*

Sweet Basil Vinaigrette

MAKES ABOUT 1 CUP

 ½ cup balsamic vinegar
     Juice of 1 lime
  5 to 7 fresh basil leaves, cut into thin strips
     Sea salt and freshly ground black pepper to taste
 ½ cup extra-virgin olive oil

Whisk the vinegar, lime juice, basil, salt, and pepper together in a small bowl. Slowly add the olive oil, whisking until all the oil is incorporated. Season with additional salt and pepper to taste. Use immediately or refrigerate in an airtight container for up to 1 week.

Roasted Beet Salad with Oranges, Fennel, and Mint

I like to use citrus in salads in the wintertime because it's a refreshing contrast during a season of richer, heavier foods. This salad is layered rather than tossed so the beets won't stain the other ingredients. WHAT TO SERVE WHEN Serve this as a first course to hearty main dishes, like Red Wine–Braised Chicken (page 226) or Port-Braised Lamb Shanks with Rosemary (page 223). If you buy beets with their leafy greens attached, the greens are delicious prepared as the collard greens (see page 112).

SERVES 6 TO 8

6 medium beets (red, golden, or any other variety, or a combination), trimmed of greens and washed well
Juice of 1 orange
¼ cup olive oil
2 tablespoons balsamic vinegar
2 tablespoons maple syrup
Sea salt and freshly ground black pepper to taste
3 navel oranges, peeled and sliced into ½-inch rounds
1 large fennel bulb, halved, cored, and sliced into thin slivers
1 small red onion, sliced into very thin rounds
3 ounces crumbled goat cheese (about ¾ cup)
2 tablespoons chopped fresh chives
2 tablespoons chopped fresh mint leaves

1. Preheat the oven to 400°F.

2. Place the beets on a baking sheet with sides or in a large, glass baking dish. If you're using a combination of red and golden beets, separate them to prevent the red from bleeding onto the golden. Pour the orange juice, olive oil, vinegar, maple syrup, and ¼ cup of water over the beets and season with salt and pepper. Cover the baking sheet tightly with foil and roast the beets until they're tender when pierced with a knife, 40 to 45 minutes. Uncover and let the beets cool to room temperature. Reserve the cooking liquid.

3. Peel the beets and slice them into ¼-inch rounds. Arrange the beets, oranges, fennel, and onion on a platter or on individual plates, placing contrasting colors and textures next to one another.

4. Pour the reserved beet liquid over the vegetables, season with salt and pepper, and top with the crumbled goat cheese, chives, and mint. This is best served just after it's dressed.

Think Outside the Recipe
- ANY PUNGENT CHEESE, SUCH AS A GOOD STILTON OR BLUE, IS DELICIOUS IN PLACE OF THE GOAT CHEESE.
- IN THE WINTER, I OFTEN ROAST THE FENNEL AND THE ONIONS AS WELL AS THE BEETS AND SERVE THE SALAD WHILE THE VEGETABLES ARE STILL WARM.

about . . .
BEETS

We typically think of beets as being deep "beet red" in color, but in fact there are many different varieties, including golden, white, and Chioggia beets, which are pink-and-white striped. You can use different varieties interchangeably. Beets also range in size. At farmers markets you often find beets as small as golf balls. I like to roast these and toss them whole in a salad. I also like golden beets both for their mellow beet flavor and their beautiful color. They don't stain the way red beets do, so they're a good choice when you're tossing them with other ingredients. I usually roast rather than boil beets because I think it brings out their earthy flavor. No matter how you cook them, you have to peel beets after they're cooked. There's no other way to do this than with your hands. The peel slips off very easily, but it's still a messy job, so it's best to peel them directly over the sink. Try to resist the temptation to rinse the beets under running water. You'll rinse away all of the wonderful flavor you just cooked into them.

> **An easy way to slice goat cheese into neat rounds is with dental floss or a piece of thin wire.**

Roasted Acorn Squash Salad with Warm Goat Cheese Rounds

When I'm making a late dinner for just my husband, Peter, and I, we often want something light, like a salad. But it has to be substantial for Peter to consider it dinner, and in the cooler months, this salad is just the thing. It's best served when the squash is still warm and the goat cheese is just pulled from the oven. WHAT TO SERVE WHEN I like this with any warm, comforting main dishes, like the Braised Tarragon Chicken (page 224) or the Herb-Roasted Rack of Lamb (page 220).

SERVES 4 TO 6

  1 acorn squash (about 2 pounds), halved and seeded
  2 tablespoons olive oil
  2 tablespoons balsamic vinegar
  1 tablespoon fresh rosemary
¼ teaspoon sea salt, plus more to taste
¼ teaspoon freshly ground black pepper, plus more to taste
¼ cup fresh bread crumbs (see "Making Bread Crumbs," page 153)
  Leaves from 3 or 4 fresh thyme sprigs (about 1 tablespoon)
  6 ounces goat cheese, sliced into ⅓-inch rounds
  4 cups baby spinach and arugula leaves or any combination of baby greens, washed and drained
  Balsamic Vinaigrette (recipe follows)

1. Preheat the oven to 400°F.

2. Remove the stem and tip ends of the squash and cut the squash crosswise into ½-inch half-moon slices. Place the squash slices on a large baking sheet with sides. Drizzle with the olive oil, vinegar, rosemary, and salt and pepper to taste and toss to coat. Spread the squash in a single layer and roast for 35 to 40 minutes, turning once halfway through the cooking time, until it is tender and golden brown around the edges. Remove from the oven.

3. Reduce the oven temperature to 350°F.

4. While the squash is cooking, combine the bread crumbs, thyme, ¼ teaspoon salt, and ¼ teaspoon pepper in a small bowl. Roll the goat cheese rounds in the bread crumbs, pressing both sides gently into the crumbs to coat the cheese well. Transfer the breaded cheese rounds to a baking sheet, cover, and chill.

5. Just before serving, place the baking sheet in the oven for 4 to 5 minutes, until the cheese is just warm but doesn't lose its shape.

6. Place the greens in a bowl, drizzle with ½ cup of the Balsamic Vinaigrette, and toss. Taste for seasoning and add more salt, pepper, or vinaigrette if desired. Mound the dressed greens on a serving platter or divide them among individual plates. Arrange the squash slices and the warm goat cheese over the greens and serve immediately.

Balsamic Vinaigrette

MAKES ABOUT 1 CUP

  4 garlic cloves
½ teaspoon sea salt, plus more to taste
  1 tablespoon Dijon mustard
¼ cup balsamic vinegar
  2 tablespoons red wine vinegar
½ cup extra-virgin olive oil
  Freshly ground black pepper to taste

Mash the garlic and salt together with a mortar and pestle (or the flat side of a chef's knife on a cutting board) to form a paste. Scrape the paste into a small bowl and stir in the mustard and vinegars. Add the olive oil in a slow, steady stream, whisking until all is incorporated. Season with the black pepper and more salt to taste. This will keep refrigerated in an airtight container for up to 1 week.

Arugula and Endive
with Shaved Parmesan

I first had this salad in a little cafe in Tuscany. I remember being struck by how something so simple could be so beautiful and so delicious. The reason it works has everything to do with the quality of each ingredient. Use the best olive oil you have for this, crack the pepper from the pepper mill directly over the salad, and use good-quality real Parmesan cheese, the kind with the stamp on the rind that you get from a good cheese counter or Italian specialty store.

SERVES 4 TO 6

2 heads Belgium endive, washed and drained
1 bunch arugula, stems removed, washed, and drained (about 3 cups leaves; see "Washing Leafy Greens," page 75)
3 ounces Parmesan cheese, shaved
1/4 cup extra-virgin olive oil
2 tablespoons white wine vinegar
Sea salt and freshly ground black pepper, to taste

1. Halve the endive lengthwise and cut out the core. Cut each half of the endive on the extreme diagonal into one-inch pieces and place in a large bowl. Add the arugula and toss gently. Place the greens on individual serving plates or a large platter. Scatter the shaved Parmesan over the endive and arugula.

2. Whisk the olive oil and vinegar together and drizzle over the salad. Season with salt and pepper.

" *Use a large sharp knife or a vegetable peeler to shave Parmesan.* **"**

Roasted Tomato, Corn, and Potato
Salad with Wilted Spinach

This salad hits just the right note between a warm vegetable dish and a refreshing summer salad. WHAT TO SERVE WHEN This makes a wonderful first course or side to Rosemary-Mint Lamb Chops (page 166), Herb-Marinated Grilled Chicken Breast (page 136), or T-Bone for Two (page 160).

SERVES 6 TO 8

4 ears sweet corn, in the husk
1 1/2 pounds plum tomatoes (6 to 7), cored and quartered
1 pound small red or white potatoes (4 to 6), halved
1/2 red onion, thinly sliced
1/4 cup olive oil
3 tablespoons balsamic vinegar
Sea salt and freshly ground black pepper to taste
6 ounces spinach washed, stems removed, and drained (about 4 cups leaves)
10 fresh basil leaves, cut into thin strips

1. Preheat the oven to 450°F.

2. Soak the unshucked corn in the sink or a big bowl full of cold water for 10 to 15 minutes.

3. Place the tomatoes, potatoes, and onion slices on a baking sheet with sides. Drizzle with the olive oil and vinegar, sprinkle with the salt and pepper, and toss to coat. Spread the vegetables in a single layer on the baking sheet and roast for about 40 minutes, stirring occasionally for even browning, until the potatoes are golden brown and soft to the squeeze or tender when pierced with a knife. Remove from the oven.

4. Reduce the oven temperature to 400°F.

5. Remove the corn from the soaking water, place it on a baking sheet with sides, and roast for 20 to 25 minutes, until the kernels are tender but still crisp to the touch. Cool slightly.

6. When the corn is cool enough to handle, pull off and discard the silks and husks. Cut the kernels off the cob straight into a large bowl. Add the spinach and scrape the roasted tomatoes, potatoes, and onion, including any remaining cooking liquid, onto the spinach. Cover the bowl tightly with foil and let the vegetables rest, covered, for 5 to 8 minutes, to wilt the spinach. Taste the salad for seasoning and add more salt or pepper to taste. Add the basil and toss gently just before serving.

Corn and Sugar Snap Pea Salad with Blue Cheese Vinaigrette

Anything we make with blue cheese flies out the door at Foster's Market. WHAT TO SERVE WHEN I like this salad best with something very simple, like Grilled Salmon with your favorite fresh salsa (page 196) or Katie's Spicy Grilled Shrimp (page 177).

SERVES 4 TO 6

2 ears sweet corn, in the husk
1 pound sugar snap peas, stem ends and strings removed and blanched (see "Blanching Vegetables," page 91)
4 cups watercress, washed and trimmed of tough stems
1/2 cup crumbled blue cheese (about 2 ounces)
2 tablespoons chopped fresh chives, plus more for garnish
Sea salt and freshly ground black pepper to taste
Blue Cheese Vinaigrette (recipe follows)

1. Preheat the oven to 400°F.

2. Soak the corn in the sink or a big bowl full of cold water for 10 to 15 minutes. Place on a baking sheet with sides and roast for 20 to 25 minutes, until the kernels are tender. Cool to room temperature.

3. Remove the husks and silks from the corn and cut off the kernels directly into a large bowl. Add the sugar snap peas, watercress, 1/4 cup of the blue cheese, 2 tablespoons chives, salt, and pepper. Drizzle with 1/2 cup of the vinaigrette and toss gently. Taste for seasoning and add more salt, pepper, or vinaigrette to taste. Transfer the salad to a platter or individual plates. Garnish with the remaining blue cheese and the chives and serve immediately.

Think Outside the Recipe

- DEPENDING ON YOUR TASTES, SUBSTITUTE SPINACH, ARUGULA, OR MIXED BABY GREENS FOR THE WATERCRESS.
- WHEN CORN IS OUT OF SEASON, USE THINLY SLICED CUCUMBERS OR AVOCADOS.

Blue Cheese Vinaigrette

MAKES ABOUT 1 1/2 CUPS

1/3 cup red wine vinegar
Juice of 1 lemon
2 tablespoons chopped fresh chives
1/4 cup extra-virgin olive oil
1/4 cup canola or safflower oil
1/2 cup crumbled blue cheese (about 2 ounces)
Sea salt and freshly ground black pepper to taste

Whisk the vinegar, lemon juice, and chives together in a small bowl. Slowly add the olive oil and canola or safflower oil, one at a time in a slow, thin stream, whisking constantly until all the oils are incorporated. Stir in the crumbled blue cheese and season with salt and pepper. Use immediately or refrigerate in an airtight container for up to 1 week.

BASICS: *Making Vinaigrettes*

If you're not used to making your own vinaigrettes, the idea can be a bit daunting. But basically, it's just a base of oil, vinegar (or lemon juice) with mustard, herbs, or spices added. You can make a very simple vinaigrette with good extra-virgin olive oil and aged sherry vinegars, or you could get more complicated, adding minced shallots or garlic, fresh herbs, or mustard. I give specific recipes for the salads in this book, but I urge you to think of them as guidelines and feel free to experiment with what you have on hand. Toasted sesame seed adds an Asian flavor to any vinaigrette. Grapeseed oil is a very mild-flavored oil that makes a great base for vinaigrettes. Experiment with nut oils, such as walnut oil, and oils infused with lemon, chili peppers, or roasted garlic. To make vinaigrettes, I usually start by mixing all the ingredients except the oil. Then I add the oil slowly, whisking constantly as I add it. This method emulsifies the vinaigrettes, which means the oil and vinegar are integrated rather than separated or just shake or stir the dressing well before using.

Apple and Avocado Salad with Fresh Mint and Lime

The first time I made this, it was out of desperation. I wanted to make a salad for dinner, but I had no lettuce in the refrigerator. Peter loves salads with apples or pears; I had fresh mint In the garden and an avocado in the fruit bowl. Voilá! I liked it even better when I made it again with crunchy watercress tossed in. Make the salad just before serving so the apple and avocado don't brown.

SERVES 4

Grated zest and juice of 1 lime
1 tablespoon white wine vinegar
¼ cup extra-virgin olive oil
1 tablespoon chopped fresh mint leaves
1 tart apple (such as Granny Smith or Pippin), peeled, cored, and sliced ¼ inch thick
1 avocado, peeled, pitted, and sliced ½ inch thick
1 cucumber, peeled, halved, seeded, and sliced ¼ inch thick
4 cups watercress, washed and trimmed of tough stems
Sea salt and freshly ground black pepper to taste
3 ounces feta, thinly sliced

1. Stir the lime zest and juice and vinegar together in a small bowl. Slowly whisk in the olive oil until all is incorporated. Stir in the mint.

2. In a separate, medium bowl, combine the apple, avocado, cucumber, and watercress. Drizzle with the vinaigrette, season with salt and pepper, and toss gently. Arrange the salad on a platter or individual plates, top with the feta slices, and serve immediately.

Think Outside the Recipe
USE CRUMBLED GOAT OR BLUE CHEESE IN PLACE OF THE FETA, OR ARUGULA OR CHOPPED ROMAINE IN PLACE OF THE WATERCRESS.

BASICS: *Seeding Cucumbers*

Seeding a cucumber isn't a must, and not necessary if you're using tender, young cucumbers or long hothouse cucumbers, which are seedless. The seeds of basic supermarket varieties tend to be big and flavorless, so I like to remove them. To seed a cucumber, cut it in half from end to end and use a spoon to scrape the seeds out, leaving a rounded hollow down the middle, like a canoe.

BASICS: *Washing Leafy Greens*

It's important to wash leafy greens well—there's nothing worse than biting down on a grain of sand. If you're working with greens that come in a bunch, like spinach, cut off all the stems in one chop while the greens are still bunched together. Fill a sink or a big bowl with water. Place the greens in the water and gently press them under the water without stirring; you want to allow the sand to fall to the bottom. Then as it's soaking, go through and pinch off any remaining large stems, especially when using greens that have tough stems, like with spinach or watercress. Let the greens soak for at least 5 or 10 minutes so the sand has a chance to sink, and then lift the greens out and into a colander. Don't just pour the greens into a colander or you'll pour the sand right back over them.

Cornbread Panzanella with Avocado

Panzanella is an Italian "bread salad" that is traditionally made with cubes of day-old rustic-style bread. At Foster's Market we use this concept as a starting point, but we make panzanella different every time. This version, using cornbread as a base, is one of the most unusual—and one of the most popular. I like it served while the cornbread croutons are still warm. WHAT TO SERVE WHEN I like this panzanella with something smoky, like Chipotle Maple Barbecue Beef Brisket (page 216).

SERVES 4 TO 6

4 cups cornbread in $1/2$-inch cubes (**Skillet Cornbread**—recipe follows—or store-bought), preferably day-old
$1/2$ cup extra-virgin olive oil
Sea salt and freshly ground black pepper to taste
2 beefsteak or large heirloom tomatoes (about 1 pound)
$1/2$ small red onion, thinly sliced
$1/4$ cup red wine vinegar
6 to 8 fresh basil leaves, cut into thin strips, plus more for garnish, or 2 tablespoons chopped fresh cilantro or flat-leaf parsley leaves
1 avocado, halved, pit removed, and cut into $1/2$-inch cubes

1. Preheat the oven to 450°F.

2. Place the cornbread cubes in a large mixing bowl and toss with 3 tablespoons of the olive oil and the salt and pepper. Spread the cornbread in a single even layer on a baking sheet and bake until toasted and golden, about 15 minutes. Let the cornbread cool slightly.

3. Return the cornbread to the bowl you tossed it in. Add the tomatoes, onion, and salt and pepper. Whisk the remaining olive oil with the vinegar and drizzle over the salad. Add the basil and the avocado cubes and toss gently, taking care not to mash the avocado. Transfer the panzanella to a serving platter or individual plates, top with the additional basil, and serve immediately.

Skillet Cornbread

This cornbread is delicious warm, with sweet butter. To use it for panzanella, allow the bread to cool completely before cutting it into cubes. You can also make the cornbread a day in advance or use leftover, letting it dry out a bit before turning it into panzanella.

MAKES ONE 10- OR 12-INCH ROUND

2 tablespoons olive oil or bacon grease
$1/2$ cups yellow cornmeal
$1/2$ cup all-purpose flour
3 tablespoons sugar
2 teaspoons baking powder
$1/2$ teaspoon baking soda
2 teaspoons salt
2 cups well-shaken buttermilk
2 large eggs, lightly beaten
2 tablespoons unsalted butter, melted and cooled to room temperature

1. Preheat the oven to 425°F.

2. Pour the olive oil or bacon grease into a 10- or 12-inch cast-iron (or other ovenproof) skillet. Tilt to coat the bottom and sides of the skillet with the oil or grease and place in the preheated oven.

3. Stir the cornmeal, flour, sugar, baking powder, baking soda, and salt together in a large mixing bowl. Add the buttermilk, eggs, and melted butter and stir just until the dry ingredients are no longer visible; don't over-mix.

4. Remove the hot skillet from the oven. Pour the batter into the skillet, return it to the oven, and bake for 20 to 25 minutes, until the cornbread is golden brown and a toothpick inserted into the center comes out clean. Let the cornbread rest for 5 to 10 minutes before cutting it.

Think Outside the Recipe
- USE ROASTED OR HERB GRILLED TOMATOES (PAGE 120) IN PLACE OF HEIRLOOM TOMATOES WHEN TOMATOES AREN'T IN SEASON.
- ADD FRESH OR SMOKED MOZZARELLA OR CRUMBLED GOAT CHEESE.

White Bean Salad with Tarragon Vinaigrette

I always have cans of beans in my pantry to make quick side dishes like this salad. I like it after the beans have marinated in the vinaigrette for a few hours. WHAT TO SERVE WHEN In the summer, this salad makes the perfect side for any lamb, chicken, or beef cooked on the outdoor grill.

SERVES 4 TO 6

- 1 large yellow onion, thinly sliced
- 2 tablespoons olive oil
- 2 15½-ounce cans navy or great northern beans, rinsed and drained, or 1¾ cups dried beans, cooked until tender (see "Quick-Cooking Dried Beans," page 58)
- ½ cup canned artichoke hearts packed in water, chopped
- ⅓ cup pitted kalamata olives, thinly sliced
- 8 pepperoncini (Italian peppers in vinegar), sliced into thin rounds
- ¼ cup chopped fresh flat-leaf parsley leaves
- Tarragon Vinaigrette (recipe follows)
- Sea salt and freshly ground black pepper to taste

1. Preheat the oven to 400°F.

2. Toss the onion and olive oil on a baking sheet with sides and roast until the onion is soft and light golden, 15 to 20 minutes. Allow to cool slightly.

3. Place the drained beans in a large bowl. Scrape the onion into the bowl with the beans; add the artichoke hearts, olives, pepperoncini, parsley, and ½ cup of the vinaigrette and toss. Season with salt and pepper and add more vinaigrette to taste.

about . . .
OLIVE OIL

I recommend you have at least two bottles of olive oil in your pantry: one bottle of really good extra-virgin olive oil and a big bottle of everyday, less expensive olive oil—it doesn't even have to be extra-virgin. It's a waste to heat a really good, green extra-virgin olive oil. One of the things that makes extra-virgin olive oil special is that it's cold-pressed, a process of extracting the oil from the olive without using heat. By heating it, you counter that process and in so doing, take the delicious green, fruity flavor out of the oil. So save the more expensive extra-virgin oil for salads. Use your special olive oils flavored with lemon, red pepper, or garlic as "finishing oils," for drizzling on salads or cooked chicken or fish.

Tarragon Vinaigrette

MAKES ABOUT 1 CUP

- ⅓ cup white wine vinegar
- Grated zest and juice of 1 lemon
- 2 garlic cloves, minced
- 2 tablespoons chopped fresh tarragon or 2 teaspoons dried (see Note)
- 2 tablespoons chopped fresh flat-leaf parsley leaves
- 1 teaspoon paprika
- ½ cup olive oil
- Sea salt and freshly ground black pepper to taste

Stir the vinegar, lemon zest and juice, garlic, tarragon, parsley, and paprika together in a small bowl. Add the oil in a slow, steady stream, whisking constantly until all is incorporated. Season with salt and pepper. Use immediately or refrigerate in an airtight container for up to 1 week.

Note: *Reconstituting dried tarragon seems to revive its flavor, so if dried tarragon is all you have, bring it to a boil in 2 tablespoons of the vinegar used in the dressing before adding it to the dressing.*

about . . .
PEPPER GRINDERS

A good pepper grinder is essential to any kitchen. I urge you to invest in a quality one; there are so many pepper grinders out there that just don't do the one job they're made for. For years I bought pepper grinders based on looks or the reputation of the brand name—and I was so often disappointed in the way they worked. I recommend you choose a pepper grinder the way I now choose all my cooking tools and equipment: go to an upscale kitchenware store and ask someone who works there to recommend one. The salesperson always knows what works.

Black-Eyed Pea Salad with Roasted Butternut Squash and Goat Cheese

We chop the squash into cubes to get crisp, caramelized edges after it's roasted. I like it best while the squash is still warm. It's delicious with diced ham added. WHAT TO SERVE WHEN With the Sweet and Spicy Vinaigrette and the tangy goat cheese crumbled over it, this salad has so many flavors, I think it's best with something as simple as a grilled chicken breast.

SERVES 6 TO 8

 1 medium butternut squash, peeled, seeded, and cut into 1-inch cubes
 3 tablespoons olive oil
   Sea salt and freshly ground black pepper to taste
 2 cups (about 12 ounces) fresh or frozen black-eyed peas
 1 red bell pepper, cored, seeded, and diced
 1 jalapeño pepper, cored, seeded, and diced
 2 tablespoons chopped fresh marjoram leaves
 2 tablespoons chopped fresh flat-leaf parsley leaves
   Sweet and Spicy Vinaigrette (recipe follows)
 2 ounces goat cheese, crumbled (about ½ cup)

1. Preheat the oven to 400°F.

2. Scatter the cubes of butternut squash in one layer on a baking sheet with sides. Drizzle the squash with the olive oil, season with salt and pepper, and toss to coat. Roast for 30 to 35 minutes, until the squash is brown around the edges and tender when pierced with a fork, stirring the squash pieces periodically so the cubes brown evenly.

3. Meanwhile, place the fresh or frozen black-eyed peas in a medium saucepan with enough water to cover by 3 inches. Salt the water and bring to a boil over high heat. Reduce the heat and simmer, stirring occasionally, for about 20 minutes, until the peas are tender but still firm. Drain in a colander, rinse under cool water, and drain thoroughly.

4. Gently scrape the warm squash into a large mixing bowl. Add the peas, bell pepper, jalapeño pepper, marjoram, parsley, salt, pepper, and ½ cup of the vinaigrette and toss gently. Season with additional salt, pepper, or vinaigrette to taste. Transfer the salad to a serving platter and sprinkle with the crumbled goat cheese.

about . . .
BLACK-EYED PEAS

Black-eyed peas are a very Southern thing. In the summertime, grocery stores carry fresh black-eyed peas, which, of course, is the best way to have them. In other parts of the country, you might be able to find fresh black-eyed peas only at farmers markets or specialty food stores, if you find them at all. Fortunately, black-eyed peas are one of those rare vegetables that are almost as good frozen as fresh. They have a starchy texture and an earthy flavor that make them perfect for dressing with a vinaigrette or in succotash with fresh corn and green beans.

Sweet and Spicy Vinaigrette

MAKES ABOUT 1 CUP

 ⅓ cup apple cider vinegar
 2 tablespoons honey
   Grated zest and juice of 1 lemon
 1 teaspoon crushed red pepper flakes
   Sea salt and freshly ground black pepper to taste
 ¼ cup extra-virgin olive oil
 ¼ cup canola or safflower oil

Stir the vinegar, honey, lemon zest and juice, red pepper flakes, salt, and pepper together in a medium bowl. Add the oils in a slow, steady stream, whisking constantly until all is incorporated. Use immediately or refrigerate in an airtight container for up to 1 week.

> **BASICS:** *Peeling Butternut Squash*
>
> For years I struggled to cut the peel off of butternut squash with a knife. That is, until one of the cooks at Foster's Market showed me that I could do the job with a vegetable peeler. It seems so obvious now, but I'd just never thought of it. I peel butternut squash only when I want to slice the squash or cut it into cubes for a salad. If I'm going to puree or mash it, I just bake the halved squash, cut side down, in the skin. When it's tender, I scoop the cooked, soft squash out of the skin. I often use butternut squash and sweet potatoes in recipes interchangeably.

Chicken Salad with Crunchy Vegetables and Sesame Ginger Vinaigrette

I'm always looking for new ways to satisfy my customers' insatiable appetites for chicken salad. This one can be made several hours in advance, so it's the perfect thing to take to the office for lunch or on a picnic. If you like to eat lots of vegetables, toss in a handful of shredded savoy or napa cabbage, snow peas, or julienned carrots for more crunch.

SERVES 4 TO 6

4 cups shredded cooked chicken (1 3½- to 4-pound roasted chicken, or Herb-Marinated Grilled Chicken Breast, page 136)
2 ribs bok choy or celery stalks, sliced on the diagonal into ¼-inch pieces
1 red bell pepper, cored, seeded, and diced
¼ cup chopped fresh cilantro leaves
2 scallions, minced (white and green parts)
Sesame Ginger Vinaigrette (recipe follows)
2 cups watercress, washed and trimmed of tough stems
Sea salt and freshly ground black pepper to taste

Combine the chicken, bok choy or celery, red pepper, cilantro, scallions, and ½ cup of the vinaigrette in a large bowl and toss to mix. Add the watercress and more vinaigrette to taste. Season with salt and pepper and toss again gently. Divide the salad evenly among individual plates or place on a large platter and serve immediately.

Note: *If you make this salad to serve later, add the watercress and toss with the dressing just before serving.*

Sesame Ginger Vinaigrette

MAKES ABOUT 1 CUP

Grated zest and juice of 1 orange
2 tablespoons light soy sauce or tamari
2 tablespoons rice wine vinegar
1 tablespoon honey
2 tablespoons grated fresh ginger (about 1 2-inch piece)
2 scallions, minced (white and green parts)
2 garlic cloves, minced
2 tablespoons toasted sesame oil
½ cup canola or safflower oil
Sea salt and freshly ground black pepper to taste
2 tablespoons toasted sesame seeds

Stir the orange zest and juice, soy sauce, vinegar, honey, ginger, scallions, and garlic together in a small bowl. Slowly whisk in the sesame and canola oils until they are incorporated. Season with salt and pepper. Stir in the sesame seeds just before serving. Refrigerate in an airtight container until ready to serve for up to 1 week.

BASICS: *Toasting Nuts and Seeds*

Toasting really brings out the flavor of nuts and seeds. I generally toast them on the stovetop rather than in the oven so they're right in front of me and I'm less likely to forget—and burn!—them. To toast nuts and seeds, place them in a dry skillet over medium-high heat. Shake the pan constantly to keep them from burning, and toast until they become fragrant and get a little color on them. Remove the pan from the heat, season with sea salt, and continue to shake the pan for about 1 minute. Transfer the nuts or seeds to a small dish until you're ready to use them; otherwise they will continue to cook in the hot pan.

Zucchini Slaw Two Ways

Anyone who's ever planted a summer vegetable garden has faced the problem of too much zucchini; it just grows like crazy. This slaw is a great way to use up extra squash in an unusual way: raw. I give two different dressings here because I find that some people like a vinegar-based dressing and others like mayonnaise. WHAT TO SERVE WHEN With either dressing, this slaw is perfect picnic food. It goes great with Peter's All-World Burgers (page 155). With the Sweet and Tart Slaw Dressing, it makes a delicious relish on a hotdog or sausage sandwich.

SERVES 4 TO 6

2 medium zucchini, ends removed and cut into 2-inch julienne

2 yellow summer squash, ends removed and cut into 2-inch julienne

2 carrots, cut into 2-inch julienne

4 scallions, julienned (white and green parts)

1 red bell pepper, cored, seeded, and julienned (optional)

¼ cup chopped fresh flat-leaf parsley leaves

Creamy Slaw Dressing or **Sweet and Tart Slaw Dressing** (recipes follow)

Sea salt and freshly ground black pepper to taste

Combine the zucchini, yellow squash, carrots, scallions, bell pepper if using, and parsley in a large bowl as you cut them. Drizzle the vegetables with the dressing, season with salt and pepper, and toss. Season with additional salt and pepper to taste. Serve immediately or refrigerate in an airtight container. With the Creamy Slaw Dressing, this slaw holds up nicely for up to 3 days. With the Sweet and Tart Slaw Dressing, the slaw should be served shortly after it's tossed with the dressing.

Note: *When we make slaw at the market, we put the scallions in a bowl of water and then in the refrigerator. In only about 15 minutes, the scallions curl up and bring a different shape and texture to the dish. You can also use this trick on scallions for garnishing soups or to top an open-face sandwich.*

Creamy Slaw Dressing

MAKES ABOUT ¾ CUP

½ cup mayonnaise

2 tablespoons Dijon mustard

2 tablespoons white wine vinegar

1 teaspoon sea salt

1 teaspoon freshly ground black pepper

Whisk the mayonnaise, mustard, vinegar, salt, and pepper together in a small bowl. Use immediately or refrigerate in an airtight container for up to 1 week.

Sweet and Tart Slaw Dressing

This dressing is also nice with the addition of poppy seeds.

MAKES ABOUT 1 CUP

½ cup white vinegar

½ cup sugar

2 teaspoons sea salt

1 teaspoon freshly ground black pepper

Combine the vinegar, sugar, salt, and pepper in a jar. Put the lid on tightly and shake the jar until the sugar dissolves. Use immediately or refrigerate in an airtight container for up to 1 week.

❝ *I'm not one for fancy tools and gadgets, unless they really make a job easier. A julienne peeler, which looks like a vegetable peeler but has a toothed blade like a mandoline, makes this slaw a breeze.* **❞**

Spicy Pad Thai Salad

No matter how many dishes I try, pad thai is my absolute favorite Thai dish. With this salad, I tried to get all those flavors into a salad we could sell at the Market. WHAT TO SERVE WHEN This salad is a meal in itself. To make it more substantial, top it with Katie's Spicy Grilled Shrimp (page 177) or toss in chopped or shredded chicken.

SERVES 4 TO 6

½ pound flat rice noodles
¼ pound snow peas or sugar snap peas, stem ends and strings removed and blanched (see "Blanching Vegetables," page 91)
1 2-inch piece fresh ginger, peeled and julienned (about 2 tablespoons)
¼ small head of savoy or napa cabbage, cored and thinly sliced (about 2 cups)
2 scallions, minced (white and green parts)
2 tablespoons chopped fresh cilantro leaves
2 tablespoons chopped fresh chives
1 cup unsalted peanuts, roasted and finely chopped
2 ounces bean sprouts or pea shoots (about 1 cup)
½ teaspoon crushed red pepper flakes
Salt and freshly ground black pepper to taste
Pad Thai Vinaigrette (recipe follows)

1. Bring 4 cups of water to a boil in a medium saucepan over high heat. Remove the pan from the heat and immerse the noodles in the hot water. Let the noodles stand in the hot water for 7 to 10 minutes, stirring occasionally, until they are tender but still firm. Drain in a colander, rinse under cold water, and drain well. Turn the drained noodles into a large bowl.

2. Julienne the snow peas and toss them into the bowl with the noodles. Add the ginger, cabbage, scallions, cilantro, chives, half of the ground peanuts, half of the sprouts, the red pepper flakes, salt, and pepper. Drizzle with the Pad Thai dressing and toss gently, taking care not to break the noodles. Serve immediately, garnished with the remaining peanuts and sprouts.

Note: *If you want to make this salad in advance, cover and refrigerate and garnish just before serving. You may also need to toss the noodles with a little more dressing because they tend to absorb the dressing.*

Pad Thai Vinaigrette

This recipe makes twice what you need for the Spicy Pad Thai Salad. There are so many ways to use what is left over: as dressing for a sandwich, salad, sliced tomatoes, or avocado slices.

MAKES ABOUT 1 CUP

2 tablespoons rice wine vinegar
2 tablespoons Thai fish sauce (*nam pla*)
2 tablespoons tamarind paste
2 tablespoons light soy sauce or tamari
2 tablespoons extra-virgin olive oil
1 tablespoon ketchup
1 tablespoon sugar
1 tablespoon grated fresh ginger (1-inch piece)
2 garlic cloves, minced
Grated zest and juice of 1 orange
Grated zest and juice of 1 lemon
1 teaspoon crushed red pepper flakes or chili paste

Whisk the vinegar, fish sauce, tamarind paste, soy sauce, olive oil, ketchup, sugar, ginger, garlic, orange zest and juice, lemon zest and juice, and crushed red pepper or chili paste in a small bowl. Use immediately or refrigerate in an airtight container for up to 1 week.

Classic California Cobb Salad

There's nothing very unusual about this traditional Cobb salad—it's just as good as they get. The combination of blue cheese and avocado is one that people can't seem to get enough of, then add the bacon and forget about it. Whether we make a Cobb wrap, sandwich, a soft taco, or this salad at the Market, it'll be the first thing to go during the lunch rush.

SERVES 4 TO 6

1 head romaine lettuce, washed and torn or chopped into 1-inch pieces

5 ounces arugula, washed, stems removed, and drained (about 3 cups leaves)

Red Wine Vinaigrette with Chives (recipe follows)

Sea salt and freshly ground black pepper to taste

4 large hard-boiled eggs, peeled and coarsely chopped

6 slices bacon, fried until crisp, drained on paper towels, and crumbled

1 cucumber, halved, seeded, and cut diagonally into ¼-inch slices

2 avocados, halved, pitted, and cut into ½-inch cubes

4 cooked boneless skinless chicken breast halves (about 1½ pounds; see Herb-Marinated Grilled Chicken Breast, page 136), sliced ¼ inch thick

2 tomatoes (about 1 pound), cored and chopped

1 cup crumbled blue cheese (about 4 ounces)

1. Place the romaine and arugula in a large bowl, drizzle with ¼ cup of the vinaigrette, and toss gently. Season with salt and pepper.

2. Heap the greens on a large platter or divide them evenly among four to six individual plates. Arrange the chopped eggs, bacon, cucumber, avocado, chicken, tomatoes, and cheese in distinct rows over the greens. Drizzle with ¼ cup of the remaining vinaigrette (or more to taste) and serve immediately.

Red Wine Vinaigrette with Chives

MAKES ABOUT ¾ CUP

⅓ cup red wine vinegar

2 teaspoons Dijon mustard

½ cup extra-virgin olive oil

2 tablespoons chopped fresh chives

Sea salt and freshly ground black pepper to taste

Whisk the vinegar and mustard together in a small bowl. Add the olive oil in a slow, steady stream, whisking constantly until all is incorporated. Stir in the chives and salt and pepper. This vinaigrette will keep for up to 1 week refrigerated in an airtight container. If you're making it for later use, add the chopped chives just before serving.

All-American Chef Salad

I took the idea of the traditional chef salad and livened it up with quality ingredients and loads of fresh herbs.

SERVES 4 TO 6

1 head Bibb lettuce, washed, drained, and chopped or torn into 1-inch pieces

4 cups mixed baby lettuce, washed and drained

2 tablespoons chopped fresh basil leaves

2 tablespoons chopped fresh flat-leaf parsley leaves

2 carrots, julienned

1 red bell pepper, cored, seeded, and julienned

½ pint grape or small heirloom tomatoes, halved

½ small red onion, sliced into thin rounds

Balsamic Vinaigrette (page 70)

Sea salt and freshly ground black pepper to taste

8 ounces cooked chicken, shredded (see Herb-Marinated Chicken Breast, page 136, or store-bought)

8 ounces black forest or smoked ham, thinly sliced

6 ounces sharp Cheddar cheese, cut into ½-inch cubes (about 1½ cups)

2 hard-boiled eggs, peeled and sliced

1. Place the lettuces, basil, parsley, carrots, bell pepper, tomatoes, and onion slices in a large bowl. Drizzle with ½ cup of the vinaigrette and toss. Season with salt and pepper to taste.

2. Divide the salad among four to six plates. Arrange the chicken, ham, and cheese on top of the greens and place the egg slices around the edges. Drizzle with ¼ cup of the remaining vinaigrette (or more to taste) and serve immediately.

Italian Chef Salad with Tangy Italian Dressing

Whenever I go to an Italian restaurant, I order the antipasto platter because Italian sliced meats are so delicious I knew they'd make a great salad.

SERVES 4 TO 6

5 ounces arugula, washed, stems removed, and drained (about 3 cups)
1/2 head radicchio, washed and drained
2 heads Belgian endive, washed and drained
1/2 cup whole fresh basil leaves
   Tangy Italian Vinaigrette (recipe follows)
   Sea salt and freshly ground black pepper to taste
1/2 pound green beans, trimmed and blanched (see "Blanching Vegetables," right)
2 plum tomatoes, cored and quartered
6 pepperoncini (Italian peppers in vinegar), halved lengthwise
2 ounces sliced prosciutto
2 ounces sliced capicola
4 ounces fresh mozzarella, cut into 1/4-inch cubes, or bocconcini
2 ounces pecorino or Parmesan cheese, shaved

1. Combine the arugula, radicchio, endive, and basil leaves in a large bowl, drizzle with 1/4 cup of the vinaigrette, and toss to mix. Season with salt and pepper.

2. Divide the salad among four to six plates and top with the green beans, tomatoes, and pepperoncini. Lay the prosciutto and capicola over the greens and sprinkle with the mozzarella cubes and shaved pecorino. Drizzle with 1/4 cup of the remaining vinaigrette. Taste for seasoning and add more salt, pepper, or vinaigrette to taste. Serve immediately.

Tangy Italian Vinaigrette

If you're making this in advance, stir in the fresh herbs just before using.

MAKES ABOUT 1 CUP

1/4 cup red wine vinegar
1 shallot, minced
   Grated zest and juice of 1 lemon
2 tablespoons chopped fresh oregano leaves
2 tablespoons chopped fresh marjoram leaves
6 fresh basil leaves, cut into thin strips
2 garlic cloves, minced
1/2 cup extra-virgin olive oil
   Sea salt and freshly ground black pepper to taste

Stir the vinegar, shallot, lemon zest and juice, oregano, marjoram, basil, and garlic together in a small bowl. Add the olive oil slowly, whisking constantly until all is incorporated. Season with salt and pepper and use immediately or refrigerate in an airtight container for up to 1 week.

BASICS: *Blanching Vegetables*

Blanching is a way of cooking vegetables to bring out their color and flavor while retaining all the crunch of the raw vegetable. Blanching is really simple, but you have to be prepared and pay attention because cooking happens very quickly. Blanching broccoli or snow peas, for instance, takes 15 to 30 seconds. You literally put them in the boiling water, they brighten up almost immediately, and you take them out. Green beans or carrots might take up to a minute, but nothing you blanch will take much longer than that. Start with vegetables that are rinsed, trimmed, peeled, and cut. Have a pot of water boiling, a colander placed in the sink, and a big bowl of ice water nearby. Salt the water for green vegetables, to retain their color. Drop the vegetables into the boiling water, watch them constantly, and when they turn bright in color, drain them in the colander. Immediately plunge the drained vegetables into the ice water bath. This is called shocking the vegetables; it stops the cooking process and keeps the vegetables bright colored and crunchy. If you're blanching more than one type of vegetable, do them separately, using a slotted spoon to lift the first batch of vegetables out of the water and into the colander so you can use the boiling water for the next batch.

Grilled Ahi Tuna Niçoise Salad with Black Olive Vinaigrette

I love a classic tuna niçoise, but I've always thought it would be better using fresh ahi tuna instead of the traditional canned. In fact, it is. But ahi is only the extraordinary, melt-in-your-mouth treat that it can be when it's not overcooked.

SERVES 4 TO 6

 2 1-pound sashimi-grade ahi tuna steaks, cut 1 inch thick
¼ cup olive oil
 3 tablespoons light soy sauce or tamari
 2 tablespoons white wine vinegar
    Juice of 1 orange
 2 garlic cloves, minced
10 fresh basil leaves, cut into thin strips
    Sea salt and freshly ground black pepper to taste
 6 cups mixed baby greens or arugula leaves, washed and drained
    Black Olive Vinaigrette (recipe follows)
½ pint grape or cherry tomatoes, quartered
 1 cup fresh shelled fava beans, green beans, or sugar snap peas, blanched (see "Blanching Vegetables," page 91), favas peeled

1. Rinse the tuna, pat it dry with paper towels, and place it in a shallow dish. Whisk the olive oil, soy sauce, vinegar, orange juice, garlic, and basil together in a small bowl and pour over the tuna. Turn the tuna to coat with the marinade. Cover with plastic wrap and marinate in the refrigerator for about 1 hour.

2. Prepare a hot fire in a charcoal or gas grill. Bring the tuna to room temperature before grilling.

3. Remove the tuna from the marinade and sprinkle both sides with salt and pepper. Place the tuna over the hot coals to grill about 1 minute per side (1 to 2 minutes longer for tuna that is less rare), turning only once, brushing with the marinade while the tuna is cooking. Set the tuna aside to cool to room temperature.

4. Place the mixed greens or arugula in a large bowl, drizzle with ¼ cup of the vinaigrette, and toss. Season with additional salt and pepper to taste. Place the dressed greens on a platter or individual plates. Slice the tuna against the grain about ¼ inch thick, and lay the tuna slices over the greens. Top with the cherry tomatoes and beans and drizzle with another ¼ cup (or more to taste) of the vinaigrette.

Black Olive Vinaigrette

MAKES ABOUT 1 CUP

 3 garlic cloves
½ teaspoon salt, plus more to taste
 3 tablespoons white wine vinegar
    Grated zest of 1 lemon
 1 tablespoon chopped fresh thyme
¾ cup extra-virgin olive oil
¼ cup kalamata olives, pitted and roughly chopped
    Freshly ground black pepper to taste

Mash the garlic and ½ teaspoon of salt in a small bowl with the tines of a fork (or use a mortar and pestle). Stir in the vinegar, lemon zest, and thyme. Add the olive oil in a slow, steady stream, whisking constantly, until all the oil is incorporated. Stir in the olives and season with salt and pepper to taste. Use immediately or refrigerate in an airtight container for up to 1 week.

Tuscan Tuna and White Bean Salad with Sun-Dried Tomatoes

SERVES 4

- 3 teaspoons extra-virgin olive oil
  Juice of 2 lemons
- 1 tablespoon red wine vinegar
- 2 tablespoons chopped fresh flat-leaf parsley leaves
- 1 teaspoon chopped fresh rosemary
- ¼ cup sun-dried tomatoes
- 1 15½-ounce can cannellini beans, rinsed and drained, or 1¾ cups dried beans, cooked until tender
- 2 6-ounce cans solid white tuna packed in water, drained
- 10 roasted garlic cloves (see "Roasting Garlic," right), peeled
  Sea salt and freshly ground black pepper to taste
- 4 Balsamic-Roasted Tomatoes (page 135)

Whisk the olive oil, lemon juice, vinegar, parsley, and rosemary together in a small bowl. Add the sun-dried tomatoes and let them marinate in the vinaigrette for 10 to 15 minutes to soften. Place the beans, tuna, and garlic in a medium bowl. Add the vinaigrette and sun-dried tomatoes, season with salt and pepper, and toss gently to mix. Cover and refrigerate to marinate for at least 1 hour or overnight. Serve at room temperature, with the Balsamic-Roasted Tomatoes on top.

BASICS: Roasting Garlic

Roasting garlic changes its flavor and texture so much it's an almost entirely different thing. The garlic becomes soft and spreadable, with a nutty, earthy, and sweet flavor and none of the burn. I toss it into vinaigrettes, add it to sautéed greens, toss the cloves whole into salads, mash them with potatoes, or spread them on crostini as an appetizer or crouton for soup.

1 head of garlic
2 tablespoons olive oil
2 tablespoons chopped fresh rosemary or thyme

1. Preheat the oven to 350°F.
2. Cut the top off the head of garlic with a serrated knife so that you can see the tips of the individual cloves. Place the garlic on a sheet of aluminum foil, drizzle with the oil, and rub into all sides of the garlic to coat. Wrap the head of garlic tightly in foil and place in the oven to roast for 50 to 60 minutes, until it is soft to the squeeze.
3. Unwrap the garlic and allow it to cool. When the garlic is cool enough to touch, squeeze the soft garlic cloves out of their skins. Use the oil that you roasted the garlic in to season whatever you're using with the garlic. The cloves will keep, refrigerated in an airtight container, for up to 1 week.

Tuna Salad with Apple, Sunflower Seeds, and Avocado

SERVES 4

- 2 6-ounce cans solid white tuna packed in water, drained
- 1/4 cup sunflower seeds
  Juice of 1 lemon
- 2 tablespoons chopped fresh dill, parsley, or basil leaves
- 1/3 cup mayonnaise
- 1 tablespoon Dijon mustard
- 1 tart apple (such as Granny Smith or Pippin), peeled and diced
  Sea salt and freshly ground black pepper to taste
- 1 avocado, peeled, pitted, halved, and cut into 1/2-inch cubes
- 1 cup alfalfa, radish, or mixed crunchy sprouts

Combine the tuna in a medium bowl with the sunflower seeds, lemon juice, dill, mayonnaise, mustard, apple, salt, and pepper and stir to mix. Cover and refrigerate for 1 hour or overnight. Just before serving, add the cubed avocado and toss very gently. Top with the sprouts.

Tuna Salad with Cilantro and Pickled Jalapeño Peppers

SERVES 4

- 2 6-ounce cans solid white tuna packed in water, drained
- 1/2 cup pickled jalapeño peppers, chopped
- 2 garlic cloves, minced
  Juice of 2 limes
- 3 tablespoons extra-virgin olive oil
- 1/4 cup chopped fresh cilantro leaves
  Sea salt and freshly ground black pepper to taste
- 2 large tomatoes
- 2 limes, cut into wedges

Place the tuna in a medium bowl with the jalapeño pepper, garlic, lime juice, olive oil, cilantro, salt, and pepper and mix gently. Cover and refrigerate 1 hour or overnight. Core and slice the tomato. Lay the tomato slices on four plates. Season with salt and pepper, spoon the tuna salad on top, and serve with lime wedges.

Southern-Style Tuna Salad with Pickles and Eggs

SERVES 4 TO 6

- 2 6-ounce cans solid white tuna packed in water, drained
- 2 large hard-boiled eggs, peeled and chopped
- 2 celery stalks, diced
- 4 small kosher dill pickles or 10 whole cornichons, chopped
- 1/3 cup mayonnaise
- 1 tablespoon Dijon mustard
- 1 tablespoon chopped fresh dill or parsley leaves
  Sea salt and freshly ground black pepper to taste

Combine the tuna in a medium bowl with the chopped hard-boiled eggs, celery, pickles, mayonnaise, mustard, dill, salt, and pepper and stir to mix. Cover and refrigerate for 1 hour or overnight.

REINVENTION

I always have canned tuna in my pantry. It's such a lifesaver when it comes to making a last-minute bite with few resources. And tuna salad doesn't have to be just for sandwiches. I use it in many ways. In addition to the serving suggestions in these recipes, here are some ways I like to serve tuna salad: as an open-faced sandwich on crusty white or whole-grain bread topped with avocado; on a bed of dressed salad greens; spooned on sliced, salted heirloom or beefsteak tomatoes, topped with roasted peppers, arugula, or sprouts; or as an hors d'oeuvre spooned into halved cherry tomatoes or endive leaves.

Chicken Salad with Apples, Grapes, and Spicy Pecans

I often put fruit and nuts in salads; I love sweet and salty flavors together. This makes a nice picnic lunch on its own or a good sandwich with watercress on toasted multi-grain bread, or in a whole-wheat pita or flour tortilla.

SERVES 4 TO 6

 1 cup mayonnaise
 2 tablespoons Dijon mustard
 $1/2$ cup fruit chutney, such as Pear Chutney (page 215) or store-bought Major Grey's chutney
 4 cooked chicken breast halves, cut into $1/2$-inch pieces (see Herb-Marinated Grilled Chicken, page 136)
 2 celery stalks, chopped
 1 tart apple (such as Granny Smith or Pippin), peeled, cored, and chopped
 1 cup red seedless grapes, halved
 $1/4$ cup chopped fresh flat-leaf parsley
   Sea salt and freshly ground black pepper to taste
 1 cup Spicy Pecans (right) or store-bought spicy pecans

Stir the mayonnaise, mustard, and chutney together in a medium bowl. Add the chicken, celery, apple, grapes, parsley, salt, and pepper and toss gently. Serve immediately or cover and refrigerate for up to 3 days. Sprinkle the salad with the pecans just before serving.

Spicy Pecans

I know from experience that you will eat a handful of these pecans before they even see the chicken salad, so I made this recipe for twice what the recipe calls for. You might want to double it again, since they're good thrown into just about any salad and also make a delicious cocktail snack.

MAKES 2 CUPS

 2 cups pecan halves
 3 tablespoons pure vanilla extract
 1 tablespoon olive oil
 2 tablespoons dried rosemary
 1 teaspoon ground cinnamon
 1 teaspoon sea salt
 $1/2$ teaspoon freshly ground black pepper
 $1/4$ teaspoon cayenne pepper

1. Preheat the oven to 350°F.

2. Combine the pecans, vanilla, and olive oil in a medium bowl and toss to mix.

3. Stir the rosemary, cinnamon, salt, pepper, and cayenne together in a separate, small bowl. Sprinkle the spices evenly over the pecans and toss again.

4. Spread the pecans in one layer on a baking sheet with sides and roast, stirring several times during the cooking process, until the nuts are crispy and brown, about 15 minutes. Let the pecans cool to room temperature on the baking sheet, stirring several times while they're cooling to prevent them from sticking together and to the pan. These will last for at least a week in a sealable bag. If you are storing them, make sure they completely cool before placing them in the bag; otherwise, they'll soften in the bag.

Egg Salad with Fresh Dill and Green Olives

Egg salad is so versatile and such a nice stand-by meal because the ingredients are those you're bound to have on hand. This slightly dressed-up version makes an easy lunch served on sourdough or whole-grain toast toped with a heaping of greens. Turn it into a breakfast sandwich by piling it on a toasted English muffin and topping with crispy bacon slices. It's also a sure-to-please filling for finger or tea sandwiches using extra-thin sliced bread with the crusts trimmed. .

MAKES 2½ CUPS

  8 large hard-boiled eggs, peeled and roughly chopped
¼ cup mayonnaise
  2 tablespoons Dijon mustard
10 pimiento-stuffed green olives, chopped
  2 teaspoons olive brine or white wine vinegar
  2 tablespoons chopped fresh flat-leaf parsley
  2 teaspoons fresh dill
    Sea salt and freshly ground black pepper to taste

Place the eggs in a large bowl with the mayonnaise, mustard, olives, brine, parsley, dill, salt, and pepper and stir to combine. Taste for salt and pepper and season to taste. Serve immediately or refrigerate in an airtight container for up to 1 day.

about . . .
BOILING EGGS

I learned how to boil eggs from my Dad when I was twelve years old and I've used his method ever since. It always works perfectly, the eggs cooked just enough but not so much that the yolks discolor or dry out. To boil eggs, place them in a saucepan with enough cold water to cover the eggs by about 2 inches. Bring the water to a low boil over medium heat. Turn the heat off, cover, and let the eggs sit in the water 10 minutes longer. Drain the eggs, rinse under cold water, and let them sit in the cold water until they have cooled completely. For easy peeling, crack both pointy ends of the shell before peeling the eggs under cool running water.

Deviled Eggs on Sliced Heirloom Tomatoes

This composed platter, with the eggs on sliced tomatoes, was a standard Sunday lunch item at my Granny Foster's house when I was growing up. The deviled eggs can be prepared through step 3 up to a day in advance. It's best to slice the tomatoes just before serving the salad. WHAT TO SERVE WHEN This refreshing salad is a nice accompaniment to Grilled Buffalo Chicken Strips (page 146) or Simple Succulent Grilled Pork Chops (page 166). The eggs on their own make a delicious side dish, garnished with thin slices of pickled okra, cornichons, baby dill pickles, or pickled onions.

SERVES 4 TO 6

  6 large hard-boiled eggs, peeled
  2 tablespoons mayonnaise
  1 teaspoon Dijon mustard
  2 teaspoons dill pickle juice or white wine vinegar
  1 tablespoon fresh chopped dill
    Sea salt and freshly ground black pepper to taste
  2 pounds large heirloom tomatoes (such as Brandywine or German Johnson), or any good ripe summer tomatoes
¼ cup extra-virgin olive oil
  2 tablespoons balsamic vinegar
  6 fresh basil leaves, cut into thin strips

1. Halve the eggs lengthwise. Scoop the yolks out into a medium bowl, being careful to keep the whites intact. Set the whites aside.

2. Add the mayonnaise, mustard, pickle juice, dill, salt, and pepper to the egg yolks, and mash to a smooth paste with a fork. Spoon about 1 tablespoon of the yolk mixture to fill each egg half.

3. Core and slice the tomatoes ½ inch thick. Arrange the tomatoes on a platter or on individual plates. Place the deviled eggs alongside or on top of the tomatoes. Drizzle both with the olive oil and balsamic vinegar, then sprinkle with the basil and additional salt and pepper to taste. Serve immediately.

four
seasonal sides

Butternut Squash and Apple Mash with Melted Sharp Cheddar ○ Turnip Apple Mash with Thyme ○ Creamy Mashed Celery Root ○ Mashed Roasted Sweet Potatoes with Parmesan ○ Roasted Radishes ○ Steamed Baby Bok Choy ○ Chili-Roasted Sweet Potatoes ○ Orange-Maple Roasted Sweet Potatoes ○ Corn on the Cob Your Way ○ Greens with Crispy Bacon ○ Garlicky Greens ○ Hoisin Roasted Green Beans ○ Italian-Style Green Beans ○ Rosemary-Caramelized Parsnips ○ Lemon Roasted Asparagus ○ Roasted Cabbage Wedges ○ Steamed Cabbage with Rosemary ○ Roasted Cauliflower with Brown Butter and Sage ○ Roasted Mushrooms with Green Peas and Tomatoes ○ Smashed Green Peas ○ Herb Grilled Tomatoes ○ Cider Roasted Root Vegetables ○ Cider-Braised Endive ○ Butter-Steamed Fingerling Potatoes with Chopped Fresh Herbs ○ Pan-Braised Carrots with Orange and Rosemary ○ Oven-Roasted Garlicky Fries ○ Smashed Roasted Potatoes with Rosemary ○ *Twice-Baked Potatoes for All Seasons—Winter:* Bacon, Blue Cheese, and Garlic-Sautéed Broccoli; *Spring:* Sweet Peas, Parmesan, and Chives; *Summer:* Roasted Red Bell Pepper, Corn, and Cheddar Cheese; *Fall:* Sautéed Spinach, Mushrooms, and Thyme ○ *Rice Pilaf for All Seasons—Winter:* Long-Grain and Wild Rice Pilaf with Quinoa, Golden Raisins, and Orange Zest; *Spring:* Jasmine Rice Pilaf with Sweet Peas, Chives, Lemon Zest, and Toasted Almonds; *Summer:* Basmati Rice Pilaf with Zucchini, Roasted Red Peppers, and Parsley; *Fall:* Brown Rice and Wheat Berry Pilaf with Roasted Acorn Squash, Spinach, and Sautéed Shallots

When I go to a restaurant, it's invariably the side dishes that dictate my order. A chicken breast, grilled shrimp, and steak—they don't change much season in and season out; it's what they're served with that makes these entrees sound appealing and unique to me. That's why I think of the recipes in this chapter as the backbone of this book.

The most important word to think about with respect to these recipes is "seasonal." When you rely on simple cooking techniques that are designed to enhance the flavor of a vegetable—not mask it—those vegetables themselves must have flavor to begin with. My hope is that you will use the seasons as a guide for choosing a recipe. That in the fall you will make Rosemary-Caramelized Parsnips, in the spring you'll gravitate toward Smashed Green Peas, and in the summer you might serve fresh-picked corn on the cob and let the flavor stand alone with butter and salt.

Once you embrace this kind of thinking, it becomes second nature. Even my customers at Foster's Market, who would have my head if I were to take blueberry muffins off the menu, have gotten used to a revolving selection of seasonal sides. I think they actually like it; it gives them something to look forward to. Finding Lemon Roasted Asparagus in the case says, "Spring is here!" as clearly as seeing the first daffodils peeking up in the garden.

Butternut Squash and Apple Mash with Melted Sharp Cheddar

This is a rich but not-too-heavy side dish that you could make with almost any winter squash. It's important to have all the ingredients ready to mash with the squash so that the cheese melts while the squash is still hot.

SERVES 4 TO 6

- 2 large butternut squash (about 5 pounds), halved lengthwise and seeded
- 4 tablespoons unsalted butter
- ½ cup shredded Cheddar cheese (about 2 ounces)
- 1 cup chunky applesauce
- 1 teaspoon sea salt, plus more to taste
- ½ teaspoon freshly ground black pepper, plus more to taste

1. Preheat the oven to 400°F.

2. Place the squash, cut side down, on a baking sheet with sides. Pour 1 cup of water over the squash and roast for 50 to 55 minutes, until the flesh at the thickest point of the squash is tender when pierced with a fork.

3. Combine the butter, cheese, applesauce, salt, and pepper in a large bowl. When the squash is just cool enough to handle but still hot, scoop the flesh into the bowl and mash with a potato masher until the butter and cheese are incorporated and the mash is smooth. Season with more salt and pepper to taste and serve warm.

REINVENTION

Stir a cup of the leftover mashed squash into any risotto (see Risotto for All Seasons, page 201); top with sage leaves and crumbled Italian sausage.

Think Outside the Recipe
USE PARMESAN OR SWISS CHEESE IN PLACE OF CHEDDAR; BAKE TWO PEELED APPLES ALONGSIDE THE SQUASH, CORE THEM, AND MASH THEM WITH THE SQUASH IN PLACE OF APPLESAUCE.

about . . .
MASHED VEGETABLES

Everyone loves mashed potatoes, but few people think to use the same method to make creamy, comforting sides with other vegetables: peas, parsnips, rutabagas, celery root, carrots, beets, eggplant, butter beans, and any winter squash. No matter what vegetable you plan to mash, start by cooking it—steam, boil, sauté, or roast—until tender. Mash the tender veggies with some kind of liquid to make them rich and creamy. But just like you're thinking outside the recipe box with regards to the potatoes, think beyond butter and milk and experiment with olive oil, buttermilk, or sour cream. Cheese is a welcome addition to any mash: Swiss, Parmesan, fresh goat cheese, or smoked Gouda. You can also add other flavors, such as roasted garlic, sautéed onions, fresh chopped spinach, or just-shucked uncooked summer corn. Add a baked apple or pear for extra sweetness and lots of fresh herbs for flavor and color. And of course sea salt and freshly ground black pepper are a must.

Turnip Apple Mash with Thyme

In the fall and winter, I could eat rich, creamy, comforting sides like this one every day. Turnips tend to be bitter, so they really benefit from the sweetness of the apple. WHAT TO SERVE WHEN I think the slight sweetness of the apples and turnips together goes nicely with pork, such as Slow-Roasted Pork Shoulder (page 212) or the Simple Succulent Grilled Pork Chops (page 166), or a whole roasted chicken.

SERVES 4 TO 6

- 2 pounds medium turnips (4 to 5 turnips), peeled and cut into 2-inch chunks
- 2 tart apples (such as Granny Smith or Pippin), peeled, cored, and cut into 2-inch chunks
- 2 tablespoons olive oil
- 4 tablespoons unsalted butter
  Leaves from 3 or 4 fresh thyme sprigs (about 1 tablespoon)
  Sea salt and freshly ground black pepper to taste

1. Place the turnips in a medium saucepan with 4 cups of cool water and bring to a boil over high heat. Reduce the heat and simmer, partially covered, for 20 minutes. Remove the lid, add the apples, olive oil, and 2 tablespoons of the butter, and continue to simmer until all the liquid has evaporated and the turnips and apples begin to sizzle, 20 to 25 minutes.

2. Remove the pan from the heat. Add the remaining 2 tablespoons butter, the thyme, salt, and pepper and mash with a potato masher. Serve warm.

Think Outside the Recipe

- USE PARSNIPS OR RUTABAGA IN PLACE OF OR IN COMBINATION WITH TURNIPS.
- TRY PEARS IN PLACE OF APPLES.
- FOR THE HERBS, USE ROSEMARY OR SAGE, OR TOP WITH SAGE FRIED CRISP IN BROWN BUTTER, POURING THE BUTTER OVER THE TOP OF THE MASH.

TRICKS OF MY TRADE

- **Prep your vegetables as you unload your groceries.** Whether it's a head of cabbage, broccoli, or carrots, rinse them, trim them, and prep them (peel carrots, cut broccoli into florets). Wrap in moist paper towels to keep them crisp and refrigerate them in plastic bags.

- **When you're cutting vegetables for a particular recipe, cut more than you need.** Store the extra cut veggies in a resealable plastic bag lined with a damp paper towel.

- **Balance the menu.** If you're making a main dish that takes a lot of effort, serve it with sides that take almost none. This almost guarantees a perfectly balanced meal in terms of flavor and richness also.

- **Make vegetable packets** of chopped or julienned vegetables for a quick stir-fry or sautée or to add to salads, risotto, or rice pilaf.

- **Save small amounts of leftover vegetables** that might be just enough to add flavor to soup, pasta, or an omelette.

- **Puree garlic in the food processor or blender in large batches** and store in the refrigerator to have on hand.

- **Have everything ready to go before you start the cooking.** Prep enough for several dishes or meals at a time. Think of it in terms of working in a production kitchen where everything is done ahead of time, except the last minute cooking.

- **Snap the beans and peel your carrots and potatoes ahead of time** and keep them in containers of water until you're ready to cook them.

Creamy Mashed Celery Root

My friend Maggie Radzwiller, a personal chef in Durham, comes to our house every few weeks and cooks dinner for Peter and me. She loves to cook and knows how much I appreciate her cooking after working a long day. She made mashed celery root one evening to go with a duck breast. I was expecting mashed potatoes, so when I tasted them, the celery root was a refreshing surprise.

SERVES 4 TO 6

- 2 pounds celery root (about 4 medium celery roots), peeled and cut into 2-inch chunks
- 1¼ pounds Yukon Gold potatoes (about 3 potatoes), peeled and cut into 2-inch chunks
- ½ cup half-and-half
- 4 tablespoons unsalted butter
  Sea salt and freshly ground black pepper to taste
- 1 tablespoon chopped fresh flat-leaf parsley leaves
- 1 tablespoon chopped fresh celery leaves

1. Place the celery root and potatoes in a saucepan with enough water to cover by 2 to 3 inches when the vegetables are pushed down with your hand. Bring to a low boil over high heat, lower the heat, and boil for 30 to 35 minutes, until the vegetables are tender when pierced with a fork.

2. Drain and return the celery root and potatoes to the pan. Add the half-and-half, butter, salt, and pepper. Mash with a potato masher or process through a food mill until the vegetables are smooth and creamy. Stir in the chopped parsley and celery leaves, taste for seasoning, and serve immediately.

Note: *If these sit for a while before serving, you may need to stir in more half-and-half to loosen the puree and make it fluffy again.*

Think Outside the Recipe
JUST AS WITH REGULAR MASHED POTATOES, THESE INVITE VARIATIONS.
- USE DIFFERENT FRESH HERBS, SUCH AS MINCED CHIVES OR ROSEMARY IN PLACE OF THE PARSLEY.
- USE A GOOD OLIVE OIL IN PLACE OF THE BUTTER; ELIMINATE THE HALF-AND-HALF OR USE BUTTERMILK OR SOUR CREAM INSTEAD.

Mashed Roasted Sweet Potatoes with Parmesan

This dish couldn't be any simpler or more delicious. After you bake the sweet potatoes, just slip the skin off, mash them, and you're done. It is one of the sides that I cook most often at home. WHAT TO SERVE WHEN Pork and sweet potatoes together—it's a comfort thing for me. These make a perfect side or bed for the Slow-Roasted Pork Shoulder (page 212) or the Simple Succulent Grilled Pork Chops (page 166).

SERVES 4 TO 6

- 2 pounds sweet potatoes (3 to 4 medium)
- 2 tablespoons olive oil
- 1½ ounces Parmesan cheese, grated (about ½ cup), plus more for garnish
  Sea salt and freshly ground black pepper to taste

1. Preheat the oven to 400°F.

2. Wash and scrub the sweet potatoes and wrap them individually in foil while they're still damp. Place the sweet potatoes directly on a rack in the oven and bake for about 1 hour, until they're soft to the squeeze. Allow the sweet potatoes to cool slightly before removing the foil.

3. While the potatoes are still warm, hold one directly over a bowl and slide the skin off, letting the potato fall into the bowl. Discard the skin and repeat with the remaining sweet potatoes. Add the olive oil, Parmesan cheese, salt, and pepper and mash with a potato masher until they're fluffy and the additions are incorporated. Garnish with a sprinkling of Parmesan cheese. These are best served just after they're mashed, but they're also delicious warmed up the next day.

REINVENTION

Measure a cupful of the mashed sweet potatoes before you add the Parmesan, then use the reserved potatoes to make Sweet Potato Buttermilk Biscuits (page 31).

Roasted Radishes

Radishes are almost always eaten raw as crudités or in a salad. But roasted, they're like a sweet young turnip. You can get radishes all year long at grocery stores, but they're especially good in the springtime, when you'll find them in all different sizes and colors at farmers markets. WHAT TO SERVE WHEN The radishes go really well as a side dish with wintry meats like Slow-Roasted Pork Shoulder (page 212) or Braised Tarragon Chicken (page 224).

SERVES 4 TO 6

1 pound radishes, such as icicle, French, or Easter
  egg-colored radishes, tops on (2 bunches)
2 tablespoons unsalted butter, melted
2 tablespoons olive oil
  Leaves from 3 or 4 fresh thyme sprigs
  (about 1 tablespoon), plus more for garnish
  Sea salt and freshly ground black pepper to taste

1. Preheat the oven to 400°F.

2. Trim the tops off the radishes, leaving about ½ inch of the green stem attached; reserve the radish greens for garnish. Rinse the radishes and the tops well.

3. Put the radishes on a baking sheet with sides or an ovenproof skillet. Drizzle with the melted butter and olive oil, sprinkle with the thyme, salt, and pepper, and toss to coat evenly. Roast for 10 to 15 minutes, until the radishes are tender but still slightly crunchy (red radishes will turn pale pink in color, lighter radishes will become pale golden). Transfer to a serving platter, garnish with the radish greens and thyme leaves, and serve warm.

REINVENTION

At the Market, we toss roasted radishes into a salad with arugula and Spicy Pecans (page 97). If you want to do the same, roast the radishes them in olive oil and vinegar instead of butter and use the pan drippings to dress the salad.

Steamed Baby Bok Choy

Tamari, like soy sauce, is made from soybeans. They taste similar, but tamari is thicker and darker. You can find it at health food and specialty food markets. Baby bok choy can be found in the produce department of specialty grocery stores. It has tender leaves and wonderful crunchy stalks.

SERVES 4 TO 6

6 heads baby bok choy, halved lengthwise,
  washed, and drained
2 tablespoons tamari or light soy sauce
2 tablespoons olive oil
  Juice of 1 tangerine, clementine, or orange
  Sea salt and freshly ground black pepper to taste

Place the bok choy in a wok or large skillet with a lid. Pour the tamari, olive oil, and tangerine juice over the greens and season with salt and pepper. Cover and steam for 2 to 3 minutes, until the bok choy is bright green and tender. Lift the bok choy out of the skillet into a shallow serving bowl, pour the liquid in the pan over it, and serve warm.

Roasted Sweet Potato Wedges Two Ways

It would be a rare event to walk into Foster's Market and not find some preparation of sweet potatoes. We're so known for them that I was asked to be on the state's sweet potato commission, which entails my doing cooking demonstrations or television segments to try to convert habitual russet potato users to use sweet potatoes instead. Both of these preparations make a nice alternative to oven fries with grilled meats, like the Tequila Lime Skirt Steak (page 162) or Sliced New York Strip Steak (page 159).

SERVES 4

Chili-Roasted Sweet Potatoes

2 pounds sweet potatoes (3 to 4 medium), peeled, halved lengthwise, and cut into 3-inch wedges
1/4 cup olive oil
Juice of 2 limes
1/2 teaspoon sea salt, plus more to taste
1/2 teaspoon freshly ground black pepper, plus more to taste
2 teaspoons chili powder
2 tablespoons chopped fresh flat-leaf parsley leaves

1. Preheat the oven to 400°F.

2. Place the sweet potatoes on a baking sheet with sides and toss with the olive oil, lime juice, salt, and pepper. Spread them in a single layer and roast for 20 to 25 minutes, until the potatoes are soft and golden brown. Stir the potatoes halfway through the cooking time so they brown evenly.

3. When the potatoes are almost done, remove them from the oven, sprinkle with the chili powder and parsley, and add salt and pepper to taste, and toss to coat. Return the potatoes to the oven for 5 to 10 minutes longer, until they are tender when pierced with the tip of a knife. Serve warm or at room temperature.

Orange-Maple Roasted Sweet Potatoes

2 pounds sweet potatoes (3 to 4 medium), peeled, halved lengthwise, and cut into 3-inch wedges
4 tablespoons unsalted butter, melted
2 tablespoons olive oil
1/4 cup maple syrup
Juice of 1 orange
Leaves from 6 or 7 fresh thyme sprigs (about 2 tablespoons)
Sea salt and freshly ground black pepper to taste

1. Preheat the oven to 400°F.

2. Place the sweet potatoes on a baking sheet with sides and toss with the butter, olive oil, maple syrup, and orange juice. Spread the sweet potatoes in a single layer and roast for 25 to 30 minutes, stirring occasionally so they brown evenly.

3. Remove the potatoes from the oven and sprinkle them with the thyme, salt, and pepper. Return them to the oven to roast for another 5 to 10 minutes, until tender when pierced with the tip of a knife. Season with more salt and pepper to taste and serve warm or at room temperature.

about . . .
SWEET POTATOES

I often use sweet potatoes in place of regular potatoes and in recipes that call for pumpkin, like bread, pie, or muffins. When I'm cooking just for myself, I'll bake a sweet potato and eat it plain, with just butter and salt. When I'm buying sweet potatoes, I look for Garnet sweet potatoes, which have dark red skin and bright orange flesh. I also like Jewel sweet potatoes, which are also orange and the kind you find most often at grocery stores. I always choose small- to medium-size sweet potatoes. The giant ones tend to be starchier and more fibrous.

Corn on the Cob Your Way

In the South, a lot of people grow their own corn. It's one of the first crops of early summer and one everyone looks forward to, like the first local peaches. When it's fresh and in season, corn on the cob is just about everyone's favorite side dish, and because it's so easy to prepare, nobody appreciates it more than the cook. I serve corn with softened butter or Herb Butter (page 29), or sprinkled with chili powder and a squeeze of fresh lime. Depending on what else I'm cooking, I prepare corn in a variety of ways, including:

Grilled Corn

Grilling corn gives it a nice smoky flavor. The best time to put corn on the grill is when the fire is still much too hot for cooking meat, so the timing works out perfectly because the corn cools enough to handle while the main course cooks. To grill corn, soak the unshucked ears in cold water for 10 to 15 minutes to prevent the husks from charring and the corn from drying out when cooked. Prepare a hot fire in a charcoal or gas grill. Keep the corn on the grill for 15 to 20 minutes, turning several times to cook evenly. Allow the corn to cool slightly, then remove the husks and silks, or pull the husks back and twist them together into a "handle."

Steamed or Boiled

Steaming and boiling corn are classic preparations—and they preserve the taste of the corn in its purest form. Place the shucked corn in a large pot of salted boiling water or in a large pot with a steamer basket, covered. Just-picked corn will take only about 1 minute to cook; 2 or 3 minutes is as long as you'll need to cook any fresh corn. To steam, place the corn in a steamer over simmering water, covered, for 2 to 3 minutes.

Wrapped in Foil

This is the perfect way to cook corn at a campfire or in your fireplace. Remove the husks and silks, smear the corn with softened butter (or brush with melted butter), season with salt and pepper, and wrap in heavy-duty foil or doubled regular foil (shiny side in). Place the wrapped corn directly on the coals for 4 to 5 minutes, turning with tongs occasionally to cook evenly.

Oven-Roasted Corn

Oven-roasting gives corn some of the smoky, charred flavor you get from an outdoor grill. Soak the unshucked ears in cold water for 10 to 15 minutes. Place the ears in a single layer on a baking sheet with sides and roast in a 400°F oven for 20 to 25 minutes, until the kernels are tender but still slightly crisp. When the corn is cool enough to touch, remove the husks and silks.

❝ The longer an ear of corn has been off the stalk, the starchier it will be and the longer it will take to cook. ❞

Greens with Crispy Bacon

I grew up eating collard greens as a side dish with just about everything but dessert. Those I grew up eating were cooked with salt pork—for no less than 4 hours to be sure. For this recipe, the collards are cooked only long enough to make them tender, so you can really taste the flavor of the greens. They release enough water to steam themselves. WHAT TO SERVE WHEN I serve these with any pork or chicken dish, or with Navy Bean Soup (page 58) and Skillet Cornbread (page 76).

SERVES 2 TO 4

4 slices thick-cut bacon, preferably peppered, cut into 1-inch pieces
2 pounds collard greens (about 2 bunches), washed, stems removed, and drained
Sea salt and freshly ground black pepper to taste

1. Cook the bacon in a large saucepan over medium-high heat until crisp. Use a slotted spoon or spatula to remove the bacon pieces from the saucepan, leaving the grease in the pan to cook the greens in; drain the bacon on a paper towel.

2. Add the greens to the pan you cooked the bacon in and season with salt and pepper. Cover, reduce the heat to very low, and simmer the greens for 25 to 30 minutes, stirring occasionally, until tender. You may want to check once or twice to see that they're not sticking to the bottom. If they are, lower the heat and add a tablespoon or so of water. Season with additional salt and pepper. Top the greens with the crispy bacon pieces and serve warm.

about . . .
GREENS

You can use big leafy greens interchangeably in recipes: collard greens, mustard greens, turnip greens, kale, *cavolo nero* (black kale), spinach, or beet greens. I try to buy the relatively small, young greens, which are more tender and have more flavor than the gigantic greens with big tough stems. Even with the young greens, you'll want to remove the stems. I usually tear the stems off with my hands while I'm soaking them in a sink full of water. Some take longer to cook than others, so whatever variety you're preparing, just cook them until they're tender, between 25 and 30 minutes for the toughest of them. Greens are really healthy; they're full of vitamins and iron and are a good source of fiber.

Garlicky Greens

This is a very Italian—and delicious—way to cook dark leafy greens. Drain the greens very briefly after washing them. The remaining moisture seems to be just the amount to steam the greens.

SERVES 4 TO 6

¼ cup olive oil
4 garlic cloves, smashed and minced
1 pound kale, washed, stems removed, and drained
1 pound mustard greens, washed, stems removed, and drained
1 pound turnip greens, washed, stems removed, and drained
Sea salt and freshly ground black pepper to taste

1. Heat 2 tablespoons of the olive oil in a soup pot or a large saucepan over low heat. Add the garlic and sauté, stirring constantly, until fragrant and just beginning to color, about 1 minute.

2. Add the kale, mustard greens, and turnip greens; season with salt and pepper and toss to coat the greens with the garlic and oil. Reduce the heat to very low, cover the pot, and simmer the greens for 20 to 25 minutes, stirring occasionally, until they are tender.

3. Uncover, drizzle the greens with the remaining 2 tablespoons of olive oil, and cook, uncovered, until the liquid evaporates, 3 to 4 minutes. Serve warm.

Think Outside the Recipe
IF YOU BUY TURNIPS BY THE BUNCH, DICE ONE TURNIP AND ADD IT TO THE PAN SO YOU'LL HAVE BITES OF TENDER TURNIP ALONG WITH THE GREENS.

Hoisin Roasted Green Beans

This is a simple way to prepare green beans that takes advantage of the rich flavor of store-bought hoisin sauce. At the Market, we blanch the beans before roasting them so they retain their bright green color. At home I skip this step, but if you want them to look as beautiful as possible, blanch them first. WHAT TO SERVE WHEN The sweetness of hoisin sauce goes well with any pork dish, like the Pan-Grilled Pork Palllards (page 168). It also spices up a simply prepared grilled chicken breast (see Herb-Marinated Grilled Chicken Breast, page 136).

SERVES 4 TO 6

- 1/3 cup hoisin sauce
- Juice of 1 orange
- 2 tablespoons light soy sauce
- 2 tablespoons olive oil
- 1 1/2 pounds green beans, stem ends removed
- Sea salt and freshly ground black pepper to taste
- 2 tablespoons chopped fresh chives or parsley
- 1 tablespoon sesame seeds, lightly toasted

1. Preheat the oven to 400°F.

2. Stir the hoisin sauce, orange juice, soy sauce, and olive oil together in a large bowl. Add the green beans, toss to coat, and season with salt and pepper. (Hoison sauce is very salty, so be careful not to over-salt the green beans.) Spread the beans in an even layer on a baking sheet with sides and roast for 15 to 20 minutes, until they are soft and slightly shriveled. Sprinkle the beans with the chives and toss gently. Transfer to a serving dish, drizzle with the pan juices, and sprinkle with the sesame seeds. Serve warm or at room temperature.

Think Outside the Recipe
USE THIS METHOD TO PREPARE TENDER ASPARAGUS SPEARS, BLANCHED BROCCOLI FLORETS, CARROTS, OR WEDGES OF GREEN CABBAGE.

Italian-Style Green Beans

You can use this recipe to prepare any kind of green beans. Haricot vert, being so thin, will cook quicker and with less water than common green beans. Large, flat broad beans (also called romano beans) take a little longer to cook, but with the same amount of water. WHAT TO SERVE WHEN These go well as a side with most any meat, like Mom's Pot Roast (page 218), T-Bone for Two (page 160), or Lemon-Curry Roasted Chicken (page 227).

SERVES 4 TO 6

- 1 1/2 pounds green beans, stem ends removed
- 2 garlic cloves, minced
- 3 tablespoons olive oil
- 1 tablespoon unsalted butter
- Sea salt and freshly ground black pepper to taste

1. Place the beans in a medium saucepan with 1 1/2 cups cold water. Sprinkle with the minced garlic, drizzle with the olive oil, and place the butter on top of the beans. Season with salt and pepper, cover and bring to a boil over high heat. Reduce the heat to medium-low and simmer the beans, covered, until the water has cooked off, 12 to 14 minutes. Check from time to time to make sure the water hasn't cooked off before the beans are done; if it has, add a splash more water.

2. When the beans are done and all the water has cooked off and you can hear the beans sizzling in the pot, let them cook about 30 seconds longer to sauté in the butter and oil; be careful not to burn them at this point. Season with more salt and pepper to taste and serve warm.

about . . .
SERVING FOOD AT ROOM TEMPERATURE

Serving food at room temperature is such a convenience, especially when you're cooking for a crowd. In a cool place, foods can sit at room temperature safely for 1 1/2 to 2 hours. My rule is that a dish cooked with only olive oil can be served room temperature without compromising the texture or flavor whatsoever, but something cooked with butter or a combination of butter and oil is best served warm. The butter will solidify as it cools, changing the texture after 30 minutes or so. The butter can also spoil if it sits out at room temperature. If you want to serve vegetables at room temperature, substitute oil in a recipe for the butter.

Rosemary-Caramelized Parsnips

At the Market we roast every vegetable you can imagine (and some you might not), from radishes to cauliflower to beets to cabbage. Root vegetables, like these parsnips, are particularly popular because the roasting makes root vegetables candy-sweet. WHAT TO SERVE WHEN Roasted root vegetables go with most anything, but I especially think of serving them with roasted meats, like the Herb-Roasted Rack of Lamb (page 220) or Standing Pork Roast (page 215).

SERVES 4 TO 6

1¹/₂ pounds parsnips, peeled, halved lengthwise, and halved again crosswise
2 tablespoons unsalted butter, melted
2 tablespoons olive oil
¹/₄ cup apple cider or unfiltered apple juice
1 tablespoon apple cider vinegar
1 tablespoon chopped fresh rosemary
Sea salt and freshly ground black pepper to taste

1. Preheat the oven to 400°F.

2. Place the parsnips on a large baking sheet with sides. Drizzle with the melted butter, olive oil, apple cider, and vinegar; sprinkle with the rosemary, salt, and pepper and toss to coat. Spread the parsnips in a single layer on the baking sheet and roast, stirring or shaking the pan occasionally, for 30 to 35 minutes, until they are tender and caramel colored. Remove the parsnips from the oven, season with additional rosemary, salt, and pepper, and serve immediately.

Think Outside the Recipe
YOU COULD COOK ALMOST ANY ROOT VEGETABLES USING THIS RECIPE, INCLUDING CARROTS, SALSIFY, TURNIPS, SLICED RUTABAGAS, OR ANY COMBINATION.

Lemon Roasted Asparagus

Our salad chef Laura Cyr created this simple but delicious asparagus dish. We get two crops of asparagus in North Carolina, one in the spring and another in the fall, so this is a staple at the Market for a good part of the year. WHAT TO SERVE WHEN I love this asparagus alongside Eggs Benedict (page 18). It also makes a healthy, easy-to-eat snack to take on picnics, or you can toss leftovers into a salad the next day.

SERVES 6 TO 8

1 pound thin asparagus, trimmed of tough ends
¹/₄ cup olive oil
Juice of 1 lemon
2 tablespoons balsamic vinegar
Sea salt and freshly ground black pepper to taste
2 tablespoons chopped chives or scallions (white and green parts of scallions)

1. Preheat the oven to 400°F.

2. Lay the asparagus on a baking sheet with sides and drizzle with the oil, lemon juice, and vinegar. Sprinkle with salt and pepper and toss to coat. Spread the asparagus in an even layer and roast, turning once, for 8 to 10 minutes, depending on the size of the asparagus, until they are bright green and just tender but still slightly crisp.

3. Arrange the asparagus spears on a serving platter, pour any remaining cooking liquid over them, and season with additional salt and pepper to taste. Serve warm or cover and refrigerate until ready to serve. Sprinkle with the chopped chives just before serving.

Cabbage Two Ways

I think cabbage is an underrated vegetable. It's easy to make, it's good for you, and it has a distinct, slightly sweet flavor that goes well with so many meats: pork, chicken, or fish. It also has a nice long growing season. Cabbage gets sweeter after it's hit by frost, so it's one of the few green vegetables that is best in the winter. I give you two distinct ways to prepare it here.

Roasted Cabbage Wedges

SERVES 4 TO 6

1 small to medium head green cabbage (about 1½ pounds), cored and cut into 6 or 8 large wedges
2 tablespoons unsalted butter, melted
3 tablespoons olive oil
    Sea salt and freshly ground black pepper to taste
2 tablespoons chopped fresh flat-leaf parsley leaves

1. Preheat the oven to 400°F.

2. Place the cabbage wedges on a baking sheet with sides. Drizzle with the butter and olive oil, sprinkle with the salt and pepper, and toss to coat. Pour ½ cup water around the cabbage and roast for 30 to 35 minutes, turning several times, until the cabbage is tender and slightly crisp and golden brown around the edges.

3. Season with more salt and pepper to taste, sprinkle with the parsley, and serve immediately.

Steamed Cabbage with Rosemary

SERVES 4 TO 6

1 small to medium head green cabbage (about 1½ pounds), cored and cut into 4 or 6 large wedges
2 fresh rosemary sprigs
3 tablespoons olive oil
    Sea salt and freshly ground black pepper to taste
½ teaspoon crushed red pepper flakes

Place the cabbage wedges in a medium saucepan over medium heat with 1½ cups water and the rosemary sprigs. Drizzle with the olive oil and season with the salt and pepper and red pepper flakes. Cover and steam for 15 to 20 minutes, until almost all the water has evaporated and the cabbage is tender. Serve immediately.

Roasted Cauliflower with Brown Butter and Sage

I'd never roasted cauliflower until recently, after I tasted some that one of the cooks at the Market had roasted. Roasting really intensifies the taste of cauliflower, and perhaps even more important, it gives it color. WHAT TO SERVE WHEN Cauliflower goes with just about any meat; I like to serve this with the Slow-Roasted Pork Shoulder (page 212) or the Lemon-Curry Roasted Chicken (page 227).

SERVES 4

1 head cauliflower, cut or broken into bite-size florets
4 tablespoons unsalted butter
2 tablespoons olive oil
2 tablespoons chopped fresh sage leaves
    Sea salt and freshly ground black pepper to taste

1. Preheat the oven to 400°F.

2. Place the cauliflower on a baking sheet with sides.

3. Melt the butter over medium heat and cook for 2 to 3 minutes, until it just browns and gives off a nutty aroma; be careful not to let it burn. Add the olive oil and sage and pour over the cauliflower. Season with salt and pepper and toss to coat.

4. Roast the cauliflower for 30 to 35 minutes, stirring midway through so it cooks evenly, until it is light brown around the edges. Season with additional salt and pepper to taste and serve warm.

about . . .
FRIED SAGE

Fried sage leaves make an elegant finish to roast chicken, turkey, or pork, or any dish containing sage. I've tried frying other herbs, but sage, maybe because the leaves are thicker than other herb leaves, fry up the best. And the flavor of sage is enhanced with cooking in a way other herbs aren't. I fry sage leaves in either butter or olive oil, depending on how I'll use them. If I just want the leaves, I fry them in oil. I fry them in brown butter when I want to use the butter, too. The leaves tend to burn very quickly, but the good news is, they're just sage leaves; you can fry another one until you get it right. The trick is to take the leaves out of the hot oil or butter as soon as they crisp, which takes just a few seconds.

Roasted Mushrooms with Green Peas and Tomatoes

Make this easy dish as a colorful, flavorful side to grilled steak or simple roasted chicken.

SERVES 4 TO 6

- 8 ounces cremini or button mushrooms (or portobello mushrooms), wiped clean, larger mushrooms cut into bite-size pieces
- 1 16-ounce bag (3 cups) frozen petite peas, rinsed and drained
- 1/2 pint grape or cherry tomatoes
- 1 small red onion, halved lengthwise and thinly sliced
- 2 tablespoons olive oil
- 2 tablespoons unsalted butter, melted
  Sea salt and freshly ground black pepper to taste
- 2 tablespoons chopped fresh flat-leaf parsley leaves

1. Preheat the oven to 400°F.

2. Place the mushrooms, peas, tomatoes, and onion on a large baking sheet with sides. Drizzle with the oil and butter, season with salt and pepper, and stir to coat. Spread the vegetables in an even layer and roast for 18 to 20 minutes, stirring often, until the mushrooms are golden brown and the tomatoes are soft. Sprinkle with the parsley and more salt and pepper, and serve warm.

Think Outside the Recipe
THIS RECIPE CAN ALSO BE MADE WITH BROCCOLI OR GREEN BEANS, THOUGH THE BEANS WILL TAKE ABOUT 5 MINUTES LONGER TO COOK. YOU CAN ALSO USE THIS RECIPE AS A BASE TO PREPARE THE VEGETABLES ON THE GRILL.

Smashed Green Peas

When I'm testing recipes, my nephew Patrick, who runs the Durham Market, eats with us several times a week. When he really likes something, he says, "I don't think this is quite right. Don't you think you should test that again?" I served these peas with the Herb-Roasted Rack of Lamb (page 220), and now he constantly suggests I test them again to get them just perfect. It's so sweet and flavorful it's hard to believe it contains almost nothing but peas. WHAT TO SERVE WHEN Their bright green color looks beautiful on the plate and makes a nice bed for any lamb dish, or grilled shrimp or fish.

SERVES 4 TO 6

- 1 16-ounce bag frozen petite peas, rinsed and drained
- 4 tablespoons unsalted butter
  Sea salt and freshly ground black pepper to taste
- 2 tablespoons heavy cream

1. Place the peas in a medium saucepan with 3/4 cup cold water, 2 tablespoons of the butter, salt, and pepper and bring to a low boil over medium heat. Cover, reduce the heat, and simmer the peas for 15 to 20 minutes, until tender but still bright green.

2. Drain off the excess water. Add the remaining 2 tablespoons butter and the heavy cream and mash the peas with a potato masher until smooth. Season with additional salt and pepper to taste and serve warm.

about . . .
SALT

I've recently started using sea salt for all my savory cooking. It's just so much more flavorful than kosher salt, which is what I used to use, so you need less of it to season your food. The other salt I always have at home is *fleur de sel,* a very special French sea salt. Buy a small container and reserve for instances where it really makes a difference: sprinkle a bit on fish after it's cooked, or on a tomato salad. At home, I use sea salt even in baked goods; it's all I keep on hand.

Herb Grilled Tomatoes

When Peter and I went on vacation in Ireland, we were served tomatoes like these with our eggs for breakfast, and we just loved them. It's such a simple concept; the tomatoes get sweeter and juicier after just a few minutes on the fire. If you don't already have the grill fired up, make them in a grill pan or under the broiler. WHAT TO SERVE WHEN Put the tomatoes on the grill when you make Sliced New York Strip Steak (page 159) or Simple Succulent Grilled Pork Chops (page 166), or serve them alongside any egg dish. On a bed of sautéed spinach and topped with finely grated Parmesan, the tomatoes can be the centerpiece of a warm, satisfying vegetarian meal.

SERVES 4 TO 6

2 tablespoons balsamic vinegar
2 tablespoons olive oil
1 garlic clove, minced
2 tablespoons chopped fresh rosemary
3 medium beefsteak tomatoes, cored
   and halved crosswise
   Sea salt and freshly ground black pepper to taste

1. Prepare a red-hot fire in a charcoal or gas grill.

2. Whisk the vinegar, oil, garlic, and rosemary together in a small bowl.

3. Place the tomatoes, cut side up, in a small shallow dish, drizzle with the vinaigrette, and roll the tomatoes in the vinaigrette to coat. Turn the tomatoes cut side down and let them marinate at room temperature for 20 to 30 minutes.

4. Just before grilling, season the tomatoes with salt and pepper. Place the tomatoes, cut side down, on the grill for 3 to 4 minutes, until they begin to darken and plump up. Remove the tomatoes from the grill and return them to the dish they marinated in. Spoon the marinade over the tomatoes and serve warm.

❝ *The only time to make these herb-grilled tomatoes is when you have sweet, vine-ripened tomatoes.* ❞

Cider Roasted Root Vegetables

This is one of my favorite ways to cook root vegetables—the sweetness of the cider really brings out their natural flavor.

SERVES 4 TO 6

1/4 cup cider vinegar
1/4 cup unfiltered apple juice or fresh apple cider
2 tablespoons olive oil
3 tablespoons unsalted butter, melted
1 tablespoon Dijon mustard
2 tablespoons chopped fresh rosemary or thyme or a combination
2 small turnips, trimmed, peeled and quartered lengthwise
4 small Yukon Gold or red potatoes, halved
1 medium sweet potato, peeled and cut into 2-inch wedges
2 carrots, peeled and cut into 2-inch pieces
2 parsnips peeled and cut into 2-inch pieces
Sea salt and freshly ground black pepper to taste
2 tablespoons chopped fresh parsley

1. Preheat the oven to 400°F.

2. Whisk the vinegar, apple juice, oil, butter, mustard, and rosemary together in a large bowl. Add the turnips, potatoes, sweet potatoes, carrots, and parsnips and toss to coat. Season with salt and pepper and scatter the vegetables in a single layer on a large baking sheet with sides. Roast for 45 to 50 minutes, turning the vegetables occasionally with a spatula, until they are tender and light golden brown around the edges. Toss with the parsley and serve warm or at room temperature.

Think Outside the Recipe
THINK OF THIS MORE AS A METHOD FOR COOKING VEGETABLES THAN AS AN EXACT RECIPE. USE WHICHEVER OF THESE ROOT VEGETABLES YOU HAVE, OR INCLUDE OTHER MORE UNUSUAL ROOT VEGETABLES, SUCH AS RUTABAGA OR SALSIFY.

Cider-Braised Endive

The sweetness of the sauce is the perfect contrast to the bitterness of the endive. WHAT TO SERVE WHEN This endive makes a nice bed for Pan-Seared Grouper (page 185) or Crispy Pan-Seared Duck Breast (page 151).

SERVES 4 TO 6

1 tablespoon unsalted butter
1 tablespoon olive oil
4 heads endive (about 1 pound), trimmed and halved
1 cup fresh apple cider or unfiltered apple juice
2 tablespoons apple cider vinegar
1 tablespoon light brown sugar
Leaves of 3 to 4 fresh thyme sprigs (about 1 tablespoon)
Sea salt and freshly ground black pepper to taste
1 tablespoon chopped fresh parsley

1. To wash the endive, cut it in half and soak it in water for 5 to 10 minutes. You want to make sure to keep the leaves together for this dish. Cut the core out of the endive.

2. Heat the butter and olive oil in a large heavy sauté pan over medium heat until the butter melts. Add the endive, cut side down, and cook about 2 minutes, until the endive is light brown.

3. Add the cider, vinegar, sugar, thyme, salt and pepper, reduce the heat to low and simmer, uncovered for about 15 minutes, until the endive is tender and the juices are thick and syrupy. Spoon the pan juices over the endive a few times while it's cooking. Remove them from the oven and serve warm, cut side up, drizzled with the pan juices and sprinkled with the chopped fresh parsley.

Think Outside the Recipe
DEPENDING ON WHAT YOU'RE SERVING IT WITH, OR WHAT YOU HAVE IN THE HOUSE, BRAISE THE ENDIVE IN FRESH ORANGE JUICE, CHICKEN BROTH, VEGETABLE BROTH, OR WINE IN PLACE OF THE APPLE CIDER.

Butter-Steamed Fingerling Potatoes with Chopped Fresh Herbs

Fingerling potatoes are so flavorful, I like them best with a simple preparation. The method in this recipe both steams and sautés the potatoes, so they turn a nice golden brown. Fingerlings are small, so they cook really quickly. I give a variety of herb options here because I change the herbs I cook them with depending on what I'm serving with the potatoes. WHAT TO SERVE WHEN These make a good, simple side with hearty grilled meats like the T-Bone for Two (page 160) or Rosemary-Mint Lamb Chops (page 166).

SERVES 4 TO 6

1 pound fingerling potatoes, scrubbed well
2 tablespoons olive oil
2 tablespoons unsalted butter
 Sea salt and freshly ground black pepper to taste
1 tablespoon chopped fresh flat-leaf parsley leaves
1 tablespoon chopped fresh tarragon, thyme, marjoram, sage, or rosemary

1. Place the potatoes in a medium saucepan with 1½ cups cool water and bring to a boil over high heat. Add the olive oil, butter, salt, and pepper; reduce the heat, cover, and simmer the potatoes for 15 to 18 minutes, until they are tender when pierced with the tip of a knife.

2. Uncover the pot and sprinkle the potatoes with the herbs. Simmer the potatoes, uncovered, 2 to 3 minutes longer, until all the water has evaporated. After the water has evaporated, the potatoes will begin to sizzle as they sauté in the pan. Let them cook this way for a few minutes, until golden brown.

Pan-Braised Carrots with Orange and Rosemary

I cook these carrots often at home, especially in the colder months; they're simple to make yet so flavorful. I buy carrots with the tops on. They're so sweet, and they're small enough that for a recipe like this, you don't need to cut them. WHAT TO SERVE WHEN These sweet carrots go nicely with any fall or wintry meats, like Mom's Pot Roast (page 218), Herb-Marinated Grilled Turkey Breasts (page 148), or Standing Pork Roast (page 215).

SERVES 4 TO 6

1 pound small carrots, with tops on (about 2 bunches) or bagged baby carrots
2 tablespoons olive oil
1 tablespoon unsalted butter
1 tablespoon chopped fresh rosemary
 Juice of 1 orange
 Sea salt and freshly ground black pepper to taste

1. Trim the tops off the carrots, leaving about ½ inch of the green stem attached, and wash thoroughly.

2. Heat the olive oil and butter in a large sauté pan over medium heat until the butter melts. Add the carrots and cook, stirring from time to time, for about 8 minutes, until the carrots are tender and have a little color.

3. Add the rosemary and cook for 1 to 2 minutes longer, stirring occasionally. Stir in the orange juice, ½ cup of cold water, salt, and pepper. Cover, reduce the heat to low, and let the carrots simmer until nearly all of the liquid has cooked off, about 10 minutes. Season with more salt and pepper to taste and serve warm.

Oven-Roasted Garlicky Fries

We can never make enough of these hot, crispy fries at the Market. They smell so good that the minute we take a batch out of the oven, our customers know—and the potatoes are gone. It doesn't help that the staff eats half of them before the potatoes leave the kitchen.

SERVES 4 TO 6

1½ pounds Yukon Gold potatoes (6 to 8 potatoes), scrubbed (not peeled) and cut lengthwise into 6 to 8 wedges (depending on the size of the potato)
¼ cup olive oil
2 tablespoons unsalted butter, melted
4 garlic cloves, minced
2 tablespoons chopped fresh rosemary or 2 teaspoons dried, crumbled
   Sea salt and freshly ground black pepper to taste

1. Preheat the oven to 400°F.

2. Place the potatoes on a baking sheet with sides and toss with the olive oil and butter, garlic, rosemary, salt, and pepper. Spread in one layer and roast for 25 to 30 minutes, until they are tender and golden brown and slightly crisp on the outside. Serve warm or at room temperature.

Think Outside the Recipe
I LIKE YUKON GOLD POTA-
TOES BECAUSE THEY HAVE
A RICH, BUTTERY TASTE
AND SUCH A NICE COLOR,
BUT I SOMETIMES MAKE
THESE POTATOES WITH
MORE UNUSUAL VARIETIES,
LIKE BLUE FINNS, FINGER-
LINGS, OR RED NEW
POTATOES.

Smashed Roasted Potatoes with Rosemary

The secret to these potatoes is using good, green, fruity olive oil and the best sea salt you have. WHAT TO SERVE WHEN These are great with Peter's All-World Burgers (page 155 or Sliced New York Strip Steak (page 159).

SERVES 4 TO 6

1½ pounds small Yukon Gold potatoes (6 to 8)
½ cup extra-virgin olive oil
   Sea salt and freshly ground black pepper to taste
2 tablespoons chopped fresh rosemary or flat-leaf parsley leaves

1. Preheat the oven to 400°F.

2. Place the potatoes in a large pot of cold, salted water and bring the water to a boil over high heat. Reduce the heat and cook the potatoes at a low boil for 15 to 20 minutes, until they have softened but are still slightly undercooked. They should feel slightly firm, not mushy, when pierced with the tip of a sharp knife. Drain the potatoes and allow them to cool slightly.

3. Pour ¼ cup of the olive oil on a large baking sheet with sides and place the potatoes on the baking sheet. When the potatoes are cool enough to touch, smash them flat with the heel of your hand. Drizzle with 2 tablespoons of the remaining olive oil, sprinkle with salt, pepper, and half the rosemary, and toss to coat. Bake the potatoes for 15 minutes, until the undersides are golden brown and crispy.

4. Remove the pan from the oven, flip the potatoes with a spatula, drizzle with the remaining 2 tablespoons olive oil and return them to the oven for another 15 minutes, until they are crisp on both sides. Sprinkle with the remaining rosemary and additional salt and pepper to taste and serve immediately.

Twice-Baked Potatoes for All Seasons

At the Market, these hearty potatoes are eaten as a meal in themselves. They're a big hit with kids and students. Below is a base recipe plus variations to make them during each season. To make them slightly less decadent, substitute equal amounts of plain low-fat yogurt or buttermilk mixed with a splash of olive oil for the butter and sour cream. My way of lowering the calories of these decadent potatoes is to use small Yukon Gold potatoes instead of the big russets—and to serve only one per person.

SERVES 8

4 large russet potatoes (about 3 pounds), scrubbed well
Olive oil for rubbing on the potatoes (about 2 tablespoons)
½ cup sour cream
6 tablespoons unsalted butter, softened
¼ cup milk
1 cup freshly grated Parmesan cheese
2 tablespoons chopped flat-leaf parsley plus more for garnish
Sea salt and freshly ground black pepper to taste

1. Preheat the oven to 400°F.

2. Pierce the potatoes in several places with a fork and rub with olive oil. Place the potatoes directly on the oven rack to bake until they are tender when pierced with a knife, about 1 hour. Remove from the oven and cool slightly.

3. Reduce the oven temperature to 375°F.

4. When the potatoes are cool enough to handle, cut them in half lengthwise and use a large spoon to scoop the flesh out into a large bowl, leaving a ½-inch-thick "shell." Add the sour cream, butter, milk, cheese, parsley, and salt and pepper and mash until all is incorporated. Scoop the filling into the shells, dividing it evenly among them.

5. Place the potatoes on a baking sheet and bake until the stuffing is golden and the potatoes are heated through, about 20 minutes. Garnish with more parsley and serve warm.

WINTER: *Bacon, Blue Cheese, and Garlic-Sautéed Broccoli*
Omit the Parmesan and parsley; add ½ head broccoli florets, broken up into bite-size pieces, blanched, and sautéed with 1 tablespoon olive oil and 2 minced garlic cloves; 8 ounces crispy fried bacon, crumbled; 1 cup crumbled blue cheese; and 2 teaspoons chopped fresh thyme leaves, plus more for garnish.

SPRING: *Sweet Peas, Parmesan, and Chives*
Omit the parsley; add 1 cup fresh or frozen petite green peas, blanched; and ¼ cup chopped fresh chives, plus more for garnish.

SUMMER: *Roasted Red Pepper, Corn, and Cheddar Cheese*
Omit the Parmesan and parsley; add kernels from 2 ears fresh corn (1 cup kernels); 1 red pepper, roasted, peeled, seeded, and chopped; 1 cup shredded sharp Cheddar cheese; and 4 teaspoons chopped fresh thyme, plus more for garnish.

FALL: *Sautéed Spinach, Mushrooms, and Thyme*
Omit the Parmesan and parsley; add 1 tablespoon olive oil; 1 tablespoon unsalted butter; 1 cup button mushrooms, thinly sliced (about ¼ pound); 2 cups spinach leaves sautéed with 2 tablespoons olive oil and 2 minced garlic cloves; 1 cup grated Swiss cheese; 1 teaspoon each chopped fresh rosemary and chopped fresh chives, plus more for garnish.

Rice Pilaf for All Seasons

Pilaf is different from other rice dishes in that you cook the rice quickly in the pan with oil or butter before adding liquid, giving the rice a rich, slightly nutty flavor. I like to toss rice with different grains and vegetables. These are some of my favorite seasonal combos.

WINTER
Long Grain and Wild Rice Pilaf with Quinoa, Golden Raisins, and Orange Zest

SERVES 4 TO 6

1 tablespoon unsalted butter
1 tablespoon olive oil
1 leek, washed well, trimmed, and julienned (white and green parts)
1 cup long grain–wild rice blend, rinsed and drained
2½ cups chicken broth, or vegetable broth or water
1 large carrot, trimmed and julienned
Grated zest and juice of 1 orange
2 teaspoons sea salt, plus more to taste
½ teaspoon freshly ground black pepper, plus more to taste
½ cup quinoa
2 tablespoons chopped fresh flat-leaf parsley leaves
1 tablespoon fresh thyme leaves
½ cup golden raisins

1. Melt the butter and olive oil together in a medium saucepan over medium-low heat. Add the leek and cook and stir for about 5 minutes to soften. Stir in the rice and cook, stirring often, for about 2 minutes, until the rice slides around easily in the pan. Stir in the broth, carrot, orange zest and juice, 2 teaspoons salt, and ½ teaspoon pepper. Reduce the heat to low, cover, and simmer for about 25 minutes.

2. While the rice simmers, rinse the quinoa in a fine-mesh strainer and drain well. Add the quinoa to the saucepan with the rice and stir to combine. Replace the lid and simmer the quinoa and rice for another 15 minutes, until all the liquid is absorbed and the grains are soft and fluffy.

3. Remove the saucepan from the heat and stir in the parsley, thyme, and raisins. Season with additional salt and pepper to taste and serve warm.

SPRING
Jasmine Rice Pilaf with Sweet Peas, Chives, Lemon Zest, and Toasted Almonds

SERVES 4 TO 6

1 tablespoon unsalted butter
1 tablespoon olive oil
1 medium onion, chopped
1½ cups jasmine rice or basmati rice, rinsed and drained
2 cups chicken broth, or vegetable broth or water
½ cup unsweetened coconut milk
2 teaspoons sea salt, plus more to taste
½ teaspoon freshly ground black pepper, plus more to taste
1 cup fresh or frozen petite peas, rinsed and drained
¼ cup chopped fresh chives
¾ cup slivered almonds, lightly toasted
Grated zest and juice of 1 lemon

1. Melt the butter and olive oil together in a medium saucepan over medium-low heat. Add the onion and cook, stirring often, for about 5 minutes, until the onion is soft and translucent. Stir in the rice and cook, stirring often, for about 2 minutes, until the rice slides easily in the pan. Stir in the broth, coconut milk, 2 teaspoons salt, ½ teaspoon pepper, and peas, and bring to a boil over medium-high heat. Reduce the heat to low, cover, and simmer for 15 to 20 minutes, until the rice is fluffy and has absorbed the liquid.

2. Remove the saucepan from the heat. Add the chives, almonds, and lemon zest and juice and gently stir to combine. Season with more salt and pepper to taste and serve warm.

SUMMER

Basmati Rice Pilaf with Zucchini, Roasted Red Peppers, and Parsley

SERVES 4 TO 6

- 1 medium zucchini or yellow crookneck or pattypan squash, cut into ½-inch cubes
- 2 tablespoons olive oil
- 2 teaspoons salt, plus more to taste
- ½ teaspoon freshly ground black pepper, plus more to taste
- 1 tablespoon unsalted butter
- 1 medium white onion, chopped
- 1½ cups basmati or jasmine rice, rinsed and drained
- 2½ cups chicken broth, or vegetable broth or water
- 2 red bell peppers, roasted, peeled, and diced (see "Peppers," page 54)
- ½ cup chopped fresh flat-leaf parsley leaves
- 4 or 5 basil leaves, cut into thin strips

1. Preheat the oven to 400°F.

2. Place the zucchini cubes on a baking sheet with sides and toss with 1 tablespoon of the olive oil and salt and pepper to taste. Roast the zucchini for about 15 minutes, stirring periodically so it browns evenly, until it is tender and golden brown. Cool to room temperature.

3. Melt the butter and the remaining 1 tablespoon of olive oil together in a medium saucepan over medium-low heat. Add the onion and cook about 5 minutes, until the onion is soft. Add the rice and continue to cook, stirring often, for about 2 minutes, until the rice slides around easily in the pan. Stir in the broth, 2 teaspoons salt, and ½ teaspoon pepper and bring to a low boil over medium-high heat. Reduce the heat to low, cover, and simmer for 15 to 20 minutes, until the rice is fluffy and has absorbed the liquid.

4. Remove the rice from the heat, add the roasted peppers, roasted zucchini, parsley, and basil, and stir gently to combine. Season with additional salt and pepper to taste and serve warm.

FALL

Brown Rice and Wheat Berry Pilaf with Roasted Acorn Squash, Spinach, and Sautéed Shallots

SERVES 4 TO 6

- ½ acorn squash (about 1 pound), peeled and seeded
- 2 tablespoons olive oil
- 2 teaspoons sea salt, plus more to taste
- ½ teaspoon freshly ground black pepper, plus more to taste
- 1 tablespoon unsalted butter
- 4 shallots, peeled and thinly sliced
- 1 cup brown rice, rinsed and drained
- ½ cup wheat berries
- 3 cups chicken broth, or vegetable broth or water
- 6 ounces spinach, washed, stems removed, and drained (about 4 cups leaves)

1. Preheat the oven to 400°F.

2. Cut the squash into ½-inch cubes and place on a baking pan with sides. Drizzle with 1 tablespoon of the olive oil, sprinkle with salt and pepper to taste, and toss to coat. Roast the squash for 35 to 40 minutes, stirring periodically, until tender and golden brown. Allow to cool slightly.

3. Melt the remaining tablespoon of olive oil and the butter together in a medium saucepan over medium-low heat. Add the shallots and cook about 5 minutes to soften. Add the rice and wheat berries and cook and stir about 2 minutes longer. Stir in the broth, 2 teaspoons salt, and ½ teaspoon pepper and bring to a boil over medium-high heat. Reduce the heat to low, cover, and simmer for 40 to 45 minutes or until all the liquid is absorbed and the grains are fluffy.

4. Remove the saucepan from the heat. Add the roasted squash and the spinach and toss gently to combine and to wilt the spinach. Season with additional salt and pepper to taste and serve warm.

five

quick and tasty meat main dishes

Crispy Pan-Roasted Chicken with Spaghetti Squash and Balsamic-Roasted Tomatoes ○ Herb-Marinated Grilled Chicken Breast Your Way ○ Greek Chicken with Tomatoes and Feta ○ Chicken Cacciatore ○ Creamy Chicken with Biscuits ○ Grilled Buffalo Chicken Strips with Chunky Blue Cheese Dip ○ Herb-Marinated Grilled Turkey Breasts ○ Crispy Pan-Seared Duck Breast with Rosemary and Dried Cranberries ○ Pan-Fried Quail with Marsala Apple Cider Sauce ○ Grilled Quail with Gremolata ○ Peter's All-World Burgers ○ Sliced New York Strip Steak with Horseradish Mustard Sauce ○ T-Bone for Two with Roasted Garlic Aïoli ○ Tequila Lime Skirt Steak with Grilled Scallions ○ Grilled Beef Filet Topped with Stilton and Crispy Shallots ○ Rosemary-Mint Lamb Chops ○ Simple Succulent Grilled Pork Chops ○ Pan-Grilled Pork Paillards with Ginger Teriyaki Glaze ○ Hoisin-Marinated Grilled Pork Tenderloin

The recipes in this chapter are some of the most important in this book. For one thing, main dishes are the centerpiece of a meal—and of a table. But what's more, they're the kinds of dishes you are likely to make after a long workday, which is most every day.

A short cooking time is not just a convenience to the home cook; it is also a way of preserving the enticing fresh flavors of your raw ingredients. Meats are given nice flavor with a glaze or marinade, salsas dress up chicken and steak, and seasonal vegetables and herbs are used to make these quick main dishes special.

This kind of clean, vibrantly flavored food is light and healthful, and yet absolutely satisfying. Dishes like Tequila Lime Skirt Steak or Crispy Pan-Roasted Chicken with Spaghetti Squash and Balsamic-Roasted Tomatoes are certainly special enough for company, but they are also the kinds recipes that might become a weeknight standby.

" Balsamic vinegar has become a
staple in my kitchen as well as
these tomatoes. I always make
extra to have on hand for salads. "

Crispy Pan-Roasted Chicken with Spaghetti Squash and Balsamic-Roasted Tomatoes

The skin side of this chicken is pan-roasted until crisp and the meat is tender and moist, a classic Italian preparation. Because the tomatoes are roasted, you can make this dish all fall and winter long with supermarket tomatoes. Spaghetti squash and tomatoes is not a combination you see often, but it is delicious. WHAT TO SERVE WHEN With all the vegetables that go in this dish, it needs nothing more than a light salad, like the Arugula and Endive Salad with Shaved Parmesan (page 72).

SERVES 4

4 boneless chicken breast halves
  (about 1½ pounds), skin on
2 tablespoons whole fresh marjoram leaves
  Sea salt and freshly ground black pepper to taste
2 tablespoons unsalted butter
2 tablespoons olive oil
  Juice of 1 lemon
1 cup dry white wine
  Roasted Spaghetti Squash (recipe follows)
  Balsamic-Roasted Tomatoes (recipe follows)

1. Rinse the chicken breasts and pat dry with paper towels. Stuff 5 or 6 leaves under the skin of each breast and season both sides with salt and pepper.

2. Melt the butter and olive oil together in a large non-stick or cast-iron skillet over medium-high heat. Place the chicken in the skillet skin side down, reduce the heat to medium, and cook until the skin is crisp and golden brown and the edges of the chicken are opaque, 7 to 8 minutes. Turn the chicken, squeeze on the lemon juice, and pour the wine over the chicken. Reduce the heat to medium-low and cook, spooning the pan liquids over the chicken, until the juices run clear when the breast is pierced with a sharp knife at the thickest part, 8 to 10 minutes. Transfer the chicken to a platter and cover loosely with foil.

3. Reduce the heat and simmer the pan juices for a few minutes to thicken slightly. Spoon the spaghetti squash onto a large platter or individual plates. Place the chicken breasts on top of the squash, top each breast with three plum tomato halves, and pour the sauce over the chicken. Serve immediately.

Roasted Spaghetti Squash

SERVES 4

1 medium spaghetti squash (about 4 pounds), halved lengthwise and seeded
3 tablespoons olive oil
2 tablespoons balsamic vinegar
1 cup grated Parmesan cheese (about 3 ounces)
1 tablespoon chopped fresh rosemary
Sea salt and freshly ground black pepper to taste

1. Preheat the oven to 400°F.

2. Place the squash on a large baking sheet with sides, cut side down. Pour 1 cup of water, 1 tablespoon of the olive oil, and the vinegar over the squash and roast for about 1 hour, until it is tender to the touch. Cool slightly.

3. When the squash is cool enough to handle, turn the halves over and run a fork through the flesh of the squash to shred it into long, spaghetti-like strands. Place the shredded squash in a large bowl. Add the remaining olive oil, grated Parmesan cheese, rosemary, and salt and pepper to taste and toss gently to combine.

Balsamic-Roasted Tomatoes

MAKES 12 TOMATO HALVES

6 plum tomatoes (about 1¹/₂ pounds), halved
1 small red onion, thinly sliced
2 tablespoons olive oil
1 tablespoon balsamic vinegar
1 tablespoon fresh rosemary
Sea salt and freshly ground black pepper to taste

1. Preheat the oven to 400°F.

2. Place the tomatoes and onion slices on a baking sheet with sides. Drizzle with the olive oil and vinegar, sprinkle with the rosemary, salt, and pepper, and toss to coat. Spread the tomatoes and onion in a single layer with the tomatoes cut side down and roast for 30 to 35 minutes, stirring occasionally, until the tomatoes are soft and shriveled and the vinegar has caramelized on the bottom of the pan.

TRICKS OF MY TRADE

○ **Marinate the night before.** It takes only about 5 minutes to assemble marinade ingredients, and having your meat or fish ready to throw on the grill or into the sauté pan the next night will make your life that much easier—and your food will taste that much better.

○ **Be prepared.** These dishes literally cook while you're standing in front of the stove or the grill; the most you have to do while they cook is baste, turn, touch, or check for doneness. So having your ingredients and your work area prepared is not just a fantasy ideal, it's the only task at hand. The temptation, especially when you're in a hurry, is to dive in and get started, but take the time to sit down and read the recipe all the way through. Then set up your work area and wash and prepare all the ingredients that go into the dish. The French culinary technical term for this is *mise en place*. In practical terms, it means you're not going to have to stop midway through cooking a piece of fish to chop a tomato that should have been added to the pan two minutes ago.

○ **Keep it simple,** especially for company. You really don't need to serve as much food as you think you do. One main dish, a side, and a salad are enough.

○ **Let it rest** Meat and chicken are much more flavorful and moist if you let them rest for 5 to 10 minutes after you take them off the heat, before cutting into them.

Herb-Marinated Grilled Chicken Breast Your Way

Skinless, boneless chicken breasts are the food I cook most often at home. They're just so convenient: I put the chicken breasts in a marinade before I leave for work and when I get home, I can have dinner on the table in 15 minutes. In addition to the sauces here and on the following pages, these chicken breasts are delicious with any fresh salsa. It's served here with Grilled Pineapple Salsa (page 196). If you don't feel like lighting your outdoor grill, cook these in a stovetop grill pan.

SERVES 4

- 4 boneless, skinless chicken breast halves (about 1½ pounds)
- ¼ cup dry white wine
- 2 tablespoons olive oil
- 2 tablespoons chopped fresh herbs (such as parsley, rosemary, thyme, tarragon, sage, marjoram, oregano, basil, chives)
- 1 shallot, minced
- 2 garlic cloves, minced
- 1 lemon, thinly sliced
- Sea salt and freshly ground black pepper to taste

1. Rinse the chicken breasts, pat them dry with paper towels, and place them in a shallow glass dish. Drizzle with the wine and olive oil, sprinkle with the herbs, shallot, and garlic, and turn several times to coat evenly. Place the lemon slices on top of the chicken, cover, and marinate in the refrigerator for several hours or overnight. Bring the chicken breasts to room temperature before cooking.

2. Prepare a hot fire in a charcoal or gas grill.

3. Remove the chicken breasts from the marinade, season with salt and pepper, and lay them on the grill over the hottest part of the fire for 5 to 7 minutes per side (depending on the thickness of the breasts), spooning the marinade over the breasts as they cook. While the chicken is cooking, grill the lemon slices for 2 to 3 minutes per side, until they're slightly charred. Transfer the lemon slices to a platter.

4. Move the chicken to the side of the grill, away from the direct heat, close the lid, and cook for another 4 to 5 minutes, until the juices run clear when the chicken

is pierced with a sharp knife. Transfer to the platter with the lemon slices. Cover loosely with foil to keep warm and let the chicken rest for about 5 minutes before serving. Serve warm, topped with the grilled lemon slices and the topping of your choice.

Rustic Tomato Concassé

Concassé is a simple, summer tomato sauce for which the tomatoes are cooked just enough so they are warmed through and begin to break down. Classic concassé calls for the tomatoes to be peeled and seeded but this is a short-cut version that takes about 10 minutes, start to finish. It freezes well, so it's a great way to cook the overload of tomatoes in your summer garden. You can toss concassé with pasta, serve it atop Creamy Cheesy Corn Grits (page 23), or spoon it over grilled fish or chicken.

MAKES ABOUT 4 CUPS

- 2 tablespoons olive oil
- 1 small onion, minced
- 2 garlic cloves, minced
- 2 pounds tomatoes, cored and chopped
- 3 tablespoons balsamic vinegar
- 8 fresh basil leaves, cut into thin strips
- Sea salt and freshly ground black pepper to taste

1. Heat the olive oil in a large skillet over medium heat. Add the onion and cook for 3 to 4 minutes, until translucent. Add the garlic and sauté for 1 minute, stirring constantly to prevent it from browning.

2. Stir in the chopped tomatoes, add the vinegar, and continue cooking for about 5 to 6 minutes, stirring constantly, until the tomatoes begin to break down and give off juices.

3. Remove the concassé from the heat. Stir in the basil and season with salt and pepper. Use immediately or refrigerate in an airtight container for up to 1 week.

Roasted Tomato Sauce with Basil

Roasting the tomatoes for this sauce gives it a smoky, earthy flavor that typical tomato sauce doesn't have. It's delicious with fish, chicken, or sausage or tossed with pasta and chunks of fresh or smoked mozzarella.

MAKES ABOUT 2 CUPS

1¼ pounds plum tomatoes (about 8 tomatoes), cored and halved
1 large yellow onion, peeled and quartered with the stem intact
3 garlic cloves, unpeeled
6 tablespoons olive oil
Sea salt and freshly ground pepper to taste
6 fresh basil leaves, cut into thin strips
1 tablespoon balsamic vinegar

1. Preheat the oven to 400°F

2. Place the tomatoes, onion, and garlic on a large baking sheet with sides. Drizzle with 3 tablespoons of the olive oil, season with salt and pepper, and toss to coat. Roast for 30 to 35 minutes, stirring occasionally, until the tomatoes are shriveled and the onion is soft and lightly brown.

3. Remove the garlic and onion from the baking sheet and scrape the tomatoes and juices from the baking sheet into the bowl of a food processor fitted with a metal blade. Peel the garlic cloves and drop them into the food processor with the tomatoes. Remove the stems from the onion and add them to the food processor. Pulse for about 1 minute, until the sauce is almost smooth but still has some texture. Add the basil, balsamic vinegar, and the remaining 3 tablespoons of olive oil and pulse to combine. Transfer the tomato sauce to a small bowl and season with additional salt and pepper to taste. Use immediately or refrigerate in an airtight container for up to 1 week or freeze for up to 3 months.

Pesto Your Way

I let the basic formula of fresh herb leaves pureed with olive oil, nuts, and cheese inspire many pesto variations.

MAKES ABOUT 1 CUP

2 cups packed basil leaves, washed, drained, and dried well
½ cup fresh flat-leaf parsley leaves
4 to 8 garlic cloves (depending on your taste and the size of the cloves)
¼ cup olive oil, or more as needed
¼ cup pine nuts
2 ounces Parmesan cheese, cut into chunks (about ⅔ cup grated)
Sea salt and freshly ground black pepper to taste

1. Place the basil, parsley, and garlic in the bowl of a food processor fitted with a metal blade and pulse to make a rough chop, scraping down the side of the bowl several times.

2. With the motor running, add the olive oil slowly through the feed tube, stopping several times to scrape down the sides of the bowl. Continue to run the food processor until the leaves are pureed.

3. Add the nuts, cheese, salt, and pepper and puree about 1 minute more, until the pesto is well blended and smooth. Add more olive oil if the pesto is too thick. Refrigerate in an airtight container until ready to serve. This will keep refrigerated for up to 2 weeks.

VARIATIONS

Herbs: In place of the basil and parsley leaves, use spinach, cilantro, arugula, mint, or a combination.

Nuts: In place of the pine nuts, use almonds, walnuts, pecans, hazelnuts, or a combination.

Cheese: In place of the Parmesan, use dry Jack, dry goat cheese, or pecorino Romano.

Some combinations I like are:

- Arugula, aged goat cheese, and almonds
- Cilantro, dry Jack, and pecans
- Spinach or arugula, Parmesan, and walnuts

Chipotle Caesar Dressing

One of our cooks at Foster's Market created this variation on a classic Caesar dressing. It's so good, we've continued to make it long after its inventor left us.

MAKES ABOUT 2½ CUPS

2 large eggs
2 tablespoons white wine vinegar
  Juice of 2 limes
4 garlic cloves
1 tablespoon chili powder
1 teaspoon crushed red pepper flakes
2 chipotle peppers in adobo
1 teaspoon sea salt, plus more to taste
½ teaspoon freshly ground black pepper, plus more
  to taste
1 teaspoon Colman's dry mustard
¼ teaspoon cayenne pepper
1 cup canola or safflower oil
½ cup extra-virgin olive oil
2 ounces Parmesan cheese, shredded or grated (about
  ½ cup)

Combine the eggs, vinegar, lime juice, garlic, chili powder, red pepper flakes, chipotle peppers, salt, pepper, mustard, and cayenne pepper in the bowl of a food processor fitted with a metal blade and pulse until the ingredients are well blended. With the motor running, add the canola and olive oils through the feed tube in a slow, steady stream until the dressing is thick and a smooth, creamy consistency. Add more oil if the dressing is too thick to use as a salad dressing. Remove the lid to add the Parmesan cheese and pulse until the cheese is incorporated. Use immediately or refrigerate in an airtight container for up to 1 week.

REINVENTION

Turn a few slices of leftover chicken into a refreshing and satisfying Caesar salad or sandwich. Toss chopped crispy hearts of romaine with Chipotle Caesar Dressing (left). Top with sliced chicken breast and shaved Parmesan.

Greek Chicken with Tomatoes and Feta

Tomato, oregano, and feta is a classic combination, and makes this simple chicken dish something special. It's one of our most popular dinner items at the Market. WHAT TO SERVE WHEN This chicken makes a healthy, satisfying supper with a green vegetable, like the Italian-Style Green Beans (page 113), and rice pilaf (see Rice Pilaf for All Seasons, page 128).

SERVES 4

```
4   boneless, skinless chicken breast halves (about
    1½ pounds)
    Grated zest and juice of 1 lemon
1   cup dry white wine
2   tablespoons chopped fresh oregano, plus more for
    garnish
½   teaspoon sea salt, plus more to taste
½   teaspoon freshly ground black pepper, plus more to
    taste
2   tablespoons olive oil
1   tablespoon unsalted butter
1   small onion, diced
4   plum tomatoes, cored and chopped
2   garlic cloves, minced
½   cup pitted Greek olives
6   fresh basil leaves cut into thin strips, plus more for
    garnish
2   ounces feta cheese, cut into ¼-inch cubes (about
    ½ cup)
```

1. Rinse the chicken breasts under cool water, pat dry with paper towels, and place them in a shallow glass baking dish.

2. Stir the lemon zest and juice, wine, oregano, salt, and pepper together in a small bowl. Pour the marinade over the chicken and rub it onto all sides. Cover and marinate the chicken in the refrigerator for several hours or overnight. Bring to room temperature before cooking.

3. Heat the olive oil and butter in a large skillet over medium-high heat until the butter melts. Remove the chicken breasts from the marinade, reserving the marinade to make the sauce, and place them in the skillet. Cook the chicken breasts, turning only once, for 4 to 5 minutes per side, until lightly brown on both sides. Transfer them to a platter loosely covered with foil to keep warm while you prepare the sauce.

4. Add the onion and tomatoes to the pan you cooked the chicken in, reduce the heat to medium, and cook, stirring frequently, 2 or 3 minutes, until the onion is soft and translucent and the tomatoes soften and release liquid. Add the garlic and sauté for 1 minute, stirring constantly. Add the reserved marinade and bring it to a boil. Reduce the heat and simmer for 2 to 3 minutes, until the liquid has reduced by half. Season with additional salt and pepper, if desired.

5. Return the chicken to the skillet with the sauce. Add the olives and basil and simmer on low heat 6 to 8 minutes, until the chicken is cooked through and feels firm to the touch.

6. Transfer the chicken breasts to a platter or individual plates. Spoon the sauce over each breast and scatter the feta cubes over the top. Garnish with the additional fresh basil and oregano leaves, and serve warm.

about . . .
MEAT MARINATOR

I'm a big fan of the instant meat marinator. It's a very simple contraption: a plastic container with a little vacuum-pump attached that takes the air out of the container, which allows meat or fish inside to marinate more quickly. Marinating for 10 minutes in one of these is the equivalent of marinating for several hours.

Chicken Cacciatore

Chicken thighs have so much flavor that they can really stand up to a rich sauce like this one. WHAT TO SERVE WHEN This wintry dish goes nicely with roasted butternut squash or Roasted Spaghetti Squash (page 135).

SERVES 4 TO 6

- 8 ounces cremini (Baby Bella) or button mushrooms, wiped clean, stems trimmed, and halved
- 5 tablespoons olive oil
- 2 tablespoons sherry vinegar
  Sea salt and freshly ground black pepper to taste
- 8 chicken thighs (about 2½ pounds)
- 2 tablespoons chopped fresh marjoram leaves
- 1 small yellow onion, diced
- 2 garlic cloves, minced
- ½ cup dry white wine
- 1 28-ounce can chopped tomatoes
- 1 cup chicken broth
- 2 tablespoons chopped fresh flat-leaf parsley leaves, plus more for garnishing the chicken
  Freshly grated Parmesan cheese, for garnish

1. Preheat the oven to 400°F.

2. Place the mushrooms, caps down, in a single layer in a small baking dish. Drizzle with 2 tablespoons of the olive oil and the vinegar, season with salt and pepper, and toss to coat. Roast the mushrooms until golden brown, about 20 minutes, stirring several times during the cooking process so they cook evenly.

3. Rinse the chicken, pat dry with paper towels, and season with salt, pepper, and 1 tablespoon of the marjoram.

4. Heat the remaining 3 tablespoons of olive oil in a large skillet over medium-high heat. Lay the chicken thighs in the skillet, reduce the heat to medium, and cook for 4 to 5 minutes per side until lightly browned on both sides. Transfer the chicken to a platter loosely covered with foil to keep warm.

5. Add the onion to the skillet you cooked the chicken in and cook over medium-high heat for about 5 minutes, stirring often, until soft and translucent. Add the garlic and sauté, stirring constantly, for 1 minute more. Add the wine and bring to a boil, scraping up all the brown bits from the bottom of the pan. Continue to boil for 2 to 3 minutes, until the wine has reduced by half. Stir in the chopped tomatoes and the chicken broth, bring to a low boil, and simmer 10 to 12 minutes, until the sauce reduces and thickens. Taste for salt and pepper and season with more if desired.

6. Return the chicken to the pan with the sauce and simmer 12 to 15 minutes, until the chicken is cooked through; the juices will run clear when the chicken is pierced with the tip of a small knife. Stir in the mushrooms, parsley, and remaining marjoram and cook for 1 to 2 minutes. Place the chicken thighs on individual plates and spoon the sauce over them. Garnish with the grated Parmesan cheese and a sprinkling of chopped parsley.

Think Outside the Recipe
IF YOU PREFER LIGHT MEAT, USE BONELESS, SKINLESS CHICKEN BREASTS IN PLACE OF THIGHS AND REDUCE THE COOKING TIME SLIGHTLY. ADD A FEW TABLESPOONS OF CAPERS OR ½ CUP OF SLICED GREEN OLIVES IF YOU LIKE THE SALTY ZING THEY GIVE TO A DISH.

Creamy Chicken with Biscuits

I don't always go to the trouble to make the biscuits that top this creamy, old-fashioned chicken dish because one of the best things about it is that it's quick and easy to make. Kids love it, so when I have out-of-town guests with kids for dinner, I make either this or Creamy Mac, Chicken, and Cheese (page 229).

SERVES 4 TO 6

 2 leeks, trimmed and chopped
 4 boneless, skinless chicken breast halves (about 1½ pounds)
¼ cup all-purpose flour
 1 teaspoon sea salt, plus more to taste
½ teaspoon freshly ground black pepper, plus more to taste
 1 tablespoon olive oil
 1 tablespoon unsalted butter
 1 bunch small carrots, trimmed and scrubbed
 1 cup heavy cream
½ cup chicken broth
 6 store-bought or homemade biscuits (see Angel Biscuits, page 28; Sweet Potato Buttermilk Biscuits, page 31)
 1 cup fresh or frozen petite green peas
 2 tablespoons chopped flat-leaf parsley leaves or chives

1. Preheat the oven to 250°F.

2. Place the leeks in large bowl or sink full of cold water and let them soak for 10 to 15 minutes to remove all the sand and dirt. Carefully skim out the leeks, leaving the grit behind. Drain well and dice.

3. Rinse the chicken breasts, pat them dry with paper towels, and cut on the diagonal into ¾-inch strips.

4. Mix the flour, 1 teaspoon salt, and ½ teaspoon pepper together in a medium bowl. Toss the chicken strips in the flour mixture to coat them evenly.

5. Warm the olive oil and butter in a large skillet over medium heat until the butter has melted and sizzles when you add a drop of flour. Add the chicken strips and sauté until they're golden brown and slightly crisp, about 3 minutes per side. Transfer to an ovenproof dish, cover loosely with foil, and place them in the oven to keep warm.

6. Add the leeks and carrots to the skillet you cooked the chicken in, reduce the heat to medium-low, and cook and stir the vegetables until the leeks are soft, about 5 minutes. Add the cream and chicken broth and bring to a low boil over medium-high heat. Simmer, stirring occasionally, for about 10 minutes or until the carrots are tender and the liquid has reduced by half.

7. Meanwhile, place the biscuits in the oven for about 10 minutes to warm through.

8. Return the chicken to the skillet, add the peas, and simmer about 5 minutes longer, until the peas are tender and the chicken is warmed through. Remove the skillet from the heat and stir in the parsley or chives. Season with additional salt and pepper to taste.

9. Slice the warmed biscuits in half and place the bottom halves on individual dinner plates. Spoon the chicken pieces and carrots over the biscuits, spoon the gravy over the chicken, and cap with the biscuit tops. Serve immediately.

Grilled Buffalo Chicken Strips with Chunky Blue Cheese Dip

I believe the real reason people love Buffalo wings is not for the wings at all, but for the combination of the spicy sauce and the blue cheese. This version, made with chicken breasts cut into thin strips, gives you all the good stuff without the hassle of those tiny bones. WHAT TO SERVE WHEN Besides being a popular hors d'oeuvre any time, these tangy chicken strips make an unexpected light dinner with Fresh Mozzarella Salad with Avocado, Roasted Corn, and Grape Tomatoes (page 64).

SERVES 4 TO 6

For the wing sauce
- 4 tablespoons unsalted butter, melted
- 3 tablespoons olive oil
- 1 tablespoon hot sauce (Tabasco or Texas Pete)
- 1 tablespoon Worcestershire sauce
- 1/2 teaspoon cayenne pepper
- 1 teaspoon paprika

For the chicken
- 4 boneless, skinless chicken breast halves (about 1 1/2 pounds)
- 1 teaspoon sea salt
- 1/2 teaspoon freshly ground black pepper
- **Chunky Blue Cheese Dip** (recipe follows)
- 1 fennel bulb, cored and cut into strips
- 2 celery stalks, halved and cut into 3-inch sticks

1. Prepare a hot fire in a charcoal or gas grill.

2. To make the wing sauce, whisk the butter, oil, hot sauce, Worcestershire sauce, cayenne pepper, and paprika together in a small bowl.

3. Rinse the chicken breasts under cool water and pat them dry with paper towels. Cut the chicken breasts diagonally into 1/2-inch-wide strips and season with salt and pepper. Place the strips in a shallow dish or bowl, pour half the wing sauce over them, and toss to coat evenly.

4. Brush the grill grates or grill pan lightly with oil. Place the chicken strips on the grill or in the grill pan and grill 2 to 3 minutes per side, depending on the thickness of the breast, until the chicken is cooked through. Remove the chicken from the grill and serve immediately with the Chunky Blue Cheese Dip, the remaining wing sauce, and the fennel and celery sticks.

Chunky Blue Cheese Dip

If you make this in advance, add the chives just before serving so they stay green and crisp. If you want to use it as a dressing for a wedge of iceberg lettuce or sliced heirloom tomatoes, thin with a bit more buttermilk.

MAKES ABOUT 1 1/2 CUPS

- 1/4 cup well-shaken buttermilk
- 1 cup mayonnaise
- 1 teaspoon white wine vinegar
- 1/2 teaspoon sea salt, plus more to taste
- 1/2 teaspoon freshly ground black pepper, plus more to taste
- 4 ounces crumbled blue cheese (about 1 cup)
- 2 tablespoons chopped fresh chives

Stir the buttermilk, mayonnaise, vinegar, 1/2 teaspoon salt, and 1/2 teaspoon pepper together in a medium bowl. Stir in the blue cheese; the dip will be creamy with small chunks of blue cheese remaining. Season with additional salt and pepper to taste, stir in the chives, and transfer the dip to a small serving bowl. Serve immediately or refrigerate in an airtight container for up to 1 week.

Herb-Marinated Grilled Turkey Breasts

Turkey is so often relegated to Thanksgiving that people don't think to cook a turkey breast by itself. I made this for friends in Lake Placid recently. Not only were they surprised to get turkey when it wasn't Thanksgiving, but I'd used a natural, free-range turkey, which is so much more moist and flavorful than conventional turkey. It's best if you plan ahead and marinate the turkey overnight. Ask your butcher to cut the bone out of the turkey breast. If you find a boneless breast, by all means, buy it. WHAT TO SERVE WHEN This succulent turkey breast is wonderful straight from the grill, served with a vibrant salad, like the Fried Green Tomato and Ripe Red Tomato Salad (page 66), or the Corn and Sugar Snap Pea Salad (page 73). You can also use the turkey meat in any of the salads that call for grilled or shredded chicken, and use the leftovers to make hot or cold sandwiches or wraps.

SERVES 8 TO 10

- 1 2½-pound turkey breast, bone removed
- 1 cup dry white wine
- ⅓ cup light soy sauce or tamari
  Grated zest and juice of 1 lemon
  Grated zest and juice of 1 orange
- ¼ cup olive oil
- ¼ cup fresh thyme leaves (leaves from about 15 sprigs)
- 8 to 10 fresh sage leaves
- 2 garlic cloves, crushed
- 1 tablespoon grated fresh ginger (1-inch piece)
- 1 teaspoon sea salt
- ½ teaspoon freshly ground black pepper

1. Rinse the turkey and pat dry with paper towels. Remove the skin and discard. To butterfly the breast into one evenly thick, flat piece, slice into the breast from the side at its thickest point, cutting about half-way into the meat. Fold the sliced part open, like a book.

2. Stir the wine, soy sauce, lemon zest and juice, orange zest and juice, olive oil, thyme, sage, garlic, and ginger together in a large bowl. Place the turkey in the bowl and turn several times to coat all sides. Cover and marinate in the refrigerator overnight or for at least several hours. Bring the turkey to room temperature before placing it on the grill.

3. Prepare a fire in a charcoal or gas grill and let the fire die to medium coals.

4. Lift the turkey out of the marinade, reserving the marinade for basting. Season with the salt and pepper and place the turkey over the direct heat for 7 to 8 minutes per side, basting frequently. Move the turkey to indirect heat, cover the grill, and cook 15 to 20 minutes longer, or until an instant-read thermometer registers 155°F.

5. Transfer the turkey to a platter or cutting board and let it rest, loosely covered with foil, for 10 minutes before slicing. Cut the turkey breast against the grain into ¼-inch slices. Serve warm or at room temperature.

about . . .
PLASTIC STORAGE BAGS

Sealable plastic bags are so handy in the kitchen. I use them for many things. If you marinate in them, you can shake to distribute the marinade over the meat evenly—and then just throw them out when you're done. They're easy to carry for a picnic; throw them in the cooler and you don't have to worry about bringing dirty containers home with you. You can also pound chicken breasts in them; the bags don't tear like waxed paper, and you can add your marinade ingredients to the bag once the chicken is pounded.

BASICS: *Outdoor Grilling*

I absolutely love to grill. I like how easy it is and how grilling brings out the natural flavors of foods without masking them in any way. If I'm grilling something that takes more than 15 minutes, like barbecued chicken or ribs, I use briquettes (Kingsford Charcoal is my favorite) because they burn for a long time. But for steaks or boneless chicken breasts, which cook quickly, I use hardwood charcoal. Hardwood is ready quicker than briquettes, it gets hotter, and more important, the hardwood charcoal imparts a smoky, wood flavor to the food. My friends who have gas grills say the convenience of the gas grill motivates them to use it much more often than they would if they had to prepare a fire in a charcoal grill. Use whatever works for you.

Preparing the Food

- Trim the meat of excess fat before placing it on the grill. Fat will drip onto the fire, causing the coals to flare up and the meat to char.
- Bring the meat to room temperature before placing it on the grill. This ensures even doneness instead of charred exteriors with cold, underdone centers.

Preparing the Grill

- Clean the grill grates with a heavy steel brush and leave them in place while you heat the charcoal; this further cleans the grates, and hot grill grates are important for searing meat. Brush the grates lightly with oil, especially if you're cooking something delicate, like fish.
- Avoid charcoal fluid; a chimney does the trick quickly and efficiently, and makes starting charcoal foolproof. If you are not using a chimney, mound the charcoal in the grill to start it; it heats faster this way.
- Add wood chips and herb stems to your charcoal; they will impart their flavor to what you're cooking.

How to Know When the Grill Is Ready

Generally speaking, when coals are ready, the flames will have subsided and the coals will be covered in gray ash with a red glow. To check the heat, hold your hand 3 to 4 inches above the grate and count how long before it's so hot you have to move it.

- 2 seconds means the fire is very hot—perfect for searing steaks or shrimp, or roasting corn on the cob in its husk.
- 3 to 4 seconds means the fire is medium-hot—perfect for cooking fish and quick-cooking vegetables, like asparagus or peppers.
- 5 to 6 seconds means the fire is medium—good for cooking chicken and longer-cooking vegetables, like eggplant or potatoes.

- Any longer means the fire is low and steady—needed for continuing to cook chicken on the bone or for cooking larger, thicker cuts of meat.

The Grilling

Grilling food over a hot fire sears in flavor and adds a slightly crisp exterior, but the best grilling means cooking the meat to perfection on the inside. Trust your instincts. Cooking times will vary depending on the charcoal you're using (or the power of your gas grill), the distance between the fire and the grill grates, the temperature outside, and which way the wind blows.

- Place meats that cook quickly, like boneless, skinless chicken breasts, thin cuts of beef or pork, or foods you want to sear, like a steak or bell peppers, over the hottest part of the fire.
- Cook larger pieces of meat, like a pork loin, turkey breast, or chicken on the bone over the hottest part of the fire to sear, then move them to the side of the grill and close the lid to finish cooking. This turns the grill into a sort of oven, distributing the heat evenly, so the inside can cook without the exterior charring.
- Move meat away from flare-ups and put out the flames with a spray bottle of water.
- Use a spatula or tongs to turn meat, not a fork. A fork pierces the meat, releasing the juices (i.e., moisture and flavor).
- Take meat off just before it has reached the desired doneness. It will continue to cook another 5 to 10 degrees once it's off the fire.
- Let all meats rest for about 5 minutes before cutting or serving them. This seals in the meats' natural juices.

Crispy Pan-Seared Duck Breast with Rosemary and Dried Cranberries

My dad was an avid duck hunter, so I grew up eating wild duck. My nephew Patrick is the hunter in the family now. After he goes hunting, he brings the duck to my house for me to cook. His mom, my sister Judy, makes duck a million different ways. But this preparation—with a nice crisp skin and a slightly reduced sauce—is my tried-and-true recipe, and the only way I prepare duck, wild or farmed. WHAT TO SERVE WHEN Duck makes me think of autumn, and I like to serve this duck with autumnal sides, like Garlicky Greens (page 112) and Creamy Mashed Celery Root (page 106) or Turnip Apple Mash with Thyme (page 105).

SERVES 4

- 2 boneless muscovy duck breast halves (about 1 pound each) or 4 Long Island duck breast halves, skin on
- 1 cup natural cranberry juice
- ½ cup port wine
- 2 tablespoons balsamic vinegar
- ½ cup dried cranberries or cherries
- 2 tablespoons fresh rosemary
- 2 shallots, thinly sliced
- 2 garlic cloves, minced
- Sea salt and freshly ground black pepper to taste

1. Rinse the duck breasts and pat dry with paper towels. Trim the duck of any excess fat and silver skin and cut off the edges of the skin so you are left with a 3-inch-wide strip down the middle of the breast. Score the skin in a diamond pattern with a sharp knife, being careful not to cut all the way through to the meat. Place the duck breasts in a shallow glass or ceramic dish and set aside.

2. Stir the cranberry juice, port, vinegar, cranberries, rosemary, shallots, and garlic together in a small bowl. Pour the marinade over the duck breasts and turn several times to coat both sides. Cover the dish with plastic wrap and marinate in the refrigerator for several hours or overnight.

3. Preheat the oven to 400°F.

4. Heat a cast-iron skillet (or other ovenproof skillet) over medium-high heat to very hot but not smoking. Remove the duck breasts from the marinade, reserving the marinade, and brush off any pieces of shallot or rosemary. Season with salt and pepper. Reduce the heat to medium-low and place the duck breasts, skin side down, in the skillet for 7 to 9 minutes, until the skin is very crisp. As you cook the duck breasts, spoon out or pour off the fat so the pan doesn't smoke excessively. Turn the duck breasts over and cook for 2 to 3 minutes on the other side. (When the duck is ready to be turned, it will loosen easily from the pan without the skin tearing.)

5. Pour the marinade into the skillet and bring to a low boil. Transfer the skillet to the oven and roast the duck for 12 to 15 minutes for medium-rare to medium (less time for smaller, Long Island duck breasts). If you prefer duck more well done, let it roast 3 to 5 minutes longer. Transfer to a serving platter loosely covered with foil and let the duck breasts rest for about 5 minutes.

6. Meanwhile, return the skillet to the stovetop, bring the marinade to a boil over high heat, and continue to boil until the liquid reduces and thickens slightly to a thin glaze.

7. Cut the duck breasts crosswise on a slight diagonal into ¼-inch slices. Place the duck slices on a platter or divide them among individual plates and spoon the sauce over them. Serve warm.

about . . .
DUCK FAT

Duck fat has more flavor than anything else I can think of. When I drain the fat from the pan I cooked duck in, I save the fat. Fortunately, it keeps for a long time in the refrigerator so I often have some on hand for cooking potatoes and other vegetables, or for browning onions. Duck fat is very rich, so you don't need much. Drizzle a little on top of Creamy Mashed Celery Root or Turnip Apple Mash for an additional taste treat.

Peter's All-World Burgers

My husband, Peter, is the burger cook in our family. When he decides it's burger night, he makes a huge production of it—all the condiments must be on the table and everyone seated the moment the patties come off the grill. He likes to use ground beef with 15 percent fat. The fat makes the burgers nice and juicy. He doesn't think saving such a small amount of fat by using lean meat is worth the compromise in flavor and texture. WHAT TO SERVE WHEN Burgers want to be served with picnicky foods, like Oven-Roasted Garlicky Fries (page 125) or Roasted Sweet Potato Wedges (page 110), and summery salads like Deviled Eggs on Sliced Heirloom Tomatoes (page 99) or Zucchini Slaw Two Ways (page 85).

SERVES 4

- 1½ pounds ground beef or ground chuck
- 2 tablespoons Worcestershire sauce
  Sea salt and freshly ground black pepper to taste
- 4 thin slices of Monterey Jack, Cheddar, or Swiss cheese (about 3 ounces)
- 4 soft deli-style rolls, split
- 2 tablespoons unsalted butter, melted
  Mom's 'Fridge Pickles (page 156)

1. Prepare a hot fire in a charcoal or gas grill.

2. Put the ground beef in a large bowl and break it up using your fingers. Pour the Worcestershire sauce over the meat and gently shape it into four burgers about 1 inch thick; take care not to work the meat any more than necessary or the burgers will become mushy when cooked. Season both sides with salt and pepper and place the burgers on the grill for 3 to 4 minutes; turn and cook another 3 to 4 minutes for medium-rare, or about 6 minutes for medium. Lay a slice of cheese on each burger, close the lid, and cook for another 2 to 3 minutes to melt the cheese. Remove the burgers from the grill and them let rest for 3 to 4 minutes, loosely covered with foil to keep warm.

3. While the meat is resting, brush both sides of the rolls with the melted butter and place on the grill to toast lightly, 2 to 3 minutes. Remove the rolls from the grill. Assemble the burgers or place on serving platters for guests to assemble their own. Serve warm.

Fast and Foolproof Fresh Herb Mayo

MAKES 1¼ CUPS

- 1 cup mayonnaise
- 1 tablespoon Dijon mustard
- 1 tablespoon lemon juice
- ¼ teaspoon cayenne pepper
- ½ teaspoon sea salt
- ½ teaspoon freshly ground black pepper
- ½ cup rough chopped mixed herbs, such as dill, basil, parsley, arugula, chervil, sorrel, or scallions

Combine all ingredients in a blender or food processor. Process until the herbs are pureed into the mayonnaise. Season with more salt and pepper if desired. Use immediately or refrigerate in an airtight container until ready to use.

about . . .
HAMBURGER FIXIN'S

Peter likes All-World Burgers with classic accompaniments: French's mustard, bottled mayonnaise, tomato slices, red onion slices—and always Mom's 'Fridge Pickles. If you want to venture out, some other burger condiments we like are Caramelized Onions (page 156), Chipotle Mustard Sauce (page 21), Horseradish Mustard Sauce (page 159), Greenest Goddess Dressing (page 195), Fast and Foolproof Fresh Herb Mayo (above), and any of the many fresh salsas (page 196).

The rolls are another important element; it's the quality and softness of the rolls that elevate Peter's burgers to "All-World" status. They shouldn't be too soft, like soft hamburger buns that fall apart in your hands. Nor quite like hard rolls that you have to tear with your teeth. Those I like best are the nice big rolls you find in the bakery section of a grocery store, like onion rolls, brioche rolls, or potato rolls.

Caramelized Onions

These sweet, jamlike onions can be used as a condiment for grilled meat or chicken, or on sandwiches. They're just great to have in your refrigerator.

MAKES ABOUT 2 CUPS

  3 tablespoons olive oil
  2 large sweet yellow onions, thinly sliced
  2 tablespoons sherry vinegar
  1 teaspoon sea salt, plus more to taste
½ teaspoon freshly ground black pepper, plus more to taste

1. Heat the olive oil in a large skillet over medium heat and add the onions. Reduce the heat to low and cook the onions, stirring from time to time, for about 20 minutes, or until they're very soft and have a little color. Turn the heat down if the onions are browning more than slightly.

2. Add the vinegar, 1 teaspoon salt, and ½ teaspoon pepper, and continue to cook, stirring occasionally, for another 20 to 25 minutes, until all of the liquid is cooked off and the onions are a rich golden brown color and have a jammy texture. You may need to add more oil or a little water (or stock if you have it) to keep the onions from sticking to the pan. Season with more salt and pepper to taste.

Mom's 'Fridge Pickles

I grew up eating these crunchy, not-too-sweet pickles. They're great just to snack on or served with a sharp Cheddar or Swiss cheese. In the summertime, I layer them on tomato sandwiches, and they're a must with Peter's All-World Burgers. You want to make them with kirby cucumbers because the seeds are small and the cucumbers are naturally crisp.

MAKES ABOUT 1 QUART

  1 cup white vinegar
¼ cup sugar
  1 tablespoon sea salt
½ teaspoon freshly ground black pepper
  6 whole cloves
  2 bay leaves
  1 teaspoon crushed red pepper flakes
  1 teaspoon dill seed
  4 to 5 small kirby (pickling) cucumbers, peeled in stripes and sliced into ⅛-inch-thick rounds
  1 small white onion, thinly sliced into rounds

1. Combine the vinegar, sugar, salt, black pepper, cloves, bay leaves, red pepper flakes, and dill seed in a quart jar. Place the lid on the jar and shake until the sugar has dissolved.

2. Layer the cucumbers and onion in the jar using a wooden spoon to press them tightly into the jar. Place the lid on the jar, shake it well, and refrigerate at least 4 hours, shaking the jar occasionally to keep the ingredients mixed. These pickles will keep in the refrigerator for at least 1 month.

Sliced New York Strip Steak with Horseradish Mustard Sauce

When I'm craving red meat but don't want to spend a lot of time cooking, I make a New York strip: it cooks quickly, goes with almost anything, and has that classic steak flavor and texture. If you don't want to fire up an outdoor grill, you can cook these in a grill pan or skillet; make sure to get the pan hot before putting the steaks in. WHAT TO SERVE WHEN I like to keep this simple, served with something like Chili-Roasted Sweet Potatoes (page 110) and a simple salad, like the Arugula and Endive Salad with Shaved Parmesan (page 72).

SERVES 4

2 14-ounce prime New York strip steaks, cut 1½ inches thick, at room temperature
¼ cup Worcestershire sauce
2 tablespoons balsamic vinegar
2 tablespoons olive oil
2 tablespoons chopped fresh rosemary
Sea salt and freshly ground black pepper to taste

1. Prepare a hot fire in a charcoal or gas grill.

2. Place the steaks in a glass baking dish, drizzle with the Worcestershire sauce, balsamic vinegar, and olive oil, and turn to coat both sides. Sprinkle the rosemary and pepper over the steaks and press them into the meat. Cover and marinate in the refrigerator for at least 1 hour and up to overnight. Bring the steaks to room temperature before putting them on the grill. Sprinkle the steaks with salt just before cooking.

3. Place the steaks on the grill for 5 to 6 minutes per side, turning only once, until an instant-read thermometer reads 110°F for rare. For medium-rare steaks, move the steaks away from the direct fire, close the lid of the grill, and cook another 7 to 8 minutes, until an instant-read thermometer reads 120°F (130°F for medium).

4. Let the steaks rest on a cutting board for about 5 minutes, loosely covered with foil, before slicing. Cut the steaks into ½-inch slices and fan the slices out on a platter or individual plates. Taste for salt and pepper and season with more if desired. Garnish with the additional rosemary and serve immediately.

Horseradish Mustard Sauce

This creamy, spicy condiment also makes a nice accompaniment to Mom's Pot Roast (page 218) or beef sandwiches. Feel free to play with the concept, using more or less horseradish, eliminating the sour cream for a spicier sauce, or using a sweet and spicy mustard in place of the Dijon.

MAKES ABOUT 1 CUP

2 tablespoons prepared horseradish
1 tablespoon Dijon mustard
¼ cup buttermilk
1 tablespoon sour cream
1 teaspoon freshly ground black pepper, plus more to taste
½ teaspoon sea salt, plus more to taste
1 teaspoon chopped rosemary

Combine the horseradish, mustard, buttermilk, sour cream, pepper, salt, and rosemary in a small bowl and stir to mix. Add more salt and pepper to taste. Serve immediately or refrigerate in an airtight container for up to 1 week.

BASICS: *Checking for Doneness*

The only trick, if there is one, to cooking a steak is learning how to tell when the meat is done. The worst thing you can do to a steak is overcook it; however, the next worst thing you can do to a steak is to cut into it while it's cooking. When you cut it open, the juices pour out—and with them, the flavor and any chance of a moist juicy steak.

The surest way to check a steak for doneness is by feeling it. Rare steak feels very fleshy and jiggly to the touch. Medium-rare feels fleshy, but not quite jiggly. If a steak feels firm and muscular, you can be sure you've cooked it to well done. Until you get the feel for cooking steak, use an instant-read meat thermometer to test for doneness. Take meat off the grill when it registers to 110° to 115°F for rare, 120°F to 125°F for medium-rare, and 130°F to 135°F for medium. This accounts for the extra 5 to 10 degrees that the meat will continue to cook after you take it off the heat.

T-Bone for Two with Roasted Garlic Aïoli

T-Bone is the perfect steak to share. If you're lucky, one of you will want the small portion, which is the tenderloin, while the other eyes the bigger, top loin portion, and everyone is happy. My grandfather and I shared T-bone this way when I was a child, with him getting the larger portion, and now Peter and I split the steak the same way. This is my grandfather's recipe, and it is very straightforward. The aïoli is my addition. WHAT TO SERVE WHEN T-bone is so rich and satisfying, it goes well with something light and refreshing, like Arugula and Endive Salad with Shaved Parmesan (page 72) and Smashed Roasted Potatoes with Rosemary (page 125), or Chili Roasted Sweet Potatoes (page 110). Wilted Spinach (page 191) or Garlicky Greens (page 112) are other good vegetable options.

    1 T-bone steak, cut about 1½ to 2 inches thick (about
      1½ pounds), at room temperature
      Sea salt and freshly ground black pepper to taste
      Roasted Garlic Aïoli (recipe follows)

1. Prepare a hot fire in a charcoal or gas grill or heat a cast-iron skillet to just below the smoking point.

2. Season the T-bone with salt and pepper and lay it on the grill over the hottest part of the fire or in the skillet to sear 3 to 4 minutes per side. Turn the steak on its side and hold it with a pair of tongs while you grill the fatty edge for about 2 minutes, until it is brown and slightly crisp. Lay the steak back on the grill away from the direct heat or reduce the heat under the skillet to low, cover, and cook for 6 to 8 minutes longer, or to an internal temperature of 110°F for rare; 8 to 10 minutes longer or to 120°F for medium-rare; 10 to 12 minutes longer or to 130°F for medium. Let the steak rest, loosely covered with foil, for 5 to 10 minutes before cutting. Cut the meat off the bone to serve in two separate pieces or cut it against the grain into ½-inch slices. Serve warm, with Roasted Garlic Aïoli.

Roasted Garlic Aïoli

I like to make aïoli by hand instead of in a food processor; it's something I just whip up—literally, but there's no reason you couldn't use a food processor or blender for this. For a radical shortcut to aïoli, whisk 1 cup of store-bought mayonnaise (try to find one that doesn't contain sugar or corn syrup) with the mustard, roasted garlic, pepper, herbs, and sea salt.

MAKES ABOUT 1½ CUPS

    1 head garlic, roasted (see "Roasting Garlic," page 95),
      at room temperature
    2 large eggs, at room temperature
    ½ teaspoon sea salt
    1 teaspoon Dijon mustard
    1 tablespoon white wine vinegar
    1 cup canola or safflower oil
    ½ teaspoon freshly ground black pepper
    2 tablespoons chopped fresh tarragon or parsley

1. Squeeze the garlic cloves out of their skins and into a small bowl and mash with the tines of a fork.

2. In a separate, medium bowl, whisk the eggs with the salt, mustard, and vinegar. Whisk in the oil, adding it drop by drop, until the mixture begins to thicken and emulsify. Once the mixture has emulsified, begin adding the oil in a slow steady stream, whisking constantly, until all the oil is incorporated.

3. Stir in the mashed roasted garlic, pepper, and tarragon. Serve immediately or refrigerate in an airtight container for up to 1 week.

about . . .
T-BONE STEAKS

T-bone is one of the most flavorful steaks you can buy. The t-shaped bone separates the small tenderloin (the most tender cut of beef) from the larger top loin, which is more flavorful and has a more steaklike texture. You can use T-bone and porterhouse interchangeably in recipes. The only difference is that porterhouse, which is considerably more expensive, has more tenderloin than T-bone.

STEAK REINVENTED

Leftover steak can be turned into so many good next-day meals. And a little goes a long way when you're using the steak as a component with a lot of other ingredients, like a salad, sandwich, or fajitas. All of these serve one and can be adjusted to serve more depending on how much meat you have left over.

Steak and Egg Scramble

Prepare Creamy Scrambled Eggs (page 16) with a cup of diced leftover steak and serve with Herb Grilled Tomatoes (page 120) or pan-fried tomatoes.

Steak and Egg Soft Taco

Thinly slice a small piece of leftover steak and sear it in a hot skillet to reheat. Heat a flour tortilla in a dry skillet about 1 minute per side, until it is warm and lightly toasted. Fry or scramble an egg to your liking and place it on top of the warm tortilla. Place the steak slices on the egg and drizzle with Horseradish Mustard Sauce (page 159) and any fresh salsa (page 196). Roll the tortilla or fold it in half and serve immediately.

Steak Sandwich

Lay a few steak slices on toasted country bread or a baguette slathered with Horseradish Mustard Sauce (page 159), Roasted Garlic Aïoli (page 160), or a tangy vinaigrette. Add slices of tomato and mozzarella if you like and pile the sandwich high with arugula.

Steak Fajitas

Slice 1 red bell pepper, 1 green bell pepper, and 1 yellow onion into strips and cook them in olive oil until tender. Add the leftover steak, cut into strips, and cook to warm through. Season with salt and pepper and serve the fajitas with warm flour or corn tortillas, Guacamole (page 162), and any fresh salsa (page 196).

Steak Quesadilla

Layer thin slices of leftover steak on a tortilla. Top with chopped fresh mozzarella, romaine, diced tomatoes, and ranch dressing and grill or sauté with butter to melt the cheese and crisp the tortilla.

Grilled Steak Salad

Cut 4 ounces of cooked steak into thin slices. Place the steak in a bowl with 2 cups mixed baby greens, spinach, or arugula; ¼ red onion, thinly sliced; ½ red bell pepper, thinly sliced; ½ cup halved cherry tomatoes; and a teaspoon of capers. Drizzle with a tangy vinaigrette, season with salt and pepper, and toss gently to mix.

Tequila Lime Skirt Steak with Grilled Scallions

I'd never heard of skirt steak until a catering client requested I make it years ago. She claimed it was more flavorful than flank steak, and she was right. Skirt steak takes only a few minutes to cook, but needs to marinate for a few hours to be tender, so try to plan ahead so you can put the meat in the marinade the night before you want to grill it. WHAT TO SERVE WHEN In keeping with the Mexican flavor of the marinade, I serve this steak with grilled flour or corn tortillas, accompanied by a fresh salsa (page 196) and Guacamole (right).

SERVES 4

2 tablespoons tequila
1 tablespoon Worcestershire sauce
1 tablespoon light soy sauce or tamari
1 jalapeño pepper, cored, seeded, and minced
2 scallions, minced (white and green part)
2 garlic cloves, minced
1 tablespoon light brown sugar
1 teaspoon freshly ground black pepper
1½ pounds skirt steak
½ teaspoon sea salt, plus more to taste
2 limes cut into wedges

1. Stir the tequila, Worcestershire sauce, soy sauce, jalapeño, scallions, garlic, brown sugar, and pepper together in a small bowl.

2. Place the skirt steak in a shallow bowl, baking dish, or sealable bag; pour the tequila marinade over the steak and turn or shake the bag to evenly coat the meat. Cover and marinate the meat in the refrigerator for at least 3 hours and up to overnight.

3. Prepare a hot fire in a charcoal or gas grill.

4. Remove the steak from the marinade and season both sides with salt and pepper. Place the steak on the grill for 3 to 4 minutes per side for medium-rare. Remove the steak from the grill, cover loosely with foil, and allow it to rest for 5 to 10 minutes.

5. Slice the meat from the corner diagonally against the grain into ½-inch-thick slices. Place the slices on a serving platter surrounded by the lime wedges and topped with the Grilled Scallions.

Grilled Scallions

2 bunches scallions, trimmed
¼ cup olive oil
   Sea salt and freshly ground black pepper to taste
1 lime, cut into quarters

1. Prepare a hot fire in a charcoal or gas grill.

2. Brush the scallions with the olive oil and season with salt and pepper. Place the scallions on the grill for 1 to 2 minutes, turning occasionally, until the bulbs are tender and golden and the greens are slightly crisp. Serve warm.

Guacamole

Guacamole is such a quick and easy way to give Mexican flair to so many dishes. Beyond chips, tacos, and quesadillas, serve guacamole with a simple grilled chicken breast, grilled fish, or scrambled eggs with warm corn or flour tortillas on the side. In the summertime, I often make a meal out of sliced tomatoes sprinkled with good sea salt and topped with guacamole.

MAKES ABOUT 2 CUPS

4 ripe Hass avocados, peeled and pitted
2 scallions (white and green parts), minced
1 jalapeño pepper, cored, seeded, and minced
¼ cup chopped fresh cilantro
   Juice of 1 lime
2 tablespoons olive oil
1 teaspoon ground cumin
⅛ teaspoon cayenne pepper
   Sea salt and freshly ground black pepper to taste

Place the avocados in a medium bowl and mash them with a fork. Add the scallions, jalapeño, cilantro, lime juice, olive oil, cumin, cayenne pepper, salt, and black pepper and stir to mix. Serve immediately, or transfer the guacamole to an airtight container, drizzle with additional olive oil, and refrigerate for up to several hours.

about . . .
SKIRT STEAK

Skirt steak is an underrated cut of meat. It's a long, flat piece of meat that can be very flavorful if prepared properly, and very tough if not. The main consideration is that it must be marinated before cooking. If your local butcher or specialty food store doesn't have it, use flank steak in its place. Serve skirt steak medium-rare.

Grilled Beef Filet Topped with Stilton and Crispy Shallots

I often make this for dinner guests when I don't have time to prepare. It's so easy to throw together, yet it feels like something special for any occasion. WHAT TO SERVE WHEN With the richness of the steaks plus the melted cheese, this needs a very simple accompaniment, like a bed of raw watercress or arugula, or a side of Wilted Spinach (page 191).

SERVES 4

4 beef tenderloin steaks, cut 2 inches thick (about 8 ounces each)
2 tablespoons balsamic vinegar
2 tablespoons olive oil
1 tablespoon chopped fresh rosemary
  Sea salt and freshly ground black pepper to taste
3 ounces Stilton cheese, cut into 4 slices
  Crispy Fried Shallots (recipe follows)

1. Preheat the oven to 400°F.

2. Rub the filets on all sides with the vinegar and oil. Sprinkle with the rosemary, salt, and pepper and press the rosemary into both sides of the filets. Cover and marinate in the refrigerator for at least 1 hour or overnight. Bring to room temperature before cooking.

3. Heat a grill pan or ovenproof cast-iron skillet over medium-high heat until it is hot, about 3 minutes. A pinch of salt will sizzle when dropped into the pan. Lay the filets in the pan, reserving the marinade. Reduce the heat to medium and sear the steaks for about 3 minutes, until the undersides are a rich brown color. Turn the steaks and pour the remaining marinade over them. Sear the other sides until they are a rich brown color, 2 to 3 minutes.

4. Transfer the grill pan to the oven and cook the steaks for 10 to 12 minutes, or until an instant-read thermometer registers 110°F for rare, 120°F for medium-rare, 130°F for medium. Remove the steaks from the oven and let them rest, loosely covered with foil, for about 5 minutes before serving.

5. Place each steak on a plate and top with a slice of Stilton. Sprinkle the shallots evenly over the filets and serve immediately.

Crispy Fried Shallots

These little "onion rings" make a tasty and elegant topping for most any meat dish. You can also roast the shallot rings (omit the flour and cornstarch coating) in a 400°F oven. Toss with olive oil and chopped fresh rosemary and roast 15 to 20 minutes.

3 tablespoons all-purpose flour
1/2 teaspoon cornstarch
  Salt and freshly ground black pepper to taste
6 shallots, peeled and sliced 1/8 inch thick
2 cups safflower or canola oil

1. Stir the flour, cornstarch, salt, and pepper together in a small bowl. Separate the shallots into individual rings and toss them lightly in the seasoned flour to coat on all sides.

2. Heat the oil in a large saucepan over high heat until it is very hot but not smoking. A pinch of flour will sizzle when dropped into the oil. Remove the shallots from the flour, shake off any excess flour, and place them in the hot oil to fry until they are golden brown and crisp, 1 to 2 minutes. Place the shallots on a paper towel to drain. Season with additional salt and pepper and serve immediately.

about . . .
MEAT THERMOMETERS

Instant-read thermometers are one of my favorite kitchen tools. They cost about $10, and they pay for themselves the first time you use one instead of cutting into, and ruining, a good piece of meat. Throughout these recipes, I give you the ideal internal temperatures to which you should cook various meats. Insert the thermometer into the deepest part of the meat and leave it there until the temperature reaches a steady number. Just remember that temperature will rise 5 to 10 degrees even after the meat is out of the oven or off the grill.

Rosemary-Mint Lamb Chops

When Peter cooks dinner, he likes it to take him no more than 20 minutes from the time he starts until we're sitting at the table eating. He refers to this as his "20-minute dinners," and these lamb chops, served with a green salad and oven-roasted vegetables, is one of his 20-minute dinner staples. When lamb is as moist and flavorful as this, a little pepper jelly or a drizzle of reduced balsamic vinegar is all the "sauce" it needs. WHAT TO SERVE WHEN I think it's fun to serve an entire meal for four, like these lamb chops, on one platter, so guests can help themselves. I'll arrange them on a bed of Wilted Spinach (page 191) or, if I want something a little richer, Creamy Mashed Celery Root (page 106) or mashed potatoes. I might brighten up the platter by surrounding the chops with whole fresh mint leaves and grilled lemon halves. (See photo on page 130.)

SERVES 4

8 loin lamb chops (about 2 pounds)
¼ cup red wine
2 tablespoons balsamic vinegar
2 tablespoons pepper or mint jelly
2 tablespoons chopped fresh rosemary,
   plus more for garnish
1 tablespoon chopped fresh mint,
   plus more for garnish
Sea salt and freshly ground black pepper to taste

1. Rinse the lamb chops, pat them dry with paper towels, and place them in a glass baking dish.

2. Stir the wine, vinegar, jelly, rosemary, and mint together in a small bowl. Pour the marinade over the lamb chops and press the herbs into the meat. Let the lamb chops marinate at room temperature for at least 1 hour or cover, refrigerate, and marinate overnight, turning them in the marinade several times. Bring the lamb chops to room temperature before grilling.

3. Prepare a hot fire in a charcoal or gas grill.

4. Remove the lamb chops from the marinade, season with salt and pepper, and place them on the hot fire for 4 to 5 minutes per side, basting with the marinade, until an instant-read thermometer reads 110°F to 120°F for medium-rare, which I recommend. The lamb will feel firm but slightly fleshy. Don't worry if the chops are slightly charred on the outside. This is the marinade caramelizing; it tastes delicious.

5. Transfer the chops to a serving platter, cover loosely with foil, and let rest for 3 to 5 minutes before serving. Sprinkle the chops with the additional fresh mint and rosemary and serve warm.

Simple Succulent Grilled Pork Chops

These pork chops are so foolproof you could cook them for company even when you're trying the recipe for the first time. Make sure to buy thick-cut pork chops of the best quality you can find. I like Niman Ranch, available online (www.nimanranch.com), or any other small farm-raised pork. If you like some heat and spice, rub a nice pork rub blend into the chops before placing them on the grill. WHAT TO SERVE WHEN Pork chops are so versatile. You could top these with Roasted Sweet Potato Salsa (page 198) or Black Bean Salsa (page 196) or serve them on a bed of Mashed Roasted Sweet Potatoes with Parmesan (page 106) or Roasted Cabbage Wedges (page 116). In the summertime, lighten up the meal by serving the pork chops with Cornbread Panzanella (page 76) or Apple and Avocado Salad (page 75).

SERVES 4

4 pork loin chops, cut 1 inch thick (2½ to 3 pounds)
   Olive oil for rubbing the pork chops (about
   2 tablespoons)
1 tablespoon chopped fresh marjoram
   Sea salt and freshly ground black pepper to taste

1. Prepare a hot fire in a charcoal or gas grill.

2. Meanwhile, place the pork chops on a platter and rub them on all sides with olive oil. Sprinkle both sides with the chopped marjoram, salt, and pepper, pressing the marjoram into the chops.

3. Place the chops on the grill for 5 minutes per side. Move the chops away from the direct heat, cover the grill with the lid, and cook the chops 8 to 10 minutes longer, until an instant-read thermometer reads 145°F. The pork will feel slightly firm and not fleshy. Let the pork chops rest, loosely covered with foil, for about 5 minutes before serving.

Pan-Grilled Pork Paillards with Ginger Teriyaki Glaze

The flavors in this marinade are most pronounced if you can marinate the paillards overnight. The marinade is reduced to make a delicious glaze for the finished pork. You can also cook these on an outdoor grill. WHAT TO SERVE WHEN These sweet, moist pork slices make a flavorful light meal simply served with something light, like Steamed Baby Bok Choy (page 109) or Swiss chard.

SERVES 4 TO 6

1½ pounds boneless pork loin or thin boneless pork chops
1½ cups sherry
 2 shallots, minced
   Grated zest and juice of 1 orange
 1 tablespoon light soy sauce or tamari
 2 tablespoons teriyaki sauce
 1 tablespoon fresh grated ginger (1-inch piece)
 2 tablespoons chopped flat-leaf parsley leaves, plus more for garnish
 1 tablespoon chopped fresh thyme, plus more for garnish
 ½ teaspoon sea salt
 1 teaspoon freshly ground black pepper
 1 tablespoon unsalted butter

1. Trim the fat and sinew from the pork loin. Rinse and pat dry with paper towels. Cut the pork into ½-inch slices and place the slices in a glass baking dish.

2. Stir the sherry, shallots, orange zest and juice, soy sauce, teriyaki sauce, ginger, parsley, thyme, salt, and pepper together in a medium bowl. Pour the marinade over the pork slices, turn to coat evenly, cover, and marinate in the refrigerator overnight or for at least 1 hour.

3. Preheat a grill pan or cast-iron skillet over medium heat until very hot but not smoking.

4. Remove the pork slices from the marinade, reserving the marinade, and lay them in the hot grill pan. Grill the pork slices for 2 to 3 minutes per side, basting with the marinade while it is grilling and after you turn them, until they are cooked through and feel firm to the touch. Transfer the pork slices to a platter and cover loosely with foil to keep warm.

5. Pour the remaining marinade into the grill pan or skillet, bring it to a boil, and let it boil for about 2 minutes to thicken. Add the butter and shake the pan until the butter melts. Pour the sauce over the pork, sprinkle with the additional thyme and parsley, and serve warm.

Hoisin-Marinated Grilled Pork Tenderloin

This pork is most flavorful if you marinate it overnight or use an instant meat marinator. Try to find a good hoisin sauce. There's no comparison in the flavor between that which you find in a standard grocery store and the more complex, authentic version you find in Asian or specialty markets. WHAT TO SERVE WHEN In keeping with the Asian theme, I like to serve this on a platter of steamed jasmine rice, surrounded by Steamed Baby Bok Choy (page 109).

SERVES 6

2 1-pound pork tenderloins
1/2 cup hoisin sauce
1/2 cup dry sherry
Grated zest and juice of 1 orange
1/4 cup light soy sauce or tamari
1/4 cup molasses
2 tablespoons rice wine vinegar
1 1-inch piece fresh ginger, peeled and julienned (about 2 tablespoons)
1 teaspoon Chinese five-spice powder
2 teaspoons crushed red pepper flakes
2 garlic cloves, minced
1/2 teaspoon sea salt
1/2 teaspoon freshly ground black pepper

1. Rinse the pork tenderloins and pat dry with paper towels. Cut the sinew from the tops of the loins. Place the tenderloins in a shallow bowl or baking dish or a large sealable bag.

2. Whisk the hoisin sauce, sherry, orange zest and juice, soy sauce, molasses, vinegar, ginger, five-spice powder, red pepper flakes, garlic, salt, and pepper in a small bowl. Pour the marinade over the pork, and turn to coat it evenly with the marinade. (Or pour the marinade into the bag, seal, and shake to coat the pork.) Cover the dish with plastic wrap and marinate in the refrigerator for at least 4 hours or overnight. Turn the pork several times to distribute the marinade evenly. Bring the pork to room temperature before grilling.

3. Prepare a fire in a charcoal or gas grill.

4. Place the pork on the grill for 15 minutes, basting all the while and turning three to four times. Close the grill or cover the pork with foil and cook the pork for

another 10 to 15 minutes, until an instant-read thermometer inserted into the tenderloin reads 145°F to 150°F for medium, which is my preference (155°F to 160°F for medium-well), basting several times during cooking.

5. Place the tenderloin on a cutting board, cover loosely with foil, and allow it to rest for 5 to 10 minutes before slicing. Slice the tenderloin 1/4 inch thick and fan the slices out on a platter. Serve immediately.

REINVENTION

Wrap leftover slices of pork and a drizzle of the dipping sauce in a flour tortilla with and Sesame Ginger Vinaigrette (page 82). Or make it into a sandwich with a Sweet Potato Buttermilk Biscuit (page 31) or a whole-wheat roll.

six

fast and fresh fish, pasta, and risotto meals

Crab Cakes with Cajun Aïoli ○ Pan-Seared Sea Scallops with Citrus Tarragon Butter ○ Katie's Spicy Grilled Shrimp with Sweet and Spicy Dipping Sauce ○ *Shrimp for All Seasons—Winter:* Sautéed Tangerine Shrimp; *Spring:* Garlic-Sautéed Shrimp with Spinach; *Summer:* Sautéed Shrimp with Corn and Tomatoes; *Fall:* Curry Coconut Shrimp ○ Pickled Shrimp ○ Pan-Roasted Halibut with Roasted Cherry Tomatoes and Butternut Squash ○ Pan-Seared Grouper with Lemon and Capers ○ Pan-Seared Red Snapper with Butter Beans, Tomatoes, and Corn ○ Steamed Sea Bass with Broccoli Rabe and Roasted Garlic Vinaigrette ○ Sautéed Sea Bass with Wilted Spinach and Lemon Chive Oil ○ Braised Salmon Fillets with Tarragon and White Wine over Warm Lentils with Crispy Pancetta ○ Grilled Salmon with Your Favorite Fresh Salsa ○ Black Bean Salsa ○ Grilled Pineapple Salsa ○ Roasted Corn Salsa ○ Roasted Red Bell Pepper Salsa ○ Roasted Sweet Potato Salsa ○ Roasted Green Tomato and Apple Salsa ○ Heirloom Tomato Salsa ○ *Risotto for All Seasons—Winter:* Wild Mushroom and Spinach Risotto; *Spring:* Risotto with Spring Peas and Asparagus; *Summer:* Risotto with Summer Corn and Tomatoes; *Fall:* Risotto with Roasted Butternut Squash and Thyme ○ Linguine with Clams

Fast and fresh could not be more appropriate for any other chapter in this book because these recipes are just that—easy ideas for combining the freshest and best ingredients available.

The procedures are nearly effortless, and the results are irresistible. These dishes literally cook while you're standing in front of the stove or the grill watching them—the most you'll have to do while your dinner cooks is to baste it, turn it, touch it, or squeeze it to check if something is perfectly done. And in no time you're going to sit down and enjoy a delicious home cooked meal.

Crab Cakes with Cajun Aïoli

The secret to good crab cakes is to use as little bread crumbs as it takes to hold the cakes together. This way they taste like crab, not bread. I often use Japanese bread crumbs, called panko, in place of traditional bread crumbs; their texture gives the crab cakes extra crunch. If you buy your crab from a fishmonger, often you can specify what part of the crab you want. I prefer the meat from either the claw or the back fin, which have the most flavor. WHAT TO SERVE WHEN Serve these with a green salad for a light, warm-weather meal or in place of the meat in Eggs Benedict (page 18).

SERVES 4 TO 6 (MAKES 10 2-INCH CAKES)

1 pound lump crabmeat
1 red bell pepper, cored, seeded, and minced
2 scallions, trimmed and minced (white and green parts)
1 jalapeño pepper, cored, seeded, and minced
  Grated zest and juice of 1 lemon
¼ cup mayonnaise
2 cups fresh bread crumbs (see "Making Bread Crumbs," page 153) or panko
2 large eggs
½ teaspoon sea salt
½ teaspoon freshly ground black pepper
  A pinch of cayenne pepper
6 basil leaves, cut into thin strips
¼ cup canola or safflower oil
½ cup **Cajun Aïoli** (recipe follows)
1 lemon, cut into 6 wedges

1. Preheat the oven to 200°F.

2. Place the crabmeat in a medium bowl and pick through to remove any shell pieces, taking care to keep the crabmeat in large chunks. Add the bell pepper, scallions, jalapeño pepper, lemon zest and juice, mayonnaise, ½ cup of the bread crumbs, the eggs, salt, black pepper, cayenne pepper, and basil and stir gently to mix.

3. Place the remaining 1½ cups of bread crumbs on a plate. Scoop the crabmeat with a ¼-cup measure or ice cream scoop and pat it out to form a cake about 2 inches around and 1½ inches thick. Roll the cake in the bread crumbs to coat lightly on both sides and shake gently to remove any excess crumbs. Place the crab cake on a large plate and repeat with the remaining crabmeat mixture to form 10 cakes. Cover with plastic wrap and refrigerate the crab for at least 1 hour or up to overnight to chill.

4. Heat the oil in a large nonstick skillet over medium-high heat. Place four to six crab cakes in the skillet, leaving about ½ inch between them, and cook for about 3 minutes per side, turning only once, until the crab cakes are golden brown on both sides. Place the crab cakes on a platter lined with paper towels to drain, cover loosely with foil, and place in the oven to keep warm while you cook the remaining crab cakes. Serve immediately with the Cajun Aïoli and lemon wedges.

Cajun Aïoli

Aïoli is a garlicky French mayonnaise. This one is slightly sweet and spicy with the addition of the roasted peppers. It's delicious spread on just about any meat or fish sandwich. Taste the aïoli before adding cayenne—it may be spicy enough for you without it.

MAKES ABOUT 1½ CUPS

1 red bell pepper, roasted, peeled, cored, and seeded (see "Peppers," page 54)
1 jalapeño pepper, roasted, peeled, cored, and seeded (see "Peppers," page 54)
5 roasted garlic cloves (see "Roasting Garlic," page 95)
1 large egg
  Juice of 1 lemon
½ teaspoon sea salt
½ teaspoon freshly ground black pepper
  A pinch of cayenne pepper
¾ cup canola or safflower oil

Place the bell pepper, jalapeño pepper, garlic, egg, lemon juice, salt, pepper, and cayenne in the bowl of a food processor fitted with a metal blade and pulse to mix. With the motor of the food processor running, add the oil through the feed tube in a very thin, slow stream until it forms an emulsion. Add the remaining oil until all is incorporated. Use the aïoli immediately or refrigerate in an airtight container for up to 4 days.

Think Outside the Recipe
INSTEAD OF AÏOLI, TRY TOPPING THE CRAB CAKES WITH THE ROASTED GREEN TOMATO AND APPLE SALSA (PAGE 199) OR ROASTED CORN SALSA (PAGE 197).

1½ pounds large sea scallops (about 24)
  3 tablespoons olive oil, or more as needed
½ teaspoon sea salt, plus more to taste
½ teaspoon freshly ground black pepper, plus more
    to taste
⅛ teaspoon cayenne pepper
  2 tablespoons unsalted butter, or more as needed
    Juice of 2 oranges
    Juice of 1 lemon
  1 tablespoon chopped fresh tarragon (or chives or
    chervil)

1. Rinse the scallops under cool water, pat dry with a paper towel, and place them in a shallow bowl or on a plate. Drizzle with 1 tablespoon of the olive oil, sprinkle with the salt, black pepper, and cayenne, and toss gently to coat.

2. Heat 1 tablespoon of the butter with the remaining 2 tablespoons of olive oil in a large nonstick skillet over medium-high heat until the butter melts and sizzles. Working in batches, place the scallops in the hot skillet, leaving about ½ inch between each scallop. Sear the scallops, undisturbed, for 1½ to 2 minutes per side, until they are opaque and light golden around the edges. The scallops will continue to cook after they're out of the pan so it's better to undercook than overcook them. Remove the scallops from the pan, place them on a platter, and cover loosely with foil to keep warm. Repeat with the second and possibly third batch of scallops, adding more butter and oil to the pan as needed.

3. When all the scallops are cooked, pour the orange juice, lemon juice, and tarragon into the skillet, scraping up the brown bits from the bottom of the pan. Add any juices that have accumulated around the scallops. Bring the liquid to a boil over medium-high heat and cook 1 to 2 minutes, until it reduces by half. Remove the pan from the heat and stir in the remaining tablespoon of butter until it melts.

4. If the scallops have cooled too much, return them to the pan with the sauce to warm very briefly over medium heat before serving. Serve the scallops warm, with the sauce spooned over them.

Pan-Seared Sea Scallops with Citrus Tarragon Butter

Scallops are light but also very flavorful, so they're ideal for simple preparations like this one. With this tangy citrus and tarragon butter, it's one of my standby dishes, something I make when I come home late from the Market and want a quick, effortless dinner. WHAT TO SERVE WHEN These scallops are so rich, you don't need much more than a mixed green salad or a steamed vegetable, like Steamed Baby Bok Choy (page 109), with them. Divided among as many as 8 or 10 people, they make a nice starter served atop Summer White Corn Soup (page 48) or Roasted Corn Salsa (page 197).

SERVES 4 TO 6

Katie's Spicy Grilled Shrimp with Sweet and Spicy Dipping Sauce

This is my friend Katie's recipe. Grilling the shrimp in their shells makes them much more flavorful than shrimp grilled without their shells. They are a bit messier and more work to eat, but they're worth it. Besides, eating with your hands is a great way for guests to relax and get to know each other. Have damp towels and lemon wedges on the table so people can clean their hands easily.

SERVES 4 TO 6

 2 pounds extra-large shrimp (16 to 20 per pound), shells on
 ¼ cup rice wine vinegar
 1 cup olive oil
   Juice of 2 limes
 ¼ cup Asian chili paste
 2 jalapeño peppers, cored, seeded, and minced
   Sweet and Spicy Dipping Sauce (recipe follows)

1. If you are using wooden skewers (as opposed to metal), place 8 skewers in a bowl of water to soak for at least 15 minutes and up to 1 hour to prevent them from burning on the grill.

2. Using kitchen shears, clip the shrimp along the backside from the head end toward the tail. Rinse under cool water and set on paper towels to drain.

3. Stir the vinegar, olive oil, lime juice, chili paste, and jalapeño peppers together in a small bowl. Add the shrimp, toss to coat, cover, and place in the refrigerator to marinate for 1 to 2 hours.

4. Prepare a hot fire in a charcoal or gas grill.

5. Skewer the shrimp through both the tail and the body (the shrimp will be in a "c" shape), putting 4 to 5 shrimp on each skewer; or place the shrimp in a grill basket. Grill the shrimp over the hot fire for 1½ to 2 minutes per side, turning only once, until the shells turn orange. Place them on a serving platter loosely covered with foil to keep warm.

6. While the shrimp are grilling, heat the remaining marinade over low heat. Drizzle the marinade over the shrimp and serve immediately with the Sweet and Spicy Dipping Sauce.

REINVENTION
Turn leftover shrimp, peeled, into a wrap with shredded cabbage and Sweet and Spicy Dipping Sauce.

Sweet and Spicy Dipping Sauce

This is a nice dipping sauce for foods with an Asian theme, like Hoisin-Marinated Grilled Pork Tenderloin (page 169).

MAKES ABOUT ½ CUP

 ¼ cup rice wine vinegar
   Grated zest and juice of 1 lime
 2 tablespoons light soy sauce or tamari
 1 teaspoon Asian chili paste
 1 tablespoon hoisin sauce
 1 scallion, minced
 1 garlic clove (white and green parts), minced
   Sea salt and freshly ground black pepper to taste

Stir the vinegar, lime zest and juice, soy sauce, chili paste, hoisin sauce, scallion, garlic, salt, and pepper together in a small bowl. Serve immediately or refrigerate in an airtight container for up to 1 week.

> **It's okay to undercook shrimp slightly; they are so small that they will cook through once they're removed from the heat. By cooking them in two batches, you can be sure to remove all the shrimp before some begin to overcook.**

Shrimp for All Seasons

Shrimp is such a convenient last-minute main dish: once you spend the little time it takes to shell them, they cook in just a few minutes. These seasonal preparations all cook quickly and in one pan. Paired with rice pilaf (see Rice Pilaf for All Seasons, page 128) or steamed jasmine rice, you have a nice light meal in no time.

WINTER
Sautéed Tangerine Shrimp

The warmed sections of tangerine in this dish are a sweet surprise with the shrimp. If you can find them, use clementines, a Mandarin orange variety that comes from Spain. Not only do they have extra flavorful tangy-sweet flesh, clementines are a breeze to peel—and they have no seeds!

SERVES 4 TO 6

    Juice of 4 tangerines or clementines
  2 tangerines peeled, sectioned, and seeds removed
  1 tablespoon grated fresh ginger (1-inch piece)
  1 garlic clove, minced
1½ pounds large shrimp (21 to 25 per pound), peeled and deveined
  1 tablespoon olive oil
  1 tablespoon unsalted butter
    Sea salt and freshly ground black pepper to taste
  2 tablespoons chopped fresh cilantro

1. Combine the tangerine juice and sections, ginger, garlic, and shrimp in a bowl and toss to coat the shrimp. Cover and refrigerate to marinate for 2 to 3 hours.

2. Heat half of the oil and half of butter in a large skillet over medium-high heat until the butter melts. Remove half the shrimp from the marinade, reserving the marinade; season with salt and pepper, and place in the skillet to sauté for 1 to 1½ minutes per side, until they turn pink. Place the shrimp on a platter covered loosely with foil to keep warm. Add the remaining butter and oil and cook the remaining shrimp.

3. When all the shrimp are cooked, pour the marinade and tangerine sections into the skillet, increase the heat to high, and boil the marinade until it has reduced by half, about 30 seconds. Turn off the heat and stir in the cilantro. Season with additional salt and pepper if needed and serve the shrimp warm with the tangerine sauce and sections spooned over them.

SPRING
Garlic-Sautéed Shrimp with Spinach

For an Italian-leaning version of shrimp and grits, serve these over Risotto with Spring Peas and Asparagus (page 202). If you find them, pea shoots are the ideal springy substitute for the spinach in this recipe.

SERVES 4 TO 6

  3 tablespoons olive oil
1½ pounds large shrimp (21 to 25 per pound), peeled and deveined
    Sea salt and freshly ground black pepper to taste
  4 basil leaves, cut into thin strips
  3 garlic cloves, minced
    Juice of 1 lemon
 ½ cup dry white wine
  2 tablespoons unsalted butter
  6 ounces spinach, washed, stems removed, and drained (about 4 cups)

1. Heat 2 tablespoons of the olive oil in a large skillet over medium-high heat until sizzling hot. Add half the shrimp and season with salt, pepper, and basil. Cook 1 to 1½ minutes per side, adding half the garlic and squeezing the juice of half a lemon over the shrimp when you turn them. When the shrimp are pink on both sides, scrape the shrimp and garlic onto a platter and cover loosely with foil to keep warm. Add the remaining tablespoon oil and repeat to cook the remaining shrimp.

2. Add the wine to the skillet you cooked the shrimp in and simmer for about 30 seconds to reduce slightly. Stir in the butter and spinach and sauté, stirring constantly, until the butter has melted and the spinach is just wilted, 1 to 2 minutes. Return the shrimp to the pan just to reheat and to toss with the spinach. Season with additional salt and pepper to taste and serve warm.

REINVENTION
To turn leftovers of this shrimp into a quesadilla, spread a layer of fresh ricotta cheese on a flour or corn tortilla, then top with chopped shrimp and spinach, chopped tomatoes, and watercress. Cover with another tortilla and grill or panfry to warm through.

SUMMER

Sautéed Shrimp with Corn and Tomatoes

In a perfect world, I would make this with Silver Queen corn and heirloom tomatoes.

SERVES 4 TO 6

```
 3  tablespoons olive oil
 1  shallot, minced
1½  pounds large shrimp (21 to 25 per pound),
    peeled and deveined
    Sea salt and freshly ground black pepper to taste
 1  tablespoon unsalted butter
 1  heirloom tomato, cored and diced
    Kernels from 2 ears fresh corn
 6  fresh basil leaves, cut into thin strips
```

1. Heat 2 tablespoons of the olive oil over medium-high heat in a large skillet. Add half of the minced shallot and sauté for about 1 minute, just to soften. Add half of the shrimp, season with salt and pepper, and sauté for 1 to 1½ minutes per side, until the shrimp turn pink. Remove the shrimp and shallots from the pan and cover loosely with foil to keep warm. Add the remaining tablespoon olive oil and repeat with the remaining shallot and shrimp.

2. Melt the butter over high heat in the skillet you cooked the shrimp in, being careful not to let the butter brown. Stir in the tomato and corn and sauté until the corn is tender, 3 to 4 minutes. Return the shrimp to the pan, sprinkle with the basil, and stir just to coat the shrimp with the sauce and warm them slightly. Season with additional salt and pepper and serve warm.

FALL

Curry Coconut Shrimp

The curry and coconut milk these shrimp are cooked with make them perfect for the fall, when the weather starts to cool and you crave richer foods.

SERVES 4 TO 6

```
 3  tablespoons olive oil
 1  small onion, minced
1½  pounds large shrimp (21 to 25 per pound),
    peeled and deveined
    Sea salt and freshly ground black pepper to taste
 2  teaspoons curry powder
 1  garlic clove, minced
 1  1-inch piece fresh ginger, julienned
    (about 2 tablespoons)
 ½  cup dry sherry
 1  cup unsweetened coconut milk
 1  cup fish stock or chicken broth
 ¼  cup chopped fresh cilantro leaves
 2  scallions, minced (white and green parts)
```

1. Heat half of the olive oil in a large skillet over medium-high heat. Add the onion and cook for 3 to 4 minutes, until soft and translucent.

2. Add half of the shrimp, season with salt and pepper, and sauté for 1 to 1½ minutes per side, until the shrimp are pink. Remove the shrimp from the pan, reserving the onion and pan juices, and place them on a serving platter covered loosely with foil to keep warm while you cook the remaining shrimp. Repeat, cooking the remaining shrimp in the remaining olive oil.

3. Stir the curry powder, garlic, and ginger into the pan you cooked the shrimp in and sauté for 1 minute. Add the sherry and cook for about 1 minute longer, scraping up any bits from the bottom of the pan. Add the coconut milk and broth and bring to a boil. Reduce the heat and cook at a low boil for 10 to 12 minutes, until the sauce thickens and reduces by two thirds. Return the shrimp to the pan and cook for about 1 minute, to coat with the curry sauce and to warm through. Remove the pan from the heat, sprinkle with the cilantro and additional salt and pepper to taste, and stir to coat the shrimp. Serve warm, garnished with the minced scallions.

Pickled Shrimp

My sister makes these often for tailgating, which is an activity of epic proportions at Ole Miss. These shrimp are ideal for any sort of picnic because you can make them a day in advance. Pickled shrimp might sound a little unusual, but think of them as marinated; the cooked shrimp are bathed in sweet and savory pickling spices overnight. **WHAT TO SERVE WHEN** Pull these marinated shrimp out of the refrigerator on a summer afternoon; lay them on a bed of salad greens and you have an instant tasty light lunch. Skewered with a toothpick, they make nice hors d'oeuvre; they absorb so much flavor from the marinade that they don't need any dipping sauce.

SERVES 4 TO 6

1$\frac{1}{2}$ teaspoons whole peppercorns
$\frac{1}{2}$ teaspoon crushed red pepper flakes
$\frac{1}{2}$ teaspoon whole cloves
$\frac{1}{2}$ teaspoon mustard seeds
5 bay leaves, crushed
1 lemon, halved
1 pound large shrimp in their shells
  (21 to 25 per pound)
$\frac{1}{4}$ cup olive oil
  Juice of 2 limes
3 tablespoons rice vinegar
8 basil leaves, cut into thin strips
2 tablespoons sugar
  Sea salt and freshly ground black pepper to taste
2 kirby cucumbers, peeled and sliced into thin rounds
4 cups watercress, washed and trimmed of
  tough stems, or mixed greens

1. Bring 2 quarts of salted water to a boil in a large saucepan over high heat. Add the peppercorns, red pepper flakes, cloves, mustard seeds, and bay leaves to the boiling water. Squeeze the lemon juice into the water and drop the squeezed lemon halves in. Add the shrimp and boil, stirring often, until the shrimp turn pink and float to the top, 2 to 2$\frac{1}{2}$ minutes. Drain in a colander and rinse under cold water until the shrimp are cool to stop the cooking process.

2. When the shrimp are completely cool, remove the shells, pull out the veins, rinse, and drain again.

3. Whisk the olive oil, lime juice, vinegar, basil, sugar, salt, and pepper together in a large bowl. Add the shrimp and toss to coat. Cover with plastic wrap and refrigerate the shrimp overnight or for at least 4 hours.

4. Just before serving, place the shrimp in a large bowl with the cucumber and watercress and toss gently. Serve chilled or at room temperature.

Pan-Roasted Halibut with Roasted Cherry Tomatoes and Butternut Squash

Butternut squash and tomatoes is a combination that reminds me of the first hint of fall, when the season's first winter squash and the last of summer's tomatoes are together for a short, transitional time.

SERVES 4

1 small butternut squash, halved lengthwise and seeds removed
5 tablespoons olive oil
1 pint cherry or grape tomatoes or other small heirloom variety, washed and stems removed
1/4 cup sherry vinegar
Sea salt and freshly ground black pepper to taste
4 halibut fillets, cut 1 inch thick (about 6 ounces each), skin on
2 tablespoons fresh marjoram leaves
Juice of 1 lemon
1/2 cup dry white wine
1/2 cup chicken broth

1. Preheat the oven to 400°F.

2. Place the squash, cut side down, on a baking sheet with sides. Pour 1 cup of water and 1 tablespoon of the olive oil in the pan around the squash and roast for 40 to 45 minutes, until the squash is soft when the long section is pierced with a small knife. Check on the squash while it's cooking and add more water if the baking sheet is dry. Remove from the oven and let the squash cool.

3. While the squash roasts, place the tomatoes in a small baking dish and drizzle with 1 tablespoon of the olive oil and 2 tablespoons of the vinegar. Sprinkle with salt and pepper and toss to coat. Roast the tomatoes alongside the squash for about 20 minutes, until they are soft and slightly brown and wrinkled. Remove from the oven.

4. Reduce the oven temperature to 300°F.

5. Meanwhile, rub the halibut with 1 tablespoon of the olive oil and season with 1 tablespoon of the marjoram, salt, and pepper. Heat the remaining 2 tablespoons of olive oil in a large nonstick skillet over medium-high heat until just before the smoking point, or until a pinch of salt sizzles when dropped in the oil. Place the halibut fillets, skin side down, in the skillet. Reduce the heat to medium and cook the fish without moving it until it is opaque halfway up the side, about 4 minutes. Carefully turn the fish over and squeeze the lemon juice over it. Cook for 2 to 3 minutes longer, until it is opaque and tender and flaky when pierced with the tip of a sharp knife. Carefully transfer the fish to a platter covered loosely with foil, and place it in the oven to keep warm while you prepare the sauce.

6. Pour the wine, broth, and remaining 2 tablespoons vinegar into the pan you cooked the fish in, increase heat to high, and bring to a boil. Boil for 2 to 3 minutes, until the sauce is bubbly and thickens slightly.

7. Remove the skin from the squash and cut it into bite-size chunks. Add the squash chunks, tomatoes, and remaining marjoram to the pan with the sauce and simmer, stirring gently, to warm. Season with salt and pepper, spoon the squash and tomatoes over and around the fish, and serve immediately.

Pan-Seared Grouper with Lemon and Capers

This classic, subtle preparation works well with any mild fish fillets, such as halibut, salmon, tilapia, or snapper. WHAT TO SERVE WHEN Serve this dish on a bed of Wilted Spinach (page 191) topped with grated Parmesan cheese or Cider-Braised Endive (page 121) and rice pilaf (see Rice Pilaf for All Seasons, page 128).

SERVES 6

6 grouper fillets, cut 1 inch thick
  (about 6 ounces each), skin on
1/2 teaspoon sea salt, plus more to taste
1/2 teaspoon freshly ground black pepper,
  plus more to taste
2 tablespoons chopped fresh chives
2 tablespoons unsalted butter
2 tablespoons olive oil
1 lemon, thinly sliced
1/4 cup capers, drained
1/4 cup caper berries (optional), drained and halved
1/4 cup dry white wine
  Juice of 1 lemon

1. Season the grouper fillets with the 1/2 teaspoon salt, 1/2 teaspoon pepper, and half of the chives, pressing the chives to adhere to the fish. Heat the butter and olive oil in a large skillet over medium-high heat until hot but not smoking. A pinch of salt will sizzle when dropped in the oil. Place the fillets in the skillet, skin side down, and cook them undisturbed for about 4 minutes, until the underside is slightly crisp and the fillets lift easily from the pan. While the fish is cooking, scatter the lemon slices, capers, and caper berries over and around the fish.

2. Turn the fillets and cook for 3 to 4 minutes on the flesh side, until they are opaque and tender and flaky when pierced with the tip of a sharp knife. Carefully lift the fish fillets from the skillet and place them on a platter covered loosely with foil to keep warm.

3. Add the wine and lemon juice to the skillet you cooked the fish in and bring to a boil over medium-high heat, scraping any brown bits from the bottom of the pan. Boil for about 1 minute, until the liquid has reduced and thickened slightly. Spoon the pan drippings, sliced lemons, and capers over the fish and serve immediately.

Crispy Capers

Cooked until crisp in brown butter, capers turn a simple fillet of fish or breast of chicken into an elegant finished dish.

2 tablespoons unsalted butter
2 tablespoons drained capers

Heat the butter in a medium saucepan over medium heat until it is just brown and gives off a nutty aroma. Add the capers and sauté until some begin to pop open, about 2 minutes. Pour the capers and butter over the warm fish fillets.

about . . .
PAN-SEARING FISH

I love pan-searing as a method for cooking fish. The direct heat of the pan gives the meat a crispy exterior, and adding liquid to the pan steams the meat, making the interior of the fish fillet moist and tender. When I pan-sear fish, I always do it over medium or medium-high heat, never high heat, which would char the delicate exterior while the inside remained raw. I think the fish is more flavorful if you sear it with the skin on, but I like to remove it after the fish is cooked, before serving. After flipping the fish during cooking, pour some of the marinade you used into the pan (or another liquid, such as wine or fruit juice) so the fish simmers and steams in the liquid; this will help keep the fish moist and flavorful. A minute or two will make a big difference in the flavor of the fish, so be careful not to overcook it. Remember that it will continue to cook after you remove it from the heat.

Pan-Seared Red Snapper with Fresh Butter Beans, Tomatoes, and Corn

This is probably my favorite fish dish to make in the summer, when fresh shell beans, corn, and tomatoes are at all the farmers markets.

SERVES 4

- 4 red snapper fillets, cut $\frac{1}{2}$ inch thick (about 6 ounces each), skin on
- 3 tablespoons olive oil
- $\frac{1}{2}$ teaspoon salt, plus more to taste
- $\frac{1}{2}$ teaspoon freshly ground black pepper, plus more to taste
- 10 basil leaves, cut into thin strips
- 1 tablespoon unsalted butter
- 1 cup dry white wine
- 1 cup fresh shelled or frozen butter beans
- 1 tomato, cored and chopped
  Kernels from 2 ears fresh corn (about 1 cup)
- 1 lime, quartered

1. Rinse the snapper fillets under cool water and pat dry with paper towels. Place the fillets, skin side down, on your work surface and rub with 1 tablespoon of the olive oil. Season with salt and pepper and press the basil strips into the flesh side of the fillets.

2. Heat the remaining 2 tablespoons olive oil and the butter in a large nonstick skillet over medium-high until the oil starts to sizzle. Place the fillets in the skillet, skin side down, and sauté for about 3 minutes, until the skin side is crisp. Turn and sauté the fish about 1 minute longer, until the undersides are light brown. Pour the wine into the skillet, reduce the heat, cover, and simmer for about 1 minute longer, or until it is opaque and tender and flaky when pierced with the tip of a sharp knife.

3. Remove the skin from the fillets and transfer the fillets, skinned side down, to a serving platter; cover loosely with foil to keep warm.

4. Add the beans, tomato, and corn to the pan you cooked the fish in and simmer for 3 to 5 minutes, until the beans are crisp-tender. Add the remaining basil and additional salt and pepper to taste and spoon the succotash over and around the red snapper fillets. Serve immediately with the lime wedges.

about . . .
BUTTER BEANS

"Butter Beans" is the Southern variety of lima beans. I think they're one of those great, almost-forgotten foods. They're delicious and can be prepared in so many ways, yet people seldom cook with them anymore. During the summer, I buy them fresh and shell them. Their flavor and texture stand up to freezing, so they're one of the vegetables, in addition to peas and corn, that I always have on hand in the freezer.

Steamed Sea Bass with Broccoli Rabe and Roasted Garlic Vinaigrette

Steaming is such a refreshing way to prepare fish. You can really taste the fish, so always make sure to use the freshest you can find. Any mild-flavored fish will work in place of the sea bass in this recipe.

SERVES 4

4 sea bass fillets, cut 1 inch thick (about 6 ounces each), skin on
½ teaspoon sea salt, plus more to taste
½ teaspoon freshly ground black pepper, plus more to taste
2 tablespoons chopped fresh chives
2 tablespoons chopped fresh chervil or flat-leaf parsley leaves
1 lemon, thinly sliced
Steamed Broccoli Rabe (recipe follows)
Roasted Garlic Vinaigrette (recipe follows)

1. Rinse the fish fillets under cool water and pat dry with paper towels. Season the fillets on both sides with a half teaspoon each of the salt and pepper and press the chives and chervil into the flesh side of the fish.

2. Bring 1 cup of water to a boil in a steamer over medium-high heat. Place the lemon slices in the steamer basket and lay the sea bass fillets on top. Cover the pot and steam the fish for 3 to 4 minutes, until it is opaque and tender and flaky when pierced with the tip of a sharp knife.

3. Place several pieces of the steamed broccoli rabe on each plate. Remove the skin from the fish fillets and place the fish, skinned side down, on the broccoli rabe. Drizzle each fillet with about a teaspoon of the Roasted Garlic Vinaigrette, season with additional salt and pepper to taste, and serve immediately.

Steamed Broccoli Rabe with Roasted Garlic Vinaigrette

Broccoli rabe is a leafy green with small, broccoli-like clusters on its stems. It is in the same family as cabbage and turnip greens. It is slightly bitter, but very tasty. In addition to serving it with this fish, it is a nice complement to a sweeter side dish, like the Butternut Squash and Apple Mash (page 104), or sweet potatoes prepared in any way.

SERVES 4

1 head broccoli rabe, trimmed of tough stems
2 tablespoons olive oil
Sea salt and freshly ground black pepper to taste
Roasted Garlic Vinaigrette (recipe follows)

Place the broccoli rabe in a medium saucepan with the olive oil, salt, pepper, and ½ cup of water. Bring to a boil over high heat, lower the heat, cover, and steam the broccoli rabe until it is tender and bright green, about 1½ minutes. Toss with the vinaigrette and serve warm.

Roasted Garlic Vinaigrette

The pureed garlic in this vinaigrette makes the vinaigrette slightly creamy. It makes a delicious dressing for sturdy greens like escarole or frisee, or for white beans.

MAKES ABOUT ¾ CUP

1 head roasted garlic (see "Roasting Garlic," page 95)
¼ cup white wine vinegar
Grated zest and juice of 1 lemon
½ cup extra-virgin olive oil
Sea salt and freshly ground black pepper to taste

Squeeze the garlic pulp out of the skins and place them in the jar of a blender with the vinegar, lemon zest and juice, olive oil, salt, and pepper and puree for 1 to 2 minutes, until the vinaigrette is smooth. Serve immediately or refrigerate in an airtight container for up to 4 days.

It's a good idea when serving fish to heat the serving platter and individual plates in the oven. Fish tends to cool so quickly, and the warm plates will help to keep it warm as long as possible.

Sautéed Sea Bass with Wilted Spinach and Lemon Chive Oil

This is a very simple and light preparation for fish, but it is still very flavorful. The Lemon Chive Oil really makes the flavors pop. You could use just about any fish you like in place of the sea bass, like halibut, cod, salmon, or snapper.

SERVES 4

4 sea bass fillets, cut 1-inch thick (about 6 ounces each), skin on
3 tablespoons olive oil
2 basil leaves, cut into thin strips
Sea salt and freshly ground black pepper to taste
1 tablespoon unsalted butter
Juice of 1 lemon
1/2 cup dry white wine
1/2 cup chicken broth or fish broth
Wilted Spinach (recipe follows)
Lemon Chive Oil (recipe follows)

1. Rub the fillets with 2 tablespoons of the olive oil and sprinkle with the basil, salt, and pepper. Press the basil into the flesh of the fish.

2. Heat the remaining 1 tablespoon of olive oil and the butter over medium-high heat in a large nonstick skillet until the butter melts and the oil sizzles when a pinch of salt is dropped in the pan.

3. Place the fish fillets in the pan, skin side down, and cook for about 4 minutes, until the skin is crispy and the edges begin to turn opaque. With a metal spatula, carefully turn the fish fillets, drizzle half the lemon juice over the fish, and cook 2 to 3 minutes longer, until the fish is flaky and tender to the touch.

4. Remove the fish fillets from the pan and cover them loosely with foil to keep them warm. Pour the wine into the pan and simmer over high heat for about 30 seconds, scraping up any brown bits from the bottom of the pan. Add the broth and remaining lemon juice and simmer for 1 to 2 minutes more, until the sauce has reduced and thickened slightly.

5. To serve, remove the skin and place the fish fillets on a bed of spinach mounded on individual plates or a large serving platter. Spoon the pan juices over the fish fillets and drizzle each fillet with about 1 teaspoon of the Lemon Chive Oil. Season with additional salt and pepper if desired and serve immediately.

Wilted Spinach

This spinach is just barely wilted. It's light and healthy but also very flavorful, so it makes a nice bed for any meat, chicken, or fish dishes. I often top it with a sprinkling of freshly grated Parmesan cheese.

2 tablespoons olive oil
2 bunches spinach, stems removed, washed, and drained (about 8 cups)
Sea salt and freshly ground black pepper, to taste

Heat the olive oil over high heat in a large skillet or wok until it is very hot but not smoking. Add the spinach and sauté, stirring so that it cooks evenly, until wilted, about 2 minutes. Remove the spinach from the pan, season with salt and pepper, and serve immediately.

Lemon Chive Oil

This infused oil is best if the oil has a chance to marinate with the herbs for at least an hour before being passed through a strainer.

MAKES ABOUT 1/2 CUP

1/2 cup chopped fresh chives
1/2 cup chopped fresh parsley
1/2 cup olive oil
Grated zest and juice of 2 lemons
Sea salt and freshly ground black pepper to taste

1. Place the chives, parsley, oil, lemon zest and juice, salt, and pepper in the jar of a blender or in the bowl of a food processor fitted with a metal blade and process, scraping down the sides if necessary, for about 2 minutes, until the mixture is smooth. Allow the mixture to sit in the blender (or transfer it to a measuring cup with a spout) for at least 1 hour.

2. Scrape the herb oil out of the blender and pass it through a strainer into a small bowl, pressing with the back of a spoon to press out all the oil and to remove all the fibrous threads of chives. Use immediately or refrigerate it in an airtight container. Bring the oil to room temperature and shake well before serving.

66 My rule for measuring spinach for cooking is to use one very large handful of cleaned, trimmed spinach leaves per person. Figure a large handful is 2 cups. 99

Braised Salmon Fillets with Tarragon and White Wine over Warm Lentils with Crispy Pancetta

This is subtle, classic preparation. I like to serve it on a bed of the Warm Lentils with Crispy Pancetta so when you take a bite of the fish, you get a little bit of the lentils. If you wanted to go further in that direction, make a bed layering Creamy Mashed Celery Root (page 106) then the lentils and the fish. A leafy green, like Garlicky Greens (page 112), would be nice on the side.

SERVES 4

4 salmon fillets, cut 1-inch thick (about 6 ounces each), skin on
3 tablespoons olive oil
2 tablespoons apple cider or unfiltered apple juice
    Juice of 1 tangerine (or orange)
½ cup dry white wine
2 tablespoon chopped fresh tarragon
    Sea salt and freshly ground black pepper to taste
3 tablespoon unsalted butter
    Warm Lentils with Crispy Pancetta (recipe follows)

1. Rinse the salmon fillets under cool water, pat them dry with paper towels, and place them in a shallow bowl or baking dish. Rub the flesh side of fillet with 1 tablespoon of the olive oil. Pour the apple juice, tangerine juice and wine over the fillets and and sprinkle them with 1 tablespoon of the tarragon. Press the tarragon into the flesh side of the salmon and leave the salmon skin-side up. Cover and refrigerate to marinate the fish for 1 hour to overnight.

2. Heat the remaining 2 tablespoons olive oil and 1 tablespoon of the butter in a large nonstick skillet over medium heat until hot, about 2 minutes. Season the salmon fillets with the salt and pepper, remove from the marinade, and place them skin-side down in the grill pan to cook for about 4 minutes. Turn the salmon over and cook for an additional 4 minutes or until the fish flakes easily when the tip of a knife is inserted in the thickest part of the fish. Remove the salmon from the pan and set it on a platter loosely covered with foil to keep warm.

3. Meanwhile, pour the marinade in the skillet and boil it over medium-high heat until it has reduced by half, 1 to 2 minutes. Taste for salt and pepper and season with more if necessary. Remove the skillet from the heat and add the remaining butter and tarragon, whisking until the sauce is smooth. Remove the skin from the fish fillets. Spoon the warm lentils onto four plates and press them down to form a bed. Place a salmon fillet on top of each bed of lentils. Pour the sauce over the salmon and serve immediately.

Warm Lentils with Crispy Pancetta

I prefer French green lentils, called *lentilles du Puy*, to regular brown lentils. They have such a deep, almost meaty flavor and they hold their shape nicely when cooked. You can find them at specialty food stores, often in a box if not in bulk. If you can't find them, brown lentils do nicely, too. WHAT TO SERVE WHEN I like to layer lentils under a mashed vegetable, like the Creamy Mashed Celery Root (page 106). Then I put a piece of salmon or a grilled chicken breast on top. It looks elegant, but I also like to serve it this way so I can get a bit of everything in each forkful.

SERVES 4 TO 6

3 ¼-inch-thick slices pancetta or 3 strips bacon, chopped
2 shallots, minced
1 cup French green lentils or brown lentils
2 teaspoons chopped fresh rosemary
1 teaspoon sea salt, plus more to taste
    Freshly ground black pepper to taste

1. Cook the chopped pancetta in a large skillet over medium-high heat until crisp. Remove the pancetta to a paper towel to drain, reserving the grease in the skillet.

2. Add the minced shallots to the skillet and sauté for about 2 minutes, until soft and translucent. Add the lentils, rosemary, 1 teaspoon salt, and 3 cups of water and bring just to a boil over high heat. Reduce the heat and simmer, uncovered, for about 35 minutes, until the lentils are tender and most of the liquid has evaporated. Add the pancetta, season with salt and pepper to taste, and toss gently to combine. Serve warm.

BASICS: *Cooking Fish*

I find many people are intimidated by cooking fish. The difficulty seems to be in knowing when the fish is done. Fish is tricky in that it doesn't drastically change in appearance when it's cooked, the way meat and chicken do. Also, because fish is so delicate, 1 minute can mean the difference between a perfectly cooked piece of fish and one that is overdone and dry. Getting this right is largely a matter of practice, but in the meantime, here are some hints.

○ Unless you're searing something like sushi grade tuna, you never want to cook fish over high heat, which chars the outside while leaving the inside raw; great for a steak, but for a delicate fillet of fish medium to medium-high heat is usually ideal.

○ If you're pan-searing fish, use either butter or oil, or a combination, which gives you the sweet taste of butter while the oil prevents the butter from burning. If you do use only butter and you find the butter just beginning to brown, lift the pan off the heat and let the butter cool before putting the pan back on the heat and adding the fish. If the butter has turned brown and nutty smelling, better to toss it and start over than to impart a burned-butter flavor to your fish. In any case, you want the butter or oil to be so hot that the fish sizzles when it hits the pan. If it spatters, reduce the heat slightly.

○ Cooking fish with the skin on enhances its flavor and also keeps the fish from falling apart when you turn it. After you cook the fish, it's easy to remove the skin; it just peels right off. With fish that has the skin on, sear the skin side first for a few minutes, until it's crisp. Then flip the fish over and sear the flesh side for just about a minute to give it color. At this point I may add some liquid to the pan (usually white wine but it varies depending on the recipe), and cover the pan to let the fish steam for about 1 minute, just enough to cook the inside while keeping the fish nice and tender.

○ The best way to test fish for doneness is to press it with a finger. It should feel firm but slightly fleshy. The fleshy feeling indicates that the fish is not cooked to the point of being dry. At first it may be difficult to know what "done" fish feels like, but after you cook fish a few times, you will develop a sense of it. In the meantime, if you're at all unsure, use a knife to open the fish just enough to peek inside. If it flakes apart easily, and is mostly opaque but still slightly translucent in the very center, it's done. Remember that the fish will continue to cook slightly once it's out of the pan. On average, a 6-ounce fillet of fish will take no more than 6 to 8 minutes to cook.

○ Two things that can spoil a fish dish for anyone are scales and bones. I have my fishmonger scale fish for me, and I buy fillets, I still use a strawberry huller or small knife to pull out any remaining bones. There's an actual tool, called fish tweezers, for this, but the main thing that distinguishes them from any other tweezers is that they're the ones you keep in the kitchen!

❝ *When fish is ready to be turned, it will release easily from the pan or grill. If it's sticking, it's probably too soon.* **❞**

Grilled Salmon with Your Favorite Fresh Salsa

Grilled fish topped with fresh salsa is satisfying and flavorful, but also light and refreshing. Grilling imparts the smoky flavor of the fire but still allows the flavor of the fish to prevail, and the salsa is just enough to finish the dish. I made salmon here because it's available all over the country, but any mild-flavored fish would work, including striped bass, red snapper, grouper, tilapia, swordfish, shark, or tuna. Note that you may need to adjust the cooking time. If you don't want to fire up the grill, use a grill pan.

SERVES 4

  4 salmon fillets, cut 1 inch thick
     (about 6 ounces each), skin on
  2 tablespoons olive oil
  2 tablespoons light soy sauce or tamari
     Juice of 1/2 orange
  6 to 8 basil leaves, cut into thin strips
     Sea salt and freshly ground black pepper to taste

1. Rinse the salmon fillets under cool water, pat dry with paper towels, and place skin side down in a shallow dish. Rub the salmon fillets with the olive oil, drizzle with the soy sauce and orange juice, and sprinkle with the basil. Turn the fillets to coat with the marinade, press the basil into the flesh side of the fillets, and turn them skin side up. Cover the dish with plastic wrap and marinate in the refrigerator for at least 1 hour or overnight.

2. Prepare a hot fire in a charcoal or gas grill (or heat a grill pan over medium heat to hot, almost to the smoking point). Remove the salmon fillets from the marinade, season with salt and pepper, and lay the fillets, skin side down, on the grill for 4 minutes, brushing the flesh side with the reserved marinade. Turn the fillets and grill for an additional 4 minutes, spooning the marinade over them as they cook, until the fish is opaque and flakes easily when pierced with the tip of a sharp knife. Remove the fillets from the grill, peel off the skin, and place them, skinned side down, on a serving platter or individual plates. Serve immediately, topped with the fresh salsa of your choice.

REINVENTION

Turn leftover salmon into a B.L.T. with Greenest Goddess Dressing (below). To make one sandwich, toast 2 pieces of whole wheat, spread with the dressing or mayonnaise, and top one piece of toast with 2 tomato slices, the salmon, and bacon. Season with salt and pepper, and top with a handful of arugula or mixed baby lettuces. Close the sandwich and slice in half.

Greenest Goddess Dressing

MAKES ABOUT 3 CUPS

   1 cup mayonnaise
   1 cup sour cream
      Grated zest and juice of 1 lemon
   2 tablespoons tarragon vinegar or white wine vinegar
 1/2 cup chopped fresh flat-leaf parsley leaves
 1/2 cup chopped fresh chives
   4 tablespoons chopped fresh dill
  20 fresh basil leaves
 1/2 teaspoon sea salt, plus more to taste
 1/2 teaspoon freshly ground black pepper, plus more to taste

Place the mayonnaise, sour cream, lemon zest and juice, vinegar, parsley, chives, dill, and basil leaves in the jar of a blender or bowl of a food processor fitted with a metal blade and process until the dressing is smooth and light green with specks of herbs remaining. Add the salt and pepper and season with more if desired. Use immediately or refrigerate for about 3 hours to thicken.

Linguine with Clams

I make this often when I'm at our summerhouse in Lake Placid, where I'm able to get fresh small Maine clams. It's a nice dinner to serve a crowd because you can do all the prep ahead of time and cook the clams and pasta at the last minute. Also your guests can eat it with their plates on their laps without a problem. WHAT TO SERVE WHEN I like to serve this with a simple salad and Toasted Garlic Bread (page 57) to dip into the sauce.

SERVES 8 TO 10

- 5 pounds Maine, littleneck, Manilla, or your local small clams
- 4 tablespoons unsalted butter
- 2 tablespoons olive oil, plus more for tossing with the linguine
- 2 large yellow onions, chopped
- 2 celery stalks, chopped
- 6 garlic cloves, minced
- 2 plum tomatoes, cored and chopped
- 1 bottle dry white wine (about 4 cups)
- 2 tablespoons sea salt, plus more to taste
- 1 pound linguine
- 1 tablespoon crushed red pepper flakes
- 1/4 cup chopped flat-leaf parsley leaves
- 10 to 12 basil leaves, cut into thin strips
  Freshly grated Parmesan cheese for serving with the pasta

1. Scrub the clams under cold water to remove the sand and drain in a colander.

2. Heat the butter and olive oil in a large stockpot over medium heat. Add the onions and cook and stir for 10 to 12 minutes, until the onions are very soft. Add the celery and cook for 2 to 3 minutes, until the celery softens. Add the garlic and cook 2 minutes more, stirring constantly so the garlic doesn't brown. Add the tomatoes and cook and stir for about 2 minutes, until they begin to break down.

3. Increase the heat to high, pour the wine into the stockpot, and bring to a boil. Reduce the heat and simmer for about 30 minutes.

4. While the wine is simmering, bring a large saucepan of water to a boil over high heat. Stir in the salt and the linguine, stirring occasionally so the strands don't stick together. Reduce the heat so the water is at a low boil and cook the linguine until just before al dente, about 5 minutes. You want to undercook the pasta slightly, as it will cook a bit more when you mix it with the clams and broth. Drain the pasta in a colander and rinse it under cool water to rinse off excess starch. Drizzle the drained pasta with a small amount of olive oil to keep it from sticking together and toss it gently to coat.

5. Add the clams to the pot with the wine, cover, and simmer just until the clams have opened, about 5 minutes. Stir in the red pepper flakes, parsley, and basil. Remove the clams from the broth and place them in a large bowl covered loosely with foil to keep warm.

6. Add the linguine to the broth and cook, stirring occasionally, for 2 to 3 minutes, until the pasta is warmed through and al dente. Return the clams to the pot with the linguine, cover, and steam for a few minutes to warm the clams. Season with additional salt to taste. Use a long fork or tongs to lift the linguine onto a large pasta bowl or individual plates, spoon the clams over the linguine, and pour the broth over the pasta. Serve immediately with the grated Parmesan cheese.

seven

meals that cook themselves

Fall-off-the-Bone Baby Back Ribs ○ Slow-Roasted Pork Shoulder with Sweet and Salty Glazed Onions ○ Standing Pork Roast with Pear Chutney ○ Chipotle Maple Barbecue Beef Brisket ○ Mom's Pot Roast ○ Sliced Leg of Lamb ○ Herb-Roasted Rack of Lamb with Red Wine–Mustard Sauce ○ Port-Braised Lamb Shanks with Rosemary ○ Braised Tarragon Chicken ○ Red Wine–Braised Chicken with Onions and Thyme ○ Lemon-Curry Roasted Chicken ○ Creamy Mac, Chicken, and Cheese

When you don't have a lot of time to cook, you have two choices: you can make something that cooks in a short time or you can make something that you put in the oven and let the oven do the rest. The recipes in this chapter fall into the latter category. They are roasts and braises that rely on long cooking times for tenderness, and on the wine, herbs, and aromatics they're cooked in for flavor.

Though none of these is quick-cooking, some take considerably longer than others. There are those, like Lemon-Curry Roasted Chicken, Herb-Roasted Rack of Lamb, or Creamy Mac, Chicken, and Cheese, that take very little preparation and cook in about an hour. They're the perfect choice for when you get home from work, since they cook themselves while you do what you need to do: check e-mail, do laundry, return phone calls, or exercise.

And then there are those, like the Slow-Roasted Pork Shoulder, Mom's Pot Roast, Port-Braised Lamb Shanks, and Chipotle Maple Barbecue Beef Brisket, that take around 3 hours to cook, but they require almost no attention after the 5 or 10 minutes you spend preparing them for the oven. I save these for a weekend afternoon. I put them in the oven when I'm going to be home all day anyway. It makes the house smell so good, plus I think there's something comforting about having a roast in the oven, especially during colder months. These fork-tender meats make large portions, and the leftovers are ideal for making tacos, quesadillas, sandwiches, and salads. I've given suggestions throughout the recipes for ways to transform these meats into next-day meals.

Fall-off-the-Bone Baby Back Ribs

For years I played around with barbecue ribs, trying to find a way to make them so that the meat was moist and tender but also relatively quick and easy. A few years ago, Shay, who worked with me since the opening of Foster's Market, gave me her recipe for ribs, and they're as good as any I've ever had. The ribs can be baked (through step 3) up to a day in advance, but you'll need to leave them on the grill a few minutes longer to make sure they heat all the way through.

SERVES 4 TO 6

2 slabs baby back ribs (about 3 1/2 pounds)
1 large onion, sliced
1 12-ounce bottle of beer
Sea salt and freshly ground pepper to taste
2 cups barbecue sauce (Chipotle Maple Barbecue Sauce, page 217) or your favorite bottled sauce

1. Preheat the oven to 325°F.

2. To remove the membrane from the back of the ribs, take a small dull knife, like an oyster or table knife, and pry the tip of the knife between the membrane and bone at the edge of the ribs in the center of the slab. Lift to separate the membrane from the bone, then grab the membrane with your fingers and pull it off and discard.

3. Spread the onion slices evenly on a baking sheet with sides and place the ribs, bone side down, on top. Pour the beer over the ribs, season with salt and pepper, and cover tightly with foil. Bake undisturbed for 2 hours.

4. Prepare a fire in a charcoal grill and let the coals burn to a gray ash with a faint red glow, or until you can hold your hand 3 to 4 inches above the fire for no more than 6 seconds.

5. Brush both sides of the ribs with the barbecue sauce and place them, meat side down, over the coals. Grill the ribs for 10 to 15 minutes, or until slightly charred, basting several times. Turn the ribs and baste the cooked side liberally. Close the lid of the grill and cook the ribs 10 to 15 minutes longer, basting often. Cut the slabs into individual ribs, pile them onto a large platter, and serve warm.

about . . .
RIBS

The term "living high on the hog" derives from the concept of eating the best meat on the pig, those cuts farthest from the ground, and thus has come to refer to living or eating well. Baby back ribs come from the back of the pig, about as high as it gets, and they're my favorites. They are smaller and leaner than spare ribs, which come from the belly or side of the pig. When they're cooked right, baby backs are very tender.

TRICKS OF MY TRADE

- **Cook slow-roasting meats** on days you don't need them. Prepare and put them in the oven while you're cooking something quick for that night's dinner. Take the roasted meat out of the oven and refrigerate it before you go to bed; the next day, all you'll have to do for dinner is reheat. This is also a good way to cook for company so you can relax and enjoy your guests.

- **When you go to the grocery store,** buy for a few nights. This doesn't mean you need to make a rigid menu plan. And it doesn't mean freezing meats, which I don't like to do. But if you buy fish for that night, plus chicken to marinate for the following night, and a roast to cook the night you make the chicken—for the night after that—you've taken care of the entire week's meals once you reinvent the leftovers.

- **Whether roasting** or braising, brush or spoon the pan juices over the meat to keep it moist and tender. Also, always check to make sure there is liquid in the bottom of the roasting pan; if not, add a cupful of water or broth to the pan.

Standing Pork Roast with Pear Chutney

If you don't want to make the chutney, serve the pork roast with bottled applesauce instead.

SERVES 4 TO 6

Stems and fronds of 1 fennel bulb, ¼ cup of the fronds chopped and reserved

4 long rosemary sprigs, plus 2 tablespoons chopped fresh rosemary

1 3½- to 4-pound pork loin center cut roast with bones, at room temperature

¼ cup olive oil

1 small white onion, minced or grated

4 garlic cloves, minced

2 tablespoons chopped fresh sage leaves

1 teaspoon sea salt

2 teaspoons freshly ground black pepper

1 cup dry white wine

Pear Chutney (recipe follows)

1. Preheat the oven to 350°F.

2. In a large roasting pan, make a bed of the fennel fronds and stems and the rosemary sprigs, and place the roast on top.

3. Stir the olive oil, onion, garlic, chopped rosemary, sage, chopped fennel fronds, salt, and pepper together in a small bowl to form a paste. Rub the paste into all sides of the pork roast and set the roast fat side up.

4. Pour the wine and 2½ cups of water around the pork roast and roast for 2 hours 30 minutes to 3 hours, or until an instant-read thermometer registers 145°F to 150°F, basting with the pan liquid and rotating the roasting pan every 30 minutes. Transfer the pork roast to a cutting board to rest, covered loosely with foil, for 10 to 15 minutes.

5. Cut the pork roast away from the bones, starting at the tip of the bone and cutting down along the backside of the loin, into ½-inch slices. Serve warm, with a dollop of Pear Chutney on the side.

Pear Chutney

Chutney is one of those things that I feel if you're going to take the time to make it, you may as well make a lot. There are so many ways to use it: spread on sandwiches or serve alongside Simple Succulent Grilled Pork Chops (page 166) or Lemon-Curry Roasted Chicken (page 227).

MAKES ABOUT 3 CUPS

4 under-ripe pears (about 1½ pounds), peeled, cored, and chopped

1 tart apple (such as Granny Smith or Pippin), peeled, cored, and chopped

1 small onion, diced

¾ cup granulated sugar

½ cup packed light brown sugar

½ cup apple cider vinegar

Juice of 1 lemon

2 garlic cloves, minced

1 red bell pepper, cored, seeded, and diced

1 cayenne pepper or jalapeño pepper, cored, seeded, and diced

1 tablespoon grated fresh ginger (1-inch piece) or 1 teaspoon ground

2 teaspoons yellow mustard seeds

2 teaspoons sea salt

1 teaspoon ground cinnamon

1 teaspoon ground cloves

2 bay leaves

⅔ cup raisins

½ cup chopped pecans

1. Combine the pears, apple, onion, granulated sugar, brown sugar, vinegar, lemon juice, garlic, bell pepper, cayenne, ginger, mustard seeds, salt, cinnamon, cloves, and bay leaves in a medium saucepan and bring to a boil over medium-high heat. Reduce the heat to low and simmer for 30 to 45 minutes, stirring frequently, until the fruit is very tender and the liquid has thickened.

2. Remove the pan from the heat, stir in the raisins and pecans, and allow the chutney to cool to room temperature. Remove the bay leaves and discard. Serve immediately or refrigerate in an airtight container for up to 2 weeks.

> **People often overcook pork because they think it's unsafe not to. For moist, tender meat, cook pork to 150°F. It will continue to cook to 160°F once it's removed from the oven.**

Chipotle Maple Barbecue Beef Brisket

At the Market, we use this saucy, sweet and spicy meat to make tacos, enchiladas, quesadillas, and sandwiches. And of course, we serve it on its own. One of the women who tests recipes for me, Wendy, fell in love with this dish when she tested it. It's now part of her regular dinner-party repertoire; she likes that she can have it cooking while she's getting the rest of the meal ready, and she says her guests invariably love it. WHAT TO SERVE WHEN I like this sweet, tangy brisket with Southern sorts of sides, like the Roasted Sweet Potato Wedges (page 110), Cornbread Panzanella (page 76), or the Black-Eyed Pea Salad with Roasted Butternut Squash and Goat Cheese (page 81).

SERVES 6 TO 8

- 1 3½- to 4-pound beef brisket, at room temperature
- 2 tablespoons **Quito's Butt Rub** (recipe follows) or store-bought barbecue rub
- ½ cup packed light brown sugar
- ¼ cup Worcestershire sauce
- 2 tablespoons balsamic vinegar
- 1 cup **Chipotle-Maple Barbecue Sauce** (recipe follows) or your favorite bottled sauce
- 1 cup beer

1. Sprinkle the brisket with the butt rub. Stir the brown sugar, Worcestershire sauce, and vinegar together in a shallow dish; pour over the brisket and turn several times to coat the meat evenly. Cover and marinate in the refrigerator for at least 6 hours or overnight. Bring the meat to room temperature before cooking.

2. Preheat the oven to 350°F and prepare a hot fire in a charcoal or gas grill.

3. Remove the brisket from the marinade and place it over the hot coals to sear until the outside is slightly charred, 4 to 6 minutes per side.

4. Place the seared brisket in a large cast-iron or other ovenproof skillet and pour the marinade over it. Stir the barbecue sauce and beer together and pour over the brisket. Turn to coat the brisket evenly on all sides.

5. Cover the skillet with aluminum foil or a lid and roast the brisket for 3 hours to 3 hours 30 minutes, until it pulls apart easily with a fork. Remove the brisket from the oven and serve warm, with additional warm barbecue sauce drizzled over the top or served on the table.

Quito's Butt Rub

The great thing about barbecue is that everyone eventually finds a recipe and a method of cooking that works best for him or her. In Tennessee, where I grew up, real barbecue is traditionally sprinkled with spices, rather than drenched in sauce, before it's put on the grill. Every barbecue aficionado invents a rub that he or she swears beats all others—and keeps it as a closely guarded secret. This one comes from Quito, whom has won all kinds of contests on the barbecue circuit. Sprinkle the rub onto any cut of pork, beef, or chicken before putting it on the grill—and thank Quito for the results.

MAKES ABOUT ½ CUP

- 2 tablespoons paprika
- 1 tablespoon freshly ground black pepper
- 1 tablespoon kosher or sea salt
- 1 tablespoon garlic powder
- 1 tablespoon chili powder
- 1 tablespoon packed brown sugar
- ¼ teaspoon cayenne pepper

Combine the paprika, black pepper, salt, garlic powder, chili powder, brown sugar, and cayenne in a small jar or an airtight container and shake to mix. This spice rub will keep in a cool dry place for up to 6 months.

Chipotle Maple Barbecue Sauce

This sauce has the complex sweetness of maple syrup and the smoky spice of chipotle peppers. If you don't want to make barbecue sauce from scratch but you still want the smoky heat of the chipotle peppers, use a blender to puree 3 chipotle peppers in adobo with your favorite bottled sauce.

MAKES ABOUT 4 CUPS

- 1 28-ounce can crushed tomatoes
- $1/2$ cup maple syrup
- $1/2$ cup packed light brown sugar
- 3 chipotle peppers in adobo, diced
- 1 cup white vinegar
- $1/4$ cup Worcestershire sauce
- $1/2$ cup apple cider or unfiltered apple juice
- Juice of 2 lemons
- 4 garlic cloves, minced
- 2 tablespoons Colman's dry mustard
- 2 teaspoons sea salt
- 2 teaspoons freshly ground black pepper

Combine the tomatoes, maple syrup, brown sugar, chipotle peppers, vinegar, Worcestershire, apple cider, lemon juice, garlic, mustard, salt, and black pepper in a heavy-bottomed saucepan and stir to mix. Bring the sauce to a boil over medium-high heat. Reduce the heat and simmer for 30 to 35 minutes, until the sauce is thick and reduced by about one quarter. This sauce will keep, refrigerated in an airtight container, for up to 2 weeks.

REINVENTION

Fold leftovers of this brisket inside a corn tortilla to make a soft taco with barbecue sauce, sliced red onion, and Roasted Sweet Potato Salsa (page 198) or any other fresh salsa. Or make a sandwich on a toasted hamburger bun with coleslaw, such as Zucchini Slaw (page 85).

Herb-Roasted Rack of Lamb with Red Wine–Mustard Sauce

I often made this for springtime dinners for my catering clients in Connecticut. It feels like a special occasion dish to me. It's not something to make for a large group, because the lamb racks stand so tall that you won't be able to fit more than enough for 8 in one oven. WHAT TO SERVE WHEN I like to serve these chops with bright green, springy vegetables, like Smashed Green Peas (page 119), Wilted Spinach (page 191), or Lemon Roasted Asparagus (page 115). For a starchy vegetable, I put them on a bed of Creamy Mashed Celery Root (page 106) or Mashed Roasted Sweet Potatoes with Parmesan (page 106).

SERVES 4 TO 6

2 1¼-pound racks of lamb (7 to 8 chops each), at room temperature
¼ cup olive oil
2 tablespoons chopped fresh rosemary
2 tablespoons chopped fresh thyme
2 tablespoons chopped fresh marjoram leaves
Grated zest and juice of 1 lemon
6 garlic cloves, minced

For the Red Wine–Mustard Sauce

1 cup dry red wine
1 tablespoon balsamic vinegar
1 tablespoon sugar
1 tablespoon Dijon mustard
1 tablespoon chopped fresh rosemary
1 teaspoon sea salt
1 teaspoon freshly ground black pepper

1. Preheat the oven to 450°F.

2. Stand the racks in a large roasting pan so they are propping each other up, rib bones interlaced and fat side facing out.

3. Stir the olive oil, rosemary, thyme, marjoram, lemon zest and juice, and garlic together in a small bowl to make a paste. Spoon the paste over the fatty part of the lamb, pressing it into the fat.

4. Roast the lamb for 10 minutes. Reduce the heat to 400°F and roast about 20 minutes longer, until the outside is crisp and golden brown and an instant-read thermometer inserted into the end of the rack reads 130°F to 135°F for medium-rare (135°F to 140°F for medium). Let the lamb rest on a cutting board for 5 to 10 minutes, loosely covered with foil.

5. While the lamb roasts, combine the red wine, vinegar, and sugar in a small saucepan to make the sauce. Bring to a boil over high heat and continue to boil until the liquid thickens and reduces by half, 3 to 4 minutes. Remove the saucepan from the heat and stir in the mustard, rosemary, and salt and pepper. Keep warm until you serve the lamb or reheat if necessary. Cut the lamb into individual chops, spoon the red wine–mustard sauce over them, and serve immediately.

Note: *For easier slicing, have your butcher "French" the rack (trim the rib bones), remove the chin bone, and crack between the chops.*

Port-Braised Lamb Shanks with Rosemary

This lamb reminds me of a dressy version of pot roast. The port and long cooking mellow the lamb. When it's cold outside, this kind of fall-off-the-bone meat in sauce is what I crave to eat and to cook. WHAT TO SERVE WHEN In keeping with the hearty, wintry feeling of this dish, I like to serve it on a bed of Creamy Mashed Celery Root (page 106) with Garlicky Greens (page 112) on the side.

SERVES 4 TO 6

2 tablespoons olive oil

4 lamb shanks (1 to 1¼ pounds each), trimmed of excess fat

1 teaspoon sea salt, plus more to taste

½ teaspoon freshly ground black pepper, plus more to taste

1 large yellow onion, thinly sliced

2 carrots, chopped

4 garlic cloves, smashed

6 fresh rosemary sprigs

2 cups port wine

2 cups chicken or beef broth

1. Preheat the oven to 350°F.

2. Heat the olive oil in a large Dutch oven or a deep, ovenproof skillet over medium-high heat. Rub the lamb with the salt and pepper and place the lamb in the pan to sear, turning occasionally, until the shanks are a rich brown color on all sides, 5 to 7 minutes. Remove the shanks from the pan and set aside.

3. Reduce the heat to medium, add the onion and carrots, and cook for about 5 minutes or until the onion is tender and light brown. Add the garlic and rosemary and sauté for about 1 minute, stirring constantly, taking care not to let the garlic brown. Return the lamb shanks to the pan. Pour the port and broth around the shanks and bring to a low boil.

4. Cover the Dutch oven or skillet and place it in the oven for 3 to 3½ hours, spooning the sauce over the meat occasionally, or until the lamb shanks are fork-tender. Add a cup of water to the pan while cooking if it looks dry.

5. Transfer the shanks to a serving platter and cover with foil to keep warm. Skim the fat from the surface of the cooking liquid with a ladle or large spoon and place the Dutch oven or skillet on the stovetop. Bring the liquid to a boil over high heat, reduce the heat, and simmer for about 5 minutes, until it has reduced and thickened slightly. Season with additional salt and pepper to taste.

6. To serve, you can either pull the meat off the bones or leave the meat on the bones and serve each person a whole shank with the port sauce spooned over it. Either way, after the sauce has thickened, put the meat or whole shanks in the pan with the sauce and warm over medium heat. Serve warm, with the sauce spooned over the meat.

Note: *To make this a day in advance, refrigerate the meat and sauce together in an airtight container. When you are ready to serve, remove the shanks from the sauce, skim the hardened fat from the surface, pour the sauce into a skillet to reduce over medium heat, and proceed with step 5.*

BASICS: Braising

Cooking meat or vegetables in a small amount of liquid for a long period of time is known as braising. The slow cooking breaks down the fibers of even tougher cuts of meat, making it tender and flavorful. I start braises by browning or "searing" the meat on the stove before moving it to the oven. This seals in the flavor and also gives the exterior a beautiful color. The liquid makes a nice sauce, with no effort. Braising is a pretty foolproof method of cooking as long as you remember a few things: When you sear the outside, you want a nice brown "crust," but you don't want to burn it, so adjust your heat if needed. Don't overcrowd the pan; there should be enough room in the pan for the braising liquid to touch all sides of the meat. And when the meat is cooking in the oven, it doesn't need a lot of attention, but don't completely ignore it, either. Look from time to time to make sure there's still liquid in the pan, brush or spoon the pan juices over the meat, and check for doneness.

Braised Tarragon Chicken

There's something very simple and satisfying about this dish, a variation on a classic French dish that's usually made with heavy cream. When cooked slowly in the oven, the sauce thickens and you don't even miss the cream. You could make this recipe with all breasts or all thighs instead of a whole cut-up chicken, but I like to give my guests the option of light or dark meat. Either way, it is most moist and flavorful when made with bone-in chicken.

SERVES 4 TO 6

- 1 3- to 3½-pound chicken, cut into 8 pieces (if the breasts are exceptionally large, cut them in half crosswise so they require the same cooking time as the thighs)
- 1 tablespoon unsalted butter
- 2 tablespoons olive oil
- 2 teaspoons sea salt, plus more to taste
- 1 teaspoon freshly ground black pepper, plus more to taste
- 2 tablespoons chopped fresh tarragon leaves or 2 teaspoons dried
- 3 shallots, minced
- 2 tablespoons brandy
- 1½ cups dry white wine or chicken broth
- 2 tablespoons Dijon mustard

1. Preheat the oven to 400°F.

2. Rinse the chicken and pat dry with paper towels. Heat the butter and olive oil in a large, heavy ovenproof skillet over medium-high heat until the butter melts and sizzles. Season the chicken with the salt, pepper, and 1 tablespoon of the tarragon and cook, skin side down, for 4 to 5 minutes, until golden brown. Reduce the heat to medium if browning too quickly. Turn the chicken and cook 4 to 5 minutes longer. Move the chicken to one side of the skillet and reduce the heat to medium.

3. Add the shallots to the pan with the chicken and cook, stirring occasionally, for 2 to 3 minutes, until soft and translucent. Add the brandy and wine and scrape the bottom of the skillet to loosen the brown bits. Whisk in the mustard until it is incorporated. Spread the chicken out in the pan, making sure it's skin side up, and bring the liquid to a low boil.

4. Place the skillet in the oven and cook the chicken, uncovered, basting several times with the pan juices, for 25 to 30 minutes, or until the juices run clear when the chicken is pierced at the thickest point with the tip of a knife.

5. Stir in the remaining tarragon and additional salt and pepper to taste. Spoon the sauce over the chicken and serve warm.

Note: *If the sauce is a little thin when you remove the chicken from the oven, transfer the chicken to a platter and return it to the oven just to keep warm. Place the pan on the stove and boil the liquid over high heat until it thickens, 2 to 3 minutes.*

REINVENTION

Use leftover shredded chicken to make a quesadilla. Spread a flour or corn tortilla with fresh goat cheese, add chopped fresh spinach, shredded chicken, Caramelized Onions (page 156), and any fresh salsa (page 196). Top with another tortilla and grill in a skillet with butter until the ingredients are warmed through.

Red Wine–Braised Chicken with Onions and Thyme

We make a red wine, onion, and thyme soup at the Market that we got from *The Greens Cookbook* by Deborah Madison, and that I just love. One day I was braising chicken at home and decided to turn those ingredients into a sauce; the result—this dish—was just delicious. WHAT TO SERVE WHEN This chicken is so rich and flavorful it's nice served over something simple, like steamed Basmati Rice Pilaf with Zucchini, Roasted Red Peppers, and Parsley (page 129), Turnip Apple Mash with Thyme (page 105), or Roasted Spaghetti Squash (page 135).

SERVES 4 TO 6

A 3¹/₂- to 4-pound chicken, cut into 8 pieces (if the chicken breasts are exceptionally large, cut them in half so they require the same cooking time as the other chicken pieces)

¹/₄ cup all-purpose flour

Leaves from 6 or 7 fresh thyme sprigs (about 3 tablespoons)

Sea salt and freshly ground black pepper to taste

2 tablespoons unsalted butter

2 tablespoons olive oil

1 red onion, halved and thinly sliced

2 large tomatoes, cored and chopped

1 cup dry red wine

1 cup chicken broth

1. Preheat the oven to 400°F.

2. Rinse the chicken pieces and pat dry with paper towels. Stir the flour and 2 tablespoons of the thyme leaves together in a shallow bowl. Dredge the chicken pieces in the seasoned flour, shake off excess flour, and season with salt and pepper.

3. Heat the butter and oil in a large, heavy ovenproof skillet over medium-high heat until the butter melts and sizzles. Place the chicken in the skillet skin side down, reduce the heat to medium, and cook for 6 to 7 minutes per side, turning only once, or until the chicken is golden brown on both sides. Lower the heat if the chicken seems to be browning too quickly. Remove the chicken from the pan and cover it loosely with foil to keep warm.

4. Add the onion to the pan you cooked the chicken in and cook, stirring often, until soft and translucent, about 5 minutes. Add the tomatoes and cook for about 3 minutes, until they begin to break down. Add the wine and stock and bring to a boil over high heat, scraping up any brown bits from the bottom of the pan. Reduce the heat and simmer for 3 to 4 minutes, until the liquid reduces slightly.

5. Turn the heat off and return the chicken pieces to the pan with the liquids, laying them skin side up in a single layer. Sprinkle with the remaining tablespoon of thyme and season with salt and pepper to taste.

6. Place the skillet in the oven to roast the chicken for 35 to 40 minutes, spooning the pan juices over the chicken several times, or until the juices run clear when the chicken is pierced with a knife. Remove the chicken from the oven and serve warm, with the sauce spooned on top.

Note: *The sauce should have reduced and thickened slightly in the oven. If it is still very thin, remove the chicken from the pan and boil the sauce over high heat for a few minutes, until it has reduced and thickened slightly.*

> **BASICS:** *Slicing Onions*
>
> The first thing you want to do when you're cutting an onion is create a flat surface so it doesn't roll around on the cutting board. Cut the onion in half from top to bottom, through the root and stem ends; peel the onion and chop off the root and stem ends. Next, lay the flat side of the onion on your work surface and cut across it into neat, easy slices.

Lemon-Curry Roasted Chicken

A whole roasted chicken is one of my standby Sunday night dinners. It's easy to do and is just such a comforting food. This is a slightly dressed-up version of a typical roasted chicken, with curry added to the basting juices and the gravy to pour over it. WHAT TO SERVE WHEN The curry makes this chicken so flavorful I like to serve it with really clean sides, like Steamed Baby Bok Choy (page 109) or Garlicky Greens (page 112) and rice pilaf (see Rice Pilaf for All Seasons, page 128).

SERVES 4

- 1 3- to 3½-pound chicken
- 2 lemons, halved
- 1 apple, halved and cored
- 2 cinnamon sticks
- 3 tablespoons olive oil
- ¼ cup curry powder
- 1 tablespoon light brown sugar
- 1 tablespoon sea salt
- 2 teaspoons freshly ground black pepper
  Leaves from 6 to 7 fresh thyme or lemon thyme sprigs (about 2 tablespoons)
- 1 cup chicken broth
- ½ cup dry white wine

1. Preheat the oven to 425°F.

2. Remove the giblets and loose fat from the cavity of the chicken. Rinse the chicken inside and out and pat it dry with paper towels. Place the chicken, breast side up, on a roasting rack set inside a large roasting pan or ovenproof skillet. Squeeze the juice from the lemons over the chicken and inside the cavity. Place 2 of the squeezed lemon halves, the apple halves, and cinnamon sticks in the cavity of the chicken and place the remaining lemon halves in the bottom of the pan.

3. Stir the olive oil, curry powder, brown sugar, salt, pepper, and thyme together in a small bowl to make a paste. Massage the paste into the skin of the chicken and let the chicken sit 20 to 30 minutes at room temperature to marinate before cooking.

4. Pour the broth and wine around the chicken and roast for 1 hour 20 minutes to 1 hour 25 minutes, basting frequently, until the juices run clear when the chicken is pierced with a knife in the thickest part of the thigh or an instant-read thermometer inserted into that point registers 170°F to 175°F. Add a cupful of water or wine to the pan if it gets dry. Let the chicken rest for 10 to 15 minutes before carving.

Creamy Mac, Chicken, and Cheese

We sell an astounding amount of this at the Market. Kids love it, and so do students. Adding shredded chicken makes the mac and cheese feel more like a complete meal. When I serve it at home, I like it with nothing more than a mixed green salad and a glass of Chianti.

SERVES 8 TO 10

 2 tablespoons unsalted butter, plus more for buttering the baking dish
 $1/2$ pound short, bite-size pasta such as penne, ziti, shells, bow ties, or orecchiette
 2 teaspoons sea salt, plus more to taste
 2 tablespoons olive oil
 1 large yellow onion, diced
 3 garlic cloves, minced
 2 cups milk
 2 cups heavy cream
 $3^{1}/2$ cups cooked shredded chicken (from $3^{1}/2$ to 4-pound roasted chicken)
 2 cups shredded sharp Cheddar cheese (about 8 ounces)
 $1/2$ cup grated Parmesan cheese (about $1^{1}/2$ ounces)
 8 ounces fresh spinach, washed, stems removed, and drained (about 4 cups)
 2 tablespoons chopped fresh marjoram leaves or 2 teaspoons dried
 1 to 2 tablespoons hot sauce (Tabasco or Texas Pete)
 1 teaspoon freshly ground black pepper, plus more to taste

1. Preheat the oven to 350°F. Lightly butter a 9 × 13-inch baking dish.

2. Bring a large pot of lightly salted water to a boil. Add the pasta, stir, and cook until al dente. Drain in a colander and transfer the pasta to a large bowl. Drizzle with 1 tablespoon of the olive oil and toss to coat.

3. Melt the butter with the remaining tablespoon of olive oil in a large skillet over medium heat. Add the onion and cook, stirring occasionally, for 3 to 4 minutes, until translucent. Add the garlic and cook for 1 minute longer, stirring constantly so the garlic doesn't brown.

4. Stir in the milk and cream, reduce the heat to low, and simmer, stirring occasionally, until the sauce is reduced by half and is thick enough to coat the back of a spoon, about 20 minutes.

5. Remove the sauce from the heat and add the chicken, Cheddar, Parmesan, spinach, marjoram, hot sauce, 2 teaspoons salt, and 1 teaspoon pepper. Stir until the cheeses have melted and the spinach is wilted. Pour into the bowl with the pasta and toss to coat the pasta with the sauce. Taste for salt and pepper and season with more to taste.

6. Transfer the pasta to the prepared baking dish, scraping all the sauce out of the bowl with a rubber spatula, and bake for about 45 minutes or until the sauce is bubbling around the edges and the pasta is slightly brown on top. Let the pasta rest for about 10 minutes before serving. Serve warm.

eight

a little something sweet

Half a Baguette Bread Pudding with Caramel Pecan Sauce ○ Port-Roasted Apricots ○ Blackberries and Cherries in Red Wine ○ Balsamic Glazed Figs ○ Maple-Vanilla Roasted Pears ○ Baked Apples with Cinnamon Whipped Cream ○ Roasted Peach Halves with Crumb Topping ○ Cornmeal Shortcakes with Juicy Peaches and Cream ○ Mom's Apple Cobbler with Buttermilk Biscuit Topping ○ Pear Cranberry Crisp ○ Molasses Sweet Potato Pie ○ Buttermilk Pie ○ Summer Blueberry Pie ○ Lemon Meringue Pie ○ Aunt June's Lemon Icebox Pie ○ Hazelnut Rum Torte ○ Margarita Float ○ Individual Tiramisu ○ Individual Chocolate Pudding Cakes ○ Say's Yellow Cake with Warm Chocolate Glaze ○ Sour Cream Cardamom Pound Cake ○ Orange Poppy Seed Pound Cake ○ Citrus Compote ○ Dark Chocolate Soufflé Cake ○ Chocolate Cupcakes with Mocha Buttercream or Pure Chocolaty Children's Frosting ○ Dark Chocolate Truffles ○ Thumbprint Cookies ○ Pumpkin White Chocolate Chunk Cookies ○ Peanut Butter Chocolate Chip Cookies ○ Chocolate Chip Oatmeal Cookies ○ White Chocolate Chunk Hazelnut Cookie ○ Mexican Wedding Cookies ○ Ice Cream Sandwiches Your Way ○ Shortbread Hearts with Fresh Strawberries and Crème Fraîche ○ Pecan Sandies ○ Hot and Creamy Cocoa with Gooey Toasted Marshmallows

I am not someone who wants to spend an entire day making an elaborate layer cake, but I always like to serve a little something sweet after dinner. When I make desserts, I want something quick: a cake that I can mix up in one bowl and bake while my guests are eating dinner, like Say's Yellow Cake; something I can make a day in advance, like tiramisu or bread pudding; or desserts built of different components, like fruit, cake, and sauce, that I can assemble the way I would a dinner.

The desserts in this chapter reflect that sensibility: that of someone who is more of a cook than a baker. They rely less on a precisely measured cup of flour and elaborate baking techniques than on the quality of the ingredients—like the chocolate you use to make the Dark Chocolate Soufflé Cake you make it with or any fruit you use. No amount of sugar will turn tasteless peaches into delicious Roasted Peach Halves with Crumb Topping.

These are homey, not fancy, desserts. Many of them, like Mom's Apple Cobbler, Summer Blueberry Pie, and Aunt June's Lemon Icebox Pie, are those I grew up eating—and you may have grown up with similar versions. Chocolate Cupcakes and Ice Cream Sandwiches are everyone's childhood favorites, but are elevated by fine ingredients to appeal to grown-up tastes. They are the kinds of dessert we all love because they are comforting and because they are homemade.

Half a Baguette Bread Pudding with Caramel Pecan Sauce

I have this theory that there's always half a baguette left after any dinner. What to do with it? Make bread pudding, of course. I grew up watching my mother make bread pudding once a week without a measuring cup in sight. This is a great dessert for a crowd because it serves so many and you can make it as much as a day in advance.

SERVES 6 TO 8

- 4 tablespoons unsalted butter, melted
- 2 tablespoons packed light brown sugar
- 6 cups 1½-inch cubes of baguette or country Italian bread, or any day-old bread, biscuits, or cake
- 2 cups milk
- 2 large eggs
- ⅓ cup granulated sugar
- 2 tablespoons unfiltered apple juice or apple cider
- 1 tablespoon pure vanilla extract
- 1 Granny Smith or other good baking apple (such as Pippin or Northern Spy), peeled, cored, and chopped (about 1 cup)
- 2 tablespoons dark rum
  Caramel Pecan Sauce (recipe follows)

1. Preheat the oven to 350°F. Brush a 13 × 9-inch glass baking dish or a 2-quart soufflé dish with 1 tablespoon of the melted butter and sprinkle the brown sugar evenly over the bottom of the dish.

2. Place the bread cubes in a large mixing bowl and pour the milk over the bread. Let the bread sit until it is mushy and has absorbed almost all of the milk, 4 to 5 minutes.

3. Whisk the eggs, granulated sugar, apple juice, vanilla, and the remaining melted butter together in a separate medium bowl. Pour this over the bread, add the apples, and stir gently until the ingredients are evenly distributed.

4. Pour the bread into the prepared baking dish using a rubber spatula or the edge of your hand to get all the liquid out of the bowl. Cover the baking dish with aluminum foil and bake the bread pudding for 50 minutes. Remove the aluminum foil and continue baking 15 to 20 minutes, until the bread pudding is fluffy with a golden brown crust. While the pudding is baking, prepare the Caramel Pecan Sauce.

5. Remove the baking dish from the oven, pour the rum over the top, and let it cool for 5 to 10 minutes before serving. You can pour the Caramel Pecan Sauce over the bread pudding while it's in the pan or over individual servings, but make sure to pour the sauce over the pudding while both the pudding and the sauce are warm.

Think Outside the Recipe
TO MAKE DIFFERENT TYPES OF CARAMEL SAUCES, IN PLACE OF THE PECANS, ADD ONE OF THE FOLLOWING:

- 2 TEASPOONS PURE VANILLA EXTRACT
- 2 OUNCES GOOD-QUALITY BITTERSWEET CHOCOLATE, MELTED
- ¼ CUP STRONGLY BREWED COFFEE OR ESPRESSO
- JUICE OF 1 ORANGE

Caramel Pecan Sauce

Caramel will bubble up the sides of the pan when you add a cold ingredient like cream, so make sure to use a long-handled wooden spoon or heatproof rubber spatula.

MAKES ABOUT 1 CUP

1 cup sugar
½ cup heavy cream
1 tablespoon unsalted butter
½ cup chopped pecans, lightly toasted

1. Stir the sugar with ¼ cup water in a small saucepan placed over low heat and cook, stirring constantly, until the sugar dissolves. Increase the heat to medium-high and bring the liquid to a boil without stirring. If sugar crystals appear on the sides of the pan, brush the sides down with a wet pastry brush. Boil the syrup for 4 to 5 minutes, or until it turns amber in color. If the syrup turns amber only in one section of the pan, swirl the pan to distribute the heat more evenly.

2. Remove the pan from the heat and add the cream by pouring it down the side of the pan, stirring constantly with a wooden spoon. If the caramel hardens when you add the cream, put the saucepan back over very low heat to soften. Add the butter and stir until all is incorporated. Stir in the pecans. Keep warm until ready to use or reheat over very low heat.

Port-Roasted Apricots

There's no better dessert than warm roasted fruit. But with something as simple as this, you need to be sure to start with fragrant, ripe apricots harvested in season. Later in the summer or early fall, use this method to roast plums or fresh figs. WHAT TO SERVE WHEN Serve the apricots over toasted pound cake, with Vanilla Bean Custard Sauce (page 239), vanilla ice cream, or fresh ricotta cheese.

SERVES 6

6 fresh ripe apricots, halved lengthwise and pitted
¼ cup port
1 tablespoon balsamic vinegar
2 tablespoons pure vanilla extract
¼ cup turbinado sugar (you can substitute light brown sugar)

1. Preheat the oven to 500°F.

2. Place the apricot halves in a shallow ovenproof baking dish, cut side up, and spoon the port into the cavities and over each apricot half. Drizzle the apricots with the vinegar and vanilla and spoon the turbinado sugar over them. Place the baking dish in the oven to roast the apricots for 15 to 20 minutes, until the apricots are soft and the liquid has thickened. Remove the apricots from the oven, spoon the pan liquid over them, and allow them to cool for about 5 minutes before serving. Serve warm.

Note: *For a more intense vanilla flavor, omit the vanilla extract and scrape the seeds of one vanilla bean into the sugar before spooning it over the apricots.*

Blackberries and Cherries in Red Wine

You rarely see cherries and blackberries together, but the combination is a natural in my mind, like strawberries and rhubarb. WHAT TO SERVE WHEN Spoon this dessert over bowls of vanilla ice cream or frozen yogurt or a slice of toasted Sour Cream Cardamom Pound Cake (page 260), or both.

SERVES 6 TO 8

1½ cups fresh blackberries
1½ cups cherries, pitted
  2 tablespoons brandy or framboise
¾ cup sugar
  2 cups dry red wine
  5 to 6 black peppercorns
  1 cinnamon stick

1. Put the berries and cherries in a medium bowl and pour the brandy over them. Set aside.

2. Combine the sugar, wine, peppercorns, and cinnamon stick in a medium saucepan over medium-high heat and bring to a boil. Reduce the heat to medium-low and simmer, stirring occasionally, for 8 to 10 minutes, or until the liquid has reduced to about 1 cup.

3. Pour the wine mixture over the cherries. Cool to room temperature before serving. This compote will keep refrigerated in an airtight container for up to 1 week.

Think Outside the Recipe

- IF YOU CAN'T FIND GOOD FRESH CHERRIES OR YOU PREFER DRIED, USE AN EQUAL AMOUNT OF DRIED CHERRIES SOAKED IN BRANDY FOR 15 MINUTES BEFORE ADDING THEM TO THE WINE. THE CHEWINESS OF THE DRIED CHERRIES IS A NICE CONTRAST TO THE SOFT BERRIES.

- DEPENDING ON WHAT LOOKS GOOD AT THE MARKET, YOU CAN MAKE THIS COMPOTE WITH OTHER BERRIES, SUCH AS RASPBERRIES, STRAWBERRIES, BLUE-BERRIES, OR CURRANTS IN PLACE OF THE BLACK-BERRIES OR CHERRIES.

Balsamic Glazed Figs

In the late summer and fall, when figs are in season, I can't wait to make this sophisticated, not too sweet dessert. The more you make them, the more ways you'll find to serve them, especially when you see how quick and easy they are to make. Really good, aged balsamic vinegar is often used to make desserts. Fig balsamic vinegar is a bit thicker and sweeter than regular balsamic and it has a floral, figgy flavor. WHAT TO SERVE WHEN It seems like I've served these a million different ways: spooned over vanilla ice cream or toasted pound cake, on buttered biscuits for breakfast, tossed into a salad of wilted greens with crumbled goat cheese. Served over fresh ricotta cheese, it's like a cheese course and dessert course combined.

SERVES 4 TO 6

  1 tablespoon unsalted butter
12 small fresh figs (such as Mission or Black Tehama), halved lengthwise
¼ cup sugar
  2 tablespoons fig balsamic or regular balsamic vinegar
¼ cup Vin Santo or other sweet dessert wine
    Freshly ground black pepper (optional)

1. Melt but do not brown the butter in a large skillet over medium-high heat until sizzling. Place the figs, cut side down, in the butter, and sauté for about 1 minute, until they just begin to soften and give off juice. Sprinkle the sugar over the figs and shake the pan to distribute the sugar evenly.

2. Add the vinegar and wine to the pan and bring to a boil over high heat. Continue to boil the liquid for 2 to 3 minutes, shaking the pan constantly, until the liquid becomes slightly thick and syrupy. Sprinkle with freshly ground pepper if desired and serve immediately.

Think Outside the Recipe

THIS COULD BE MADE WITH ANY DELICATE FRUIT THAT BARELY NEEDS COOK-ING, LIKE APRICOTS, CHER-RIES, OR STRAWBERRIES.

Maple-Vanilla Roasted Pears

Our brunch chef, Eric, makes these pears to serve at the Market with French toast and warm maple syrup, but I like them for dessert. It's an easy last-minute dessert that cooks in the oven while you're sitting down to dinner. I'm not particular about what kind of pears I use: I find that, unlike apples, all varieties of pears—bosc, Anjou, Comice, Bartlett—hold their shape nicely when baked. WHAT TO SERVE WHEN These pears are delicious served with warm Vanilla Bean Custard Sauce (right) or vanilla ice cream. If you're up for something a little different, try them with fresh ricotta cheese or creamy fresh goat cheese at room temperature, and cracked black pepper.

SERVES 6

  2 tablespoons unsalted butter, softened
 ½ cup sugar
  3 pears
 ¼ cup pure maple syrup
  1 tablespoon pure vanilla extract

1. Preheat the oven to 400°F. Rub the butter over the bottom of a baking sheet with sides and sprinkle with the sugar.

2. Peel the pears and cut them in half lengthwise. Cut the cores out with a melon scoop or a small paring knife and place the pears, cut side down, on the baking pan. Stir the maple syrup and vanilla together in a measuring cup and drizzle evenly over the pears.

3. Roast the pears until tender when pierced with the tip of a knife and the sugar is caramelized, 40 to 45 minutes, spooning the sauce in the pan over the pears while they cook; this keeps them moist and gives them a nice glaze. Serve warm with the sauce spooned over them.

REINVENTION

Use a leftover pear half to make an unusual and delicious quesadilla for the following day's lunch. Spread farmer cheese on a flour tortilla. Top with pear slices, drizzle with honey, and sprinkle with black pepper. Top with another tortilla and grill in a skillet with butter until the quesadilla is golden and the ingredients warmed through. Serve the pears on a salad of mixed greens with crumbled blue cheese.

Vanilla Bean Custard Sauce

You can make this ahead of time and have it on hand for up to a week to serve with poached, roasted, or grilled fruit, like the Maple-Vanilla Roasted Pears (left) or any pound cake.

MAKES ABOUT 2¼ CUPS

  6 large egg yolks
 ⅓ cup sugar
  1 cup milk
  1 cup heavy cream
  1 vanilla bean, split lengthwise
  1 tablespoon unsalted butter

1. Beat the egg yolks and sugar together in a medium bowl with an electric mixer on high speed until pale yellow and thick, about 3 minutes.

2. Stir the milk and cream together in a heavy-bottomed non-aluminum saucepan and bring to a simmer over low heat. Add the vanilla bean to the saucepan. Remove from the heat and slowly pour the milk mixture into the bowl with the eggs, whisking while you pour. Pour the custard and vanilla bean back into the saucepan, scraping the sides down with a rubber spatula. Cook over very low heat, stirring constantly with a wooden spoon or heatproof rubber spatula so the eggs don't curdle, for 8 to 10 minutes, until the custard is thick enough to coat the back of a spoon.

3. Remove from the heat, remove the vanilla bean, and stir in the butter. Serve warm or chilled. This will keep, refrigerated in an airtight container, for up to 1 week.

about . . .
VANILLA BEANS

The flavor of vanilla beans is so much more intense than vanilla extract. Plus, the seeds make pretty little dots in whatever you add them to. The beans keep in a sealable bag in the refrigerator for as long as year. When using them as in this custard recipe, you don't even have to scrape the seeds out of the pod; as the custard simmers, the seeds fall out on their own. You can put the leftover whole bean in a container of sugar to make vanilla sugar, which you can use to flavor cream, or whipped cream or to sprinkle on anything from cookies to oatmeal.

Baked Apples with Cinnamon Whipped Cream

This is the kind of just-a-little-something-sweet dessert that I like more than any other. If you have leftovers of these apples, they make a delicious breakfast spread on peanut butter toast the next morning. If the apples split while you are coring them, just bake them as halves, they are equally as good. WHAT TO SERVE WHEN Serve the apples fresh from the oven, with warm Vanilla Bean Custard Sauce (page 239) or vanilla ice cream, in addition to or instead of the Cinnamon Whipped Cream.

SERVES 6

1/4 cup sugar
2 teaspoons ground cinnamon
6 tart apples (such as Granny Smith, Pippin, Cortland or Jonagolds), peeled and cored
1/4 cup chopped walnuts or pecans
2 tablespoons unsalted butter, sliced evenly into 6 pieces
1/2 cup fresh apple cider or unfiltered apple juice
2 tablespoons dark rum
1 tablespoon pure vanilla extract
Cinnamon Whipped Cream (see "Flavored Whipped Cream," page 263)

1. Preheat the oven to 350°F.

2. Stir the sugar and cinnamon together in a small shallow bowl. Roll each apple in the cinnamon-sugar to coat the outside and then sprinkle some of the cinnamon-sugar inside the cavity of each apple. Place the apples upright in a shallow ovenproof baking dish, leaving about an inch between them in the baking dish. Pour the remaining cinnamon-sugar over the apples. Fill the apple centers with the chopped nuts and top each apple with 1 piece of the butter. Pour the apple cider, rum, and vanilla around the apples in the bottom of the baking dish. Bake the apples for 45 to 50 minutes, until they are tender and golden brown, spooning the pan juices over them several times during the cooking process. Remove the apples from the oven and serve warm, with the cooking juices spooned over them and a dollop of Cinnamon Whipped Cream on top.

Roasted Peach Halves with Crumb Topping

My friend Jolly's daughter, Jesse, says eating these peaches is "Like eating breakfast!" because the crispy crumb topping reminds her of granola. You can make this recipe with apples, pears, apricots, or plums. WHAT TO SERVE WHEN These are best served warm, just from the oven with vanilla ice cream, Vanilla Bean Custard Sauce (page 239), or chilled heavy cream.

SERVES 6

4 tablespoons (1/2 stick) unsalted butter, plus more for greasing the skillet
3 ripe peaches, peeled, halved, and pit removed
1/4 cup all-purpose flour
1/4 cup packed light brown sugar
1/4 cup rolled oats
1/4 cup chopped pecans
1/2 teaspoon ground cinnamon
1/4 teaspoon salt

1. Preheat the oven to 350°F. Lightly grease the bottom of a 6-inch skillet with butter.

2. Place the peaches in the skillet, cut side up. They should fit snugly enough to stand upright. If not, cut a small slice off the rounded bottom of each peach to give it a flat surface to rest on.

3. Stir the flour, sugar, oats, pecans, cinnamon, and salt together in a small bowl. Add the butter and work it into the mixture using a pastry blender or your fingers until the dry ingredients are no longer visible and the mixture is combined but still chunky. Sprinkle the crumb mixture in the cavity and mound it on the top of each peach, pressing lightly to keep the crumb mixture in place.

4. Bake the peaches on a center rack for 25 to 30 minutes, until the topping is golden brown and the peaches are bubbling around the edges. Let rest for about 5 minutes before serving. Serve warm.

Mom's Apple Cobbler with Buttermilk Biscuit Topping

My mom sautés the apples before assembling this cobbler to give them a necessary head start over the biscuits, which need little time in the oven. WHAT TO SERVE WHEN This is an old-fashioned, comforting dessert. I can't imagine it with anything other than a scoop of vanilla ice cream.

SERVES 6 TO 8

4 tablespoons unsalted butter, plus more
    for buttering the baking dish
6 large tart apples (such as Granny Smith,
    Pippin, or Northern Spy), peeled, cored, and
    cut into 1/2-inch chunks
1/2 cup sugar
1/2 cup fresh apple cider or unfiltered apple juice
    Grated zest and juice of 1 lemon
1 teaspoon ground cinnamon
1/2 teaspoon freshly grated or ground nutmeg
    Mom's Buttermilk Biscuit Topping (recipe follows)

1. Preheat the oven to 400°F. Butter a 7 × 11-inch or 9-inch square baking dish.

2. Melt but do not brown the 4 tablespoons of butter in a heavy-bottomed saucepan over medium heat. Add the apples, sugar, cider, and lemon zest and juice and cook, stirring occasionally, for about 5 minutes, until the apples are tender. Remove the pan from the heat and stir in the cinnamon and nutmeg.

3. Pour the apples into the prepared baking dish, scraping all the juices out of the saucepan with a rubber spatula. Let the fruit sit while you prepare the topping.

4. Arrange the biscuits over the fruit, leaving about 1/4 inch between them. Bake the cobbler on a center rack for 25 to 30 minutes, or until the biscuit topping is golden brown and the apples are bubbling around the sides of the pan. Allow the cobbler to cool for at least 10 minutes before serving. Serve warm.

Mom's Buttermilk Biscuit Topping

You can use this biscuit topping to make a fruit cobbler with any seasonal fruit: peaches, nectarines, plums, pears, mixed berries, or strawberry and rhubarb.

MAKES 12 TO 14 BISCUITS

1 cup self-rising flour or 1 cup all-purpose
    flour mixed with 1 teaspoon baking powder,
    plus more for dusting
2 tablespoons sugar
1/4 teaspoon salt
3 tablespoons cold unsalted butter,
    cut into 1/4-inch cubes
1/3 cup cold, well-shaken buttermilk

1. Stir the flour, sugar, and salt together in a large mixing bowl. Add the butter and use a pastry blender or 2 knives to cut the butter into the flour until it resembles the texture of cornmeal. Pour in the cold buttermilk and stir until the dough just comes together. Turn the dough out onto your work surface and bring it together with your hands, kneading it lightly to form a ball.

2. Lightly dust your work surface and a rolling pin with flour and roll the dough out to 1/4 inch thick. Use a 2-inch biscuit cutter (or a cookie cutter or the rim of a glass) to cut the dough into rounds and place on top of the apples.

Buttermilk Pie

During the holiday season, I make this pie using eggnog in place of buttermilk. WHAT TO SERVE WHEN Top this light custardy pie with a dollop of whipped cream, sliced summer peaches, or fresh berries.

MAKES ONE 9-INCH PIE (SERVES 8 TO 10)

    8 tablespoons (1 stick) unsalted butter
1½ cups sugar
    4 large eggs
    3 tablespoons yellow cornmeal
1½ cups well-shaken buttermilk
    2 teaspoons pure vanilla extract
 ½ teaspoon freshly grated or ground nutmeg
 ½ teaspoon ground cloves
    Pinch of salt
    1 unbaked 9-inch pie shell (see page 250)

1. Preheat the oven to 325°F.

2. Beat the butter and sugar together in a large bowl with an electric mixer on high speed until fluffy. Add the eggs, one at a time, scraping down the sides of the bowl between each addition, and making sure each egg is incorporated before adding another. Stir in the corn-meal, buttermilk, vanilla, nutmeg, cloves, and salt.

3. Pour the pie filling into the unbaked pie shell and bake the pie on a center rack for 50 to 60 minutes, until the custard is set around the edges but still slightly jiggly in the center. It will firm up completely, or "set," as it cools. Let the pie cool for at least 1 hour before slicing. Serve chilled or at room temperature.

about . . .
EGGNOG

During the holidays, I've always made eggnog because home-made is so rich and creamy, it's in another category altogether from mass-produced eggnog. Over the last few years, though, during the holidays, I've found eggnog produced by small dairies at specialty food stores and farmers markets that's so good I don't bother making my own nearly as often. In addition to drinking it, I like to drizzle eggnog over or around a slice of pumpkin or pecan pie, ice cream, or grilled or roasted fruit.

Summer Blueberry Pie

My grandmother was an expert pie baker. She made pies every weekend using whatever fruit was in season. Blue-berry was the pie I looked forward to the most.

MAKES ONE 9-INCH PIE (SERVES 8 TO 10)

    1 recipe Judy's Flaky Pie Crust (page 250)
    2 pints fresh blueberries, rinsed, drained, and stems removed
    2 tablespoons cornstarch
      Grated zest and juice of ½ lemon
    1 cup sugar, plus more for sprinkling on the pie crust (about 1 tablespoon)
    1 teaspoon freshly grated or ground nutmeg
    3 tablespoons unsalted butter, cut into ¼-inch pieces
    1 large egg
    1 tablespoon milk

1. Preheat the oven to 400°F.

2. Roll each disk of dough on a lightly floured surface into a 12-inch circle about ⅛ inch thick. Place one cir-cle into a 9-inch pie pan with the edges draping over it. Place the other circle on a baking sheet and put both in the refrigerator to chill for at least 30 minutes and up to several hours.

3. Combine the blueberries, cornstarch, lemon zest and juice, 1 cup of the sugar, and the nutmeg in a bowl and stir gently to mix. Pour the blueberry filling into the chilled bottom crust, scraping all the sugar out of the bowl with a rubber spatula.

4. Place the pie pan on a baking sheet and dot the blue-berries with the butter. Whisk the egg and milk together and brush over the edges of the pie. Place the top crust over the filling and use a pair of kitchen shears to trim the edges of both pieces of dough, leav-ing about ½ inch hanging over the rim. Fold both edges under, creating a thick lip around the pie. Use your fin-gers or a fork to crimp or press the edges of the pie. Cut 4 slits in the top crust for air vents and sprinkle the top liberally with sugar.

5. Place the baking sheet with the pie on a center rack in the oven to bake for 25 minutes. Reduce the heat to 350°F and continue baking until the juices are bubbling and the crust is golden brown, 40 to 45 more minutes. Let the pie cool at least 1 hour before serving.

Judy's Flaky Pie Crust

This is my sister's recipe for the best, flakiest pie crust I know. The egg, which is an unusual addition, makes the dough really easy to work with.

MAKES TWO 9-INCH PIE CRUSTS

   3 cups all-purpose flour, plus more for dusting
   1 teaspoon salt
   1 cup plus 3 tablespoons vegetable shortening
   1 large egg
   ⅓ cup ice water, plus 2 to 3 tablespoons as needed
   1 tablespoon white vinegar

1. Stir the flour and salt together in a large bowl. Add the shortening and cut it into the flour with a pastry cutter until the mixture resembles coarse meal.

2. In a separate small bowl, beat the egg with ⅓ cup ice water and the vinegar. Pour this into the bowl with the flour mixture, stirring with a fork just until it comes together. Do not mix any more than necessary. If the dough is dry and crumbly, add more water, 1 tablespoon at a time, until it comes together, but don't add so much water that the dough becomes wet or sticky.

3. Lightly dust your hands and work surface with flour. Turn the dough out onto the work surface and form it into a ball with your hands. Divide the dough ball into two pieces and form each piece into a flat disk about 1½ inches thick. Wrap each disk in plastic wrap and refrigerate it for at least 30 minutes, or up to 3 days.

4. For an unbaked pie shell Take the chilled dough out of the refrigerator and place it on a lightly floured surface. Dust a rolling pin with flour and roll the dough to form a 12-inch circle. Fold the dough in half or gently roll it up onto the rolling pin and lift it up to put in the 9-inch pie pan. Press the dough lightly into the bottom and up the sides of the pan.

Trim the edges of the dough with a pair of kitchen shears or a knife, leaving about 1½ inches of dough draped over the edge of the pan. Fold the extra dough under itself to form a lip around the edge of the pan. Crimp the edge of the pie with your fingers or press with the tines of a fork. Cover the crust with plastic wrap and refrigerate it for at least 1 hour or up to 3 days before baking.

For a pre-baked pie crust Preheat the oven to 425°F.

Line the bottom of the shell with aluminum foil or parchment paper and fill it with dried beans or pie weights. Place the pie shell in the oven to bake 15 to 20 minutes. Remove the beans and foil and bake for 5 to 8 minutes more, until the crust is golden brown and flaky.

about . . .
PASTRY CUTTERS

I recently rediscovered an old-fashioned kitchen tool that I find invaluable: a pastry cutter. Using a pastry cutter to cut butter into flour takes a lot less time than using two knives, and it distributes the butter more evenly than using your fingers, which is how I used to do it. Most important, it helps keep the butter from warming from the warmth of your fingers. I don't like making dough in the food processor; it's too easy to over-mix it that way because it happens so fast and you're not feeling the dough.

BASICS: *Making Pie Crust*

If you're haven't made pie crust many times, you probably think it's harder than it is. But in fact, it's just a matter of mixing flour with shortening or butter (or both) and just enough water so the dough comes together to form a ball—but not so much that the dough becomes sticky or wet. Here are some tips:

- When rolling out dough, dust your work surface and rolling pin with flour. Start with the pin in the center of the disk and roll outwards. You don't need to press down hard; simply apply light pressure and let the rolling pin do the rest. Pick up and rotate the dough periodically for even rolling and add a little more flour if needed.

- *Crimping* refers to the process of finishing the pie edge. First you fold the dough under itself to form a double-thickness lip (or quadruple-thickness for a double-crust pie) around the edge of the crust. Then put the index finger of your right hand (if you're right handed) under the dough lip to lift it while pinching around that finger with the thumb and index finger of your left hand. It's easier than it sounds, but if it sounds like more than you want to take on, just press down around the edges with the tines of a fork.

- If you rip the dough while you're rolling it or lifting it into the pie pan, it's not the end of the world. Use a scrap of dough to patch up the hole, pressing it together as best you can.

- I often make extra pie dough to have on hand, particularly during the holidays or in the summer when berries and peaches are plentiful, which is when I'm most likely to make a pie. The dough will keep, wrapped tightly in plastic, in the refrigerator for up to 3 days, or in the freezer for up to 3 months. Form the dough into a flat disk before refrigerating or freezing it. It's easier to roll out that way. You can also roll the dough out and form it into a pie pan, and freeze it at that stage: a homemade frozen pie shell. There's no need to thaw the pie shell before baking it.

- Pre-baking, also called blind baking, refers to the process of baking a pie shell before filling it. You pre-bake a crust when you are filling it with something that cooks quickly, or that is cooked before being put in a pie shell, like lemon custard. This way the crust is already cooked. When you bake the filled crust, it is just to set the filling, or in the case of Lemon Meringue Pie (page 253), to brown the meringue. You fill the empty pie shell with pie weights before you bake it to prevent it from puffing up when baked. You can buy special pie weights for this, or you can use dried beans, and keep the designated dried beans to use as pie weights next time.

- If while a pie is baking the crust starts to burn before the filling is done, cover the dark areas (usually the edges) with foil. There's a special little gadget called a piecrust guard, for just this purpose, but adding a patch of foil where you need it works perfectly fine.

- Rotate the pie halfway through the cooking process. Most ovens cook unevenly.

Lemon Meringue Pie

This is one of my aunt Ginny's many dessert specialties. I still think it's one of the prettiest desserts of all time, and it's a favorite of so many people. You can make this pie up to a day in advance through step 5. Top with meringue and bake an hour or two before serving.

MAKES ONE 9-INCH PIE OR TART (SERVES 8 TO 10)

1½ cups sugar
⅓ cup cornstarch
½ teaspoon salt
3 lemons (grated zest of 2, juice of 3 lemons)
6 large eggs, separated
4 tablespoons cold butter, cut into pieces
1 pre-baked pie shell (page 250)
¼ cup confectioners' sugar

1. Preheat the oven to 375°F.

2. Combine the sugar, cornstarch, salt, lemon juice, and 1½ cups water in a heavy-bottomed saucepan placed over medium heat and stir with a heatproof spatula or wooden spoon to combine. Stir constantly until the mixture begins to boil, 6 to 7 minutes, and continue to boil, stirring constantly, or until it is thick and glossy, about 1 minute more.

3. Lightly beat the egg yolks in a small mixing bowl. Whisk about ½ cup of the hot sugar mixture into the egg yolks and whisk until smooth. Pour the warmed egg yolks back into the saucepan with the remaining sugar mixture and whisk constantly over very low heat for about 4 minutes, until it thickens to the consistency of pudding. Be careful not to overcook the custard; it will curdle if it cooks too long or the heat is too high.

4. Remove the custard from the heat, whisk in the butter and lemon zest, and pour into the pre-baked pie crust.

5. To make the meringue, place the egg whites in a large mixing bowl and beat with an electric mixer on low speed for about 1 minute, until they begin to thicken. Increase the mixer speed to high and continue beating until the egg whites are frothy. Add the confectioners' sugar and beat until the whites form soft peaks. The peaks will hold their shape when you lift the beaters out of the bowl.

6. Spread the meringue over the lemon pie filling, making sure it touches the crust all around; otherwise the meringue will shrink away from the sides when baked, leaving a gap around the pie edges. Bake the pie on a center rack for 10 to 12 minutes, or until the peaks of the meringue are golden brown. Cool on a rack for at least 1 hour before serving. Serve at room temperature.

RUBBER SPATULAS

Heatproof rubber spatulas are among my favorite kitchen tools, especially for things that need to be stirred on the stovetop. They function as two tools in one, a rubber spatula and a wooden spoon. The flexible spatula gets in the corners, so they're ideal for getting into the crevice around a skillet or saucepan, as when making scrambled eggs, stirring custard or pudding, or melting chocolate.

" Do not over-beat egg whites or they will separate and become grainy. "

Aunt June's Lemon Icebox Pie

This is my mom's late sister June's pie. It was my dad's favorite pie, so she always brought one when she came to visit. She topped hers with meringue, but I prefer whipped cream. The gingersnap crust was also my addition because I love gingersnaps with lemon.

MAKES ONE 9-INCH PIE (SERVES 8 TO 10)

> Grated zest and juice of 3 lemons
> 3 large egg yolks, lightly beaten
> 1 14-ounce can sweetened condensed milk
> 1 tablespoon sugar
> 1 pre-baked **Gingersnap Pie Crust** (recipe follows)

For the whipped cream

> 1 cup heavy cream
> ¼ cup sugar

1. Preheat the oven to 350°F.

2. Stir the lemon zest and juice and the egg yolks together in a medium bowl. Add the condensed milk and sugar and whisk until they are thoroughly incorporated.

3. Pour the filling into the pre-baked Gingersnap Crust and bake on a center rack in the oven for 10 minutes. Allow the pie to cool to room temperature. Cover with plastic wrap and refrigerate for at least 4 hours, until it is firm and chilled.

4. Beat the whipping cream in a medium bowl with an electric mixer on high speed until soft peaks form. Add the ¼ cup sugar and beat just to combine. Remove the pie from the refrigerator. Top with the whipped cream and slice. Serve chilled.

Gingersnap Pie Crust

MAKES ONE 9-INCH PIE CRUST

> 4 ounces gingersnap cookies, finely ground (1 cup crumbs)
> ½ cup finely ground almonds or pecans
> 5 tablespoons unsalted butter, melted

1. Preheat the oven to 325°F.

2. Stir the gingersnap crumbs and almonds together in a medium bowl. Add the melted butter and stir until the crumbs are moistened. Turn the crumbs into a 9-inch pie shell and press them evenly over the bottom and up the sides of the pan to form the crust.

3. Bake the pie crust on a center rack for 8 to 10 minutes, until it feels dry and firm. It will still feel slightly soft but it will firm up more when it cools. Let the crust cool to room temperature before filling.

Hazelnut Rum Torte

I often make this torte for dinner parties because I can make it a day or more in advance. It doesn't contain flour, only bread crumbs. WHAT TO SERVE WHEN This makes an elegant dessert with mocha-flavored whipped cream (see Flavored Whipped Cream, page 263), or served with Maple-Vanilla Roasted Pears (page 239), or Blackberries and Cherries in Red Wine (page 236).

SERVES 8 TO 10

All-purpose flour for dusting the baking pan
2 cups hazelnuts
1/2 cup fresh bread crumbs (see
  "Making Bread Crumbs," page 153)
4 large eggs, separated
3 tablespoons sweet dark rum, brandy, or Frangelico
2/3 cup sugar
1/2 teaspoon salt
8 tablespoons (1 stick) unsalted butter, melted
  and cooled to room temperature, plus
  more for greasing the pan
  Confectioners' sugar or good-quality unsweetened
  cocoa powder for dusting the cake

1. Preheat the oven to 350°F. Butter an 8-inch round cake pan and dust lightly with flour.

2. Place the hazelnuts on a baking sheet with sides and toast in the oven until fragrant and lightly brown, about 10 minutes. Pour the nuts on a clean tea towel and rub them in the towel to remove the skins. Don't worry if a small amount of skin remains on the nuts. Cool to room temperature.

3. Place the cooled hazelnuts in the bowl of a food processor fitted with a metal blade and pulse until they are finely ground. Turn the hazelnuts out into a large bowl and stir in the bread crumbs.

4. In a separate medium bowl, combine the egg yolks, rum, and 1/3 cup of the sugar and beat with an electric mixer on medium-high speed until thick and pale yellow, about 3 minutes.

5. In a separate large bowl, beat the egg whites and salt with an electric mixer on high speed until they form soft peaks. The peaks should retain their shape when you lift the beaters out. Beat in the remaining 1/3 cup sugar.

6. Fold the egg yolk mixture into the whipped whites with a sturdy rubber spatula until partially combined; you will still see plenty of white streaks from the egg whites. Fold in the hazelnuts and bread crumbs, just until lightly mixed with some streaks of egg white remaining. Do not over-mix. Continue folding the mixture as you pour the melted butter down the side of the bowl and fold gently just until the batter is smooth and no white streaks remain.

7. Scrape the batter into the prepared cake pan and bake on a center rack for about 30 minutes, or until the center is firm to the touch and a wooden skewer inserted in the center comes out clean. Cool on a wire rack for 5 minutes, then turn the cake out onto the rack to cool completely.

8. Dust the cake lightly with confectioners' sugar or cocoa powder passed through a fine sieve. Serve while the cake is still slightly warm or at room temperature. This cake will keep, covered tightly in plastic wrap, refrigerated for several days. Bring to room temperature before serving.

Margarita Float

This is a grown-up beverage that I came up with to marry my love of margaritas and root beer floats. I like to prepare the glasses with the lime, salt, and sugar and freeze them for at least an hour so they're nice and frosty when I make the floats. WHAT TO SERVE WHEN These floats make a refreshing finish to any outdoor summer meal, like Peter's All-World Burgers (page 155), or Fall-off-the-Bone Baby Back Ribs (page 211).

SERVES 4

  1 lime, halved
  1 tablespoon sea salt or kosher salt
  1 tablespoon sugar
  1 pint vanilla or lemon ice cream
$1/4$ cup gold tequila
  2 tablespoons triple sec, such as Cointreau
  2 20-ounce lemon-lime sodas, such as 7-Up or Sprite

Run the cut sides of the lime around the rim of four tall glasses. Combine the salt and sugar on a small plate and dip the rims of glasses in the salt-sugar mixture. Divide the ice cream among the glasses. Add 1 tablespoon of tequila and 1½ teaspoons triple sec to each glass, then fill with the soda. Serve immediately with straws and spoons.

Individual Tiramisu

Tiramisu means "pick me up" for the espresso it contains. It's what I make when I'm craving a rich dessert. It looks very elegant made in individual wineglasses, but if you prefer to make one large dessert, a medium glass bowl works nicely so you can still see the layers.

SERVES 6

  1 cup heavy cream
$1/2$ cup sugar
  8 ounces mascarpone cheese
$1/4$ cup Marsala
  1 to $1/2$ cups strong coffee or espresso
$1/4$ cup brandy or Frangelico
18 store-bought ladyfingers
  2 ounces good-quality bittersweet chocolate, finely chopped or shaved
    Good-quality unsweetened cocoa powder for dusting the tiramisu

1. Place 6 large wineglasses in the freezer or refrigerator to chill.

2. Whip the heavy cream to soft peaks in a large bowl. Add the sugar and whip 10 to 15 seconds longer, just until the sugar is thoroughly integrated.

3. In a separate large bowl, whisk the mascarpone and Marsala together until smooth and creamy. Gently fold a third of the whipped cream into the mascarpone to lighten. Fold in the remaining whipped cream to combine.

4. Remove the wineglasses from the freezer or refrigerator. Stir the coffee and brandy together in a small bowl. One at a time, dip the ladyfingers into the coffee-brandy twice, taking care not to leave them in more than 5 seconds or they may fall apart. Place one ladyfinger into each wineglass, pressing down so it fits snugly into the bottom of the glass. You may need to break it in half to make it fit. Spoon a third of the mascarpone-cream over the ladyfinger and sprinkle with a third of the chocolate. Top with another layer of soaked ladyfinger, and repeat two more times, ending with a layer of cream. Dust lightly with cocoa powder passed through a fine sieve. Cover each glass with plastic wrap and chill for at least 3 hours or overnight.

Individual Chocolate Pudding Cakes

These warm, soft-centered chocolate cakes are a hit with just about everyone. They're essentially under-baked cakes—so the outside is the texture of a moist cake and inside is like a warm chocolate pudding that spills out when cut into. I make them in individual soufflé cups so that each person gets to break open their own cake. They seem a lot more involved than they are, so they're just the thing for that sort of dinner party where you want to impress your friends.

MAKES 6 INDIVIDUAL CAKES

8 tablespoons (1 stick) unsalted butter, plus more for buttering the soufflé cups
   Granulated sugar for dusting the soufflé cups
3 ounces good-quality semisweet chocolate
3 ounces good-quality unsweetened chocolate
3 large eggs
3 large egg yolks
1 cup confectioners' sugar
1/2 cup all-purpose flour

1. Preheat the oven to 400°F.

2. Generously butter six individual (3/4-cup) soufflé or custard cups. Dust them lightly with granulated sugar and place them on a baking sheet.

3. Melt the chocolates with the butter in a heavy-bottomed saucepan over medium-low heat. Remove the saucepan from the heat and allow the chocolate-butter to cool to lukewarm.

4. Meanwhile, whisk the eggs and egg yolks together in a large bowl. Add the confectioners' sugar and whisk to combine. Add the chocolate-butter mixture and the flour to the bowl with the eggs and stir just until the chocolate is incorporated and no flour is visible. Pour the batter, dividing it equally between the 6 cups.

5. Place the baking sheet with the soufflé cups in the oven to bake the cakes for 12 to 15 minutes, until the sides are set but the center is still very soft and jiggly. Remove from the oven and let the cakes cool for 3 to 5 minutes before turning them out onto individual dessert plates. Serve immediately.

What to Serve When
THESE ARE SO PUDDING-LIKE AND RICH, A SCOOP OF VANILLA ICE CREAM OR FLA-VORED WHIPPED CREAM (PAGE 263) IS ALL YOU'D WANT.

Say's Yellow Cake with Warm Chocolate Glaze

When I was growing up, my mom used to make this for us between commercials while we were watching TV. It's a very simple, single-pan yellow cake that takes about 45 minutes from start to finish. You pour the chocolate glaze over it while the cake is still warm and in the pan, and serve it right away. When my mom makes it at the Market, it smells so good that a whole sheet pan disappears in minutes.

SERVES 6 TO 8 (MAKES ONE 9-INCH CAKE)

  6 tablespoons unsalted butter, plus
    more for buttering the cake pan
  1 cup sugar
  2 large eggs
  1 cup all-purpose flour
  1/2 teaspoon baking powder
  1/4 teaspoon baking soda
  1/4 teaspoon salt
  1/2 cup well-shaken buttermilk
  1 teaspoon pure vanilla extract

For the chocolate glaze

  6 ounces good-quality semisweet
    chocolate, finely chopped or shaved
  1/4 cup sugar
  1/3 cup milk
  2 tablespoons unsalted butter

1. Preheat the oven to 350°F. Lightly butter a 9-inch round cake pan or 9-inch square baking dish.

2. Cream the butter and sugar together in a large bowl with an electric mixer on high speed until fluffy. Add the eggs, one at a time, mixing well and scraping down the sides of the bowl after each addition.

3. In a separate large bowl, combine the flour, baking powder, baking soda, and salt and stir to mix. Stir the buttermilk and vanilla together in a small bowl or liquid measuring cup.

4. Add a third of the flour mixture to the bowl with the butter-sugar mixture and stir until incorporated. Stir in a third of the buttermilk mixture. Continue this process alternating between flour mixture and buttermilk mixture until all the ingredients are combined and no flour is visible.

5. Pour the batter into the prepared pan and bake for 25 to 30 minutes, until a wooden skewer inserted in the center of the cake comes out clean.

6. While the cake is baking, to prepare the glaze, stir the milk, chocolate, and sugar together in a small, heavy-bottomed saucepan over medium-low heat to melt the chocolate. Continue to cook and stir at a low boil until the sauce thickens slightly, about 3 minutes. Remove from the heat, add the butter, and stir until the butter melts. If the glaze cools before the cake is out of the oven, warm it over medium heat, stirring constantly.

7. Use a skewer or the tines of a fork to poke several holes in the top of the cake. While it is still in the pan, pour 1/2 cup of the glaze over the cake and let it sit in the pan for 5 to 10 minutes for it to seep into the cake. Slice the cake and serve warm, with more glaze spooned over each slice.

Sour Cream Cardamom Pound Cake

This is a perfect, moist and dense sour cream pound cake with the addition of cardamom, an aromatic spice used in a lot in Scandinavian baking. WHAT TO SERVE WHEN The warm scent of spice in this cake invites the addition of cooked fruit, like the Balsamic Glazed Figs (page 236) or Blackberries and Cherries in Red Wine (page 236).

SERVES 10 TO 12 (MAKES ONE 10-INCH TUBE OR BUNDT CAKE)

3/4 pound (3 sticks) unsalted butter, softened, plus more for buttering the pan
3 cups all-purpose flour, plus more for dusting
1 1/2 teaspoons ground cardamom
1 teaspoon baking powder
1/2 teaspoon baking soda
1/4 teaspoon salt
3 cups sugar
6 large eggs
2 teaspoons pure vanilla extract
1 cup sour cream

1. Preheat the oven to 325°F. Butter a 10-inch tube or Bundt pan and dust lightly with flour.

2. Stir the flour, cardamom, baking powder, baking soda, and salt together in a large bowl.

3. In a separate large bowl, cream the butter and sugar together with an electric mixer on high speed until fluffy. Add the eggs one at a time, mixing well after each addition, and stopping to scrape down the sides of the bowl from time to time. Stir the vanilla and sour cream together in a small bowl or glass measuring cup.

4. Add a third of the flour mixture to the butter mixture. Mix in half of the sour cream. Repeat, alternating between the flour mixture and the sour cream and ending with the flour mixture until all the ingredients are combined. Scrape down the sides of the bowl with a rubber spatula after each addition and mix only until all the ingredients are incorporated and no flour is visible.

5. Scrape the batter into the prepared pan with a rubber spatula and smooth to even out the top. Bake the cake on the center rack of the oven for 1 hour 15 minutes to 1 hour 25 minutes, until a wooden skewer inserted into the center comes out clean. Let the cake cool in the pan for about 20 minutes, then turn the cake out of the pan onto a baking rack to cool completely. Serve warm or at room temperature. This cake will keep, tightly wrapped in plastic, for several days or in the freezer for up to 3 months.

REINVENTION

Turn leftover slices of pound cake into a free-form trifle with Vanilla Bean Custard Sauce. Place each slice of pound cake on an individual plate and top with fresh strawberries, raspberries, blueberries, blackberries, peaches, nectarines, plums, or a combination. Pour a large spoonful of the custard sauce over the fruit, top with more fruit, and serve immediately.

❝ Over-mixing the batter may cause a cake to fall in the center. ❞

½ teaspoon salt
   Grated zest of 2 oranges
⅓ cup poppy seeds
 1 cup milk
 1 tablespoon pure vanilla extract

For the glaze
 1 cup sugar
   Juice of 2 oranges

1. Preheat the oven to 325°F. Lightly butter a 10-inch tube or Bundt pan and dust lightly with flour.

2. Cream the butter and sugar together in a large bowl with an electric mixer on high speed until fluffy, about 2 minutes. Add the eggs, one at a time, beating until each egg is incorporated before adding the next one and stopping several times to scrape down the sides of the bowl.

3. In a separate medium bowl, stir the flour, baking powder, salt, orange zest, and poppy seeds together to combine. In a small bowl or a liquid measuring cup, combine the milk and vanilla.

4. Add a quarter of the flour mixture to the creamed butter-sugar, stirring until the flour is incorporated. Stir in one third of the milk and continue this process, alternating between the flour mixture and the milk and ending with the flour mixture, until all the ingredients are combined and no flour is visible.

5. Scrape the batter into the prepared pan with a rubber spatula and smooth out the top. Bake on a center rack for about 1 hour, until a toothpick inserted into the center comes out clean. (The cake may take a little less time if you make it in a tube pan rather than a Bundt pan). Cool in the pan for 10 to 15 minutes.

6. Meanwhile, to prepare the glaze, bring the sugar and orange juice to a low boil in a saucepan over medium-high heat. Continue to boil, stirring occasionally, for about 5 minutes, until the sugar dissolves and the sauce thickens slightly.

7. Turn the cake out onto a wire cooling rack. Place a sheet of waxed paper or parchment paper under the rack and pour the glaze evenly over the cake while both the cake and the glaze are still warm. (If the glaze cools before you pour it over the cake, warm it over low heat.) Let the cake rest for 30 to 40 minutes before slicing. Serve warm or at room temperature.

Orange Poppy Seed Pound Cake

This is like a classic lemon poppy seed cake, made with orange for a surprising twist. You can make it using a combination of lemon and orange or lemon and lime in place of the orange zest and juice. WHAT TO SERVE WHEN In keeping with the citrus theme, I like to serve this with Citrus Compote (page 263) and ice cream.

SERVES 10 TO 12 (MAKES ONE 10-INCH TUBE OR BUNDT CAKE)

2½ sticks unsalted butter, softened, plus
   more for buttering the pan
 3 cups all-purpose flour, plus more for dusting
 2 cups sugar
 6 large eggs
 1 tablespoon baking powder

Citrus Compote

Citrus makes the perfect refreshing dessert, especially in the winter months. I like to make the compote before dinner, so the citrus sections have a chance to soften in the warm syrup. WHAT TO SERVE WHEN Serve this sweet and tart compote with Orange Poppy Seed Pound Cake (page 262) and lemon or champagne sorbet.

SERVES 4 TO 6

  2 navel oranges
  2 lemons
  1 cup dry white wine
  1/2 cup sugar
  1 cinnamon stick
  6 whole cloves
  2 tangerines or clementines
  1 ruby red grapefruit

1. Zest 1 orange with a citrus zester or cut off the zest (the outer layer of the skin only, not the white pith underneath, which is bitter), and cut the zest into very thin strips. Halve the orange and 1 lemon, then juice them into a medium saucepan. Add the wine, sugar, cinnamon stick, and cloves and bring to a boil over medium-high heat. Continue to boil, stirring constantly, until the sugar dissolves. Reduce the heat and simmer the juices for about 5 minutes, or until they become thick and syrupy. Remove the saucepan from the heat and let the syrup cool slightly.

2. While the syrup cools, peel and section the tangerines, grapefruit, and the remaining orange and lemon, and place the sections in a medium heatproof bowl.

3. Pour the warm liquid over the sectioned fruit and serve warm or cool to room temperature and refrigerate in an airtight container until ready to serve. Reheat the compote in a saucepan over medium heat before serving. The compote will keep refrigerated in an airtight container for up to 1 week.

Think Outside the Recipe
MAKE THIS RECIPE WITH
ANY CITRUS YOU LIKE,
SUCH AS MEYER LEMONS,
KEY LIMES, BLOOD
ORANGES, OR ANY VARIETY
OF GRAPEFRUIT OR
ORANGES.

Flavored Whipped Cream

Whipped cream dresses up any dessert. During the holidays or if I'm having company, I'll always grab a pint of heavy whipping cream to have handy. Here are some of my favorite ways to individualize whipped cream to serve in different ways. Each is for 1 cup of heavy cream, whipped.

Eggnog Whipped Cream
Fold in 1/4 cup of eggnog to stir into coffee or to serve on Molasses Sweet Potato Pie (page 247) or Mom's Apple Cobbler (page 244).

Mocha Whipped Cream
Add 1 tablespoon instant espresso and 1 tablespoon cocoa powder to stir into coffee or serve with the Hazelnut Rum Torte (page 255) or the Dark Chocolate Soufflé Cake (page 265).

Cinnamon Whipped Cream
Stir in 1 tablespoon ground cinnamon and 1/4 cup light brown or turbinado sugar to serve with the Baked Apples (page 240), or the Maple-Vanilla Roasted Pears (page 239).

Zesty Whipped Cream
Add the grated zest of 1 orange or lemon to dollop on any citrus-inspired dessert, including the Citrus Compote (left) and the Orange Poppy Seed Pound Cake (page 262).

Vanilla-Spice Whipped Cream
Add 1 tablespoon pure vanilla extract and 1/2 teaspoon freshly grated nutmeg to serve with any warm fruit dessert, like the Pear Cranberry Crisp (page 246), Buttermilk Pie (page 248) or Summer Blueberry Pie (page 248).

Fruity Whipped Cream
Add 2 tablespoons pumpkin butter, apple butter, strawberry jam, or raspberry jam to serve with the Buttermilk Pie (page 248) or any pound cake.

Maple Whipped Cream
Add 2 tablespoons maple syrup to serve with the Hazelnut Rum Torte (page 255) or any cooked fruit dessert.

Dark Chocolate Soufflé Cake

This cake is very easy to make, and just fancy enough to make the ideal dinner party dessert. WHAT TO SERVE WHEN This cake is so rich and moist it's very good on its own. But if you do want to dress it up, try serving it with Vanilla Bean Custard Sauce (page 239) or with the Blackberries and Cherries in Red Wine (page 236) pooled around each slice.

SERVES 8 TO 10

- 8 tablespoons (1 stick) cold, unsalted butter, cut into 1-inch pieces, plus more for buttering the pan
- 1/2 cup sugar, plus more for dusting the pan
- 8 ounces good-quality semisweet chocolate, finely chopped or shaved
- 2 tablespoons Kahlúa or other coffee-flavored liqueur
- 1 teaspoon pure vanilla extract
- 1 teaspoon ground cinnamon
- 6 large eggs, separated

1. Preheat the oven to 350°F. Butter a 9-inch springform pan and dust lightly with sugar.

2. Melt the butter and chocolate together in a heavy-bottomed saucepan over low heat, stirring constantly. Remove from the heat; stir in the Kahlúa, vanilla, and cinnamon, and set aside to cool to room temperature.

3. Beat the egg yolks and sugar together in a medium bowl with an electric mixer on high speed until pale yellow and thick enough to hold a ribbon, about 3 minutes. The ribbons will remain visible when you lift up the beaters. Gently fold a quarter of the beaten eggs into the chocolate mixture. Pour the chocolate with the added eggs into the bowl with the remaining eggs and fold gently to combine.

4. In a separate, large bowl, beat the egg whites to soft peaks. Fold a quarter of the egg whites into the chocolate batter to lighten it, then gently fold in the remaining whites until incorporated. Do not over-mix the batter; better that you still see little traces of the egg whites than that you overwork the batter and end up with a leaden cake.

5. Pour the batter into the prepared pan and smooth it with a rubber spatula to make even. Bake on a center rack for 30 to 35 minutes, until the edges of the cake are set but the center is still soft. It will set completely as it cools. Cool the cake on a wire rack for about 5 minutes. Run a knife around the edge to loosen the cake. Open the springform pan to release the sides and transfer the cake onto a serving plate. Slice and serve immediately.

Note: *Lightening the chocolate with a little of the beaten egg whites makes the chocolate lighter and easier to work with. If you dump all the egg whites in at once, the tendency is to over-mix the batter in order to fold in the whites. If you over-mix this batter, the fluffy egg whites will collapse and you'll end up with a flat dense cake instead of a light airy one.*

about . . . CHOCOLATE

The quality of the chocolate you use in your desserts makes a big difference in taste, especially where chocolate is the main ingredient. Which chocolate you prefer is a matter of personal preference. Scharffenberger, El Rey, and Valrhôna are the three solid baking chocolates I like most. For cocoa powder, I use Scharffenberger and Lake Champlain, but I urge you to find and use whatever good-quality chocolate or cocoa you like. Some helpful hints about chocolate:

- The difference between bittersweet and semisweet chocolate is the percent of cacao (the bean from which chocolate and cocoa are made) each contains. (Bittersweet has the higher percentage of the two.) You can use the two interchangeably in recipes.

- Use a large knife or a vegetable peeler to shave chocolate either for a garnish or to prepare it for melting.

- To avoid burned, bitter-tasting chocolate, melt it slowly, stirring constantly over very low heat, ideally in a double boiler over simmering water. Many people use a microwave for melting chocolate, and they swear by it. I don't use a microwave for anything except reheating coffee, but if it works for you, do it.

Chocolate Cupcakes with Mocha Buttercream or Pure Chocolaty Children's Frosting

Everyone loves cupcakes, I think because they remind us of some of the finer moments from childhood: birthday parties! This chocolate cake is moist and chocolaty, as it should be. I give you two recipes for icing them: the buttercream with espresso added is more appealing to grown-ups; the other is a more traditional cupcake frosting that kids love.

MAKES 2 DOZEN CUPCAKES

 3 ounces good-quality unsweetened chocolate, finely chopped or shaved
$1/2$ pound (2 sticks) unsalted butter
 1 cup granulated sugar
$2/3$ cup packed light brown sugar
 4 large eggs, at room temperature
$2^1/4$ cups all-purpose flour
 1 teaspoon baking soda
$1/2$ teaspoon baking powder
$1/2$ teaspoon salt
$1/3$ cup good-quality cocoa powder
$1^1/4$ cups well-shaken buttermilk
 1 teaspoon pure vanilla extract

1. Preheat the oven to 350°F. Place 24 paper baking cups in muffin tins and spray the top, exposed part of the tins with vegetable oil spray or grease lightly with butter.

2. Place the chocolate in the top of a double boiler or in a heatproof bowl set over a pot of simmering water over low heat, stirring until the chocolate is melted. Remove from the heat and let cool to room temperature.

3. In a large bowl, cream the butter, granulated sugar, and brown sugar together with an electric mixer on high speed, scraping down the bowl frequently, until creamy. Add the eggs, one at a time, beating well after each addition. Stir in the cooled chocolate.

4. In a separate large bowl, stir the flour, baking soda, baking powder, salt, and cocoa powder together. Stir the buttermilk and vanilla together in a small bowl or liquid measuring cup.

5. Add a quarter of the flour mixture to the butter-chocolate mixture and stir to mix. Stir in a third of the buttermilk and continue this process, alternating between the flour mixture and the buttermilk and ending with the flour mixture, stirring just until the dry ingredients are moist and no longer visible.

6. Fill the prepared muffin cups three-fourths full with batter and bake on a center rack for 20 to 25 minutes, until a toothpick inserted into the center of a cupcake comes out clean and the top springs back when pressed lightly. Let the cupcakes rest in the tins for about 5 minutes before turning them out on a wire cooling rack. Cool completely before frosting.

Mocha Buttercream

This is a foolproof recipe for buttercream made easy. I have used it since I had my catering business in Connecticut and we use it to make buttercream by the gallons for wedding cakes. No matter what I add to this buttercream, it always turns out. The espresso turns these into grown-up cupcakes.

MAKES ABOUT 3 CUPS (ENOUGH FOR 24 CUPCAKES)

 2 ounces good-quality bittersweet chocolate, finely chopped or shaved
 5 egg yolks, at room temperature
$1/2$ cup sugar
$1/2$ cup dark corn syrup
$3/4$ pound (3 sticks) unsalted butter, softened
 2 tablespoons very strongly brewed espresso (1 tablespoons instant espresso mixed with 2 tablespoons hot coffee or water)

1. Place the chocolate in the top of a double boiler or in a heatproof bowl set over a pot of simmering water on low heat. Stir occasionally until the chocolate is melted. Remove from the heat and let cool to room temperature. (The chocolate should not solidify.)

2. Place the egg yolks in a large bowl and beat with an electric mixer on high speed until light yellow, about 3 to 4 minutes.

3. Combine the sugar and corn syrup in a small sauce pan and cook over medium-high heat, stirring constantly, until the sugar dissolves and the syrup is boiling. Continue to boil and stir for about 30 seconds.

4. With the beaters running, immediately pour the syrup and sugar mixture in a slow steady stream down the side of the bowl containing the egg yolks (being careful not to let the mixture hit the beaters or the syrup will spin onto the bowl and not in the yolks) until all is combined. Stop the mixer and scrape down the sides of the bowl, then continue beating until the mixture has cooled to room temperature, about 5 minutes.

5. With the mixer on high speed, add the butter 1 tablespoon at a time, beating until each tablespoon of the butter has been incorporated before adding another. The buttercream should be smooth and fluffy. Add the espresso and melted chocolate and mix until no streaks remain. Use immediately or store refrigerated in an airtight container for up to 5 days. Bring the refrigerated buttercream to room temperature and beat to a smooth consistency before using.

Note: *Pouring the syrup immediately into the yolks prevents the sugar from continuing to cook in the pan and burning even slightly, which would impart a burnt-sugar taste to your frosting.*

Pure Chocolaty Children's Frosting

This is a variation on a recipe in *The Foster's Market Cookbook*; it's a favorite of our youngest customers. Make the frosting just as you need it—refrigerated, it will become too stiff to use.

MAKES ABOUT 4 CUPS (ENOUGH FOR 24 CUPCAKES)

    5 ounces good-quality semisweet chocolate, finely
      chopped or shaved
    1 large egg white
 ¼ cup heavy cream, or more as needed
    1 tablespoon pure vanilla extract
 ½ pound (2 sticks) unsalted butter, softened
4½ cups confectioners' sugar

1. Place the chocolate in the top of a double boiler or in a heatproof bowl set over a pot of simmering water over low heat, stirring until the chocolate is melted. Remove from the heat and let cool to room temperature.

2. Combine the egg white, cream, and vanilla in a small bowl and stir to mix.

3. In a separate large bowl, beat the butter with an electric mixer on high speed until soft and creamy. Add the confectioners' sugar, about ¼ cup at a time, beating constantly until the confectioners' sugar is incorporated.

4. Slowly pour a quarter of the melted chocolate into the butter, beating constantly. Add a quarter of the egg white–cream mixture and continue, alternating between the chocolate and the egg whites mixture, until all is incorporated and the frosting is smooth and fluffy. Beat in 1 to 3 tablespoons additional heavy cream if the frosting is too stiff. Leave the frosting at room temperature until ready to use.

Dark Chocolate Truffles

Chocolate truffles are much easier to make than many people think. In fact, they require only three ingredients and two steps; they just couldn't be any easier. You can make them as much as two weeks ahead of time, then put them out with coffee when you want just a little something sweet after a meal. What more could you want? I give you a basic recipe here, with options listed below for ways to flavor truffles as you like.

MAKES ABOUT 28 TRUFFLES

8 ounces good-quality bittersweet chocolate, finely chopped or shaved
$1/2$ cup heavy cream
$1/3$ cup good-quality unsweetened powdered cocoa for coating the truffles

1. Place the chocolate in a medium metal bowl and set aside.

2. Bring the cream just to a boil in a small saucepan over high heat. Immediately remove the pan from the heat, pour the cream over the chocolate, and stir until all the chocolate has melted and the mixture is smooth. If you are adding a liquid flavoring, stir it in. Cover and refrigerate for 2 to 3 hours, or until the chocolate is firm.

3. Scoop the chocolate with a tablespoon, small ice cream scoop, or melon-baller and form into 1-inch rounds with the palms of your hands. Place the balls on a piece of waxed paper or aluminum foil.

4. Pass the cocoa powder through a fine sieve or sifter onto a plate. Toss each truffle gently in the cocoa powder (or other coating) to coat evenly. Place the coated truffles on a plate and continue until all the truffles are coated. Refrigerate until ready to serve or store in an airtight container for up to 2 weeks. Bring the truffles to room temperature before serving.

CUSTOMIZING YOUR TRUFFLES

Liquid flavorings: 2 tablespoons rum, bourbon, Kahlúa, coffee extract, almond extract, orange extract, or honey

Coatings: finely ground pistachios, walnuts, almonds, or pecans; turbinado sugar; or confectioner's sugar

Add other flavors to the coating: a pinch of cinnamon, black pepper, or cayenne pepper

Thumbprint Cookies

These are classics, and just so good. Use whatever jam you like, or make half the cookies with one jam and half with another for a colorful platter of cookies. You can make the dough in advance and refrigerate it for up to 4 days.

MAKES ABOUT 2 DOZEN COOKIES

$1/2$ cup blanched almonds
$1/2$ cup confectioners' sugar
$1^1/2$ cups all-purpose flour, plus more for dusting the work surface
$1/2$ teaspoon salt
10 tablespoons (1 stick plus 2 tablespoons) unsalted butter, cut into small pieces
1 large egg
1 teaspoon pure vanilla extract
$1/2$ cup peach preserves (or raspberry, strawberry, or apricot jam or preserves)

1. Preheat the oven to 350°F.

2. Combine the almonds and sugar in the bowl of a food processor fitted with a metal blade and pulse until almonds are finely ground, about 1 minute.

3. Add the flour and salt and pulse several times to combine. Add the butter pieces and pulse until the mixture resembles coarse meal.

4. Whisk the egg and vanilla together in a small bowl and pour this into the food processor with the almond-butter mixture. Pulse until the dough begins to stick together.

5. Turn the dough out onto a lightly floured work surface and knead several times to form a ball. Pinch off small pieces of the dough and roll them into 1-inch balls.

6. Place the balls on an ungreased baking sheet, leaving 2 inches between each. Using your thumb, press into the center of each cookie to flatten and make an indentation for the preserves.

7. Spoon $1/2$ teaspoon of the preserves into the indentation of each cookie. Place the baking sheet in the oven to bake for 16 to 18 minutes, rotating the pans halfway through for even baking, until the cookies are firm to the touch and the edges lightly brown. Remove the cookies from the oven. Allow them to cool on the baking sheet for about 5 minutes before transferring to a baking rack to cool completely.

Pumpkin White Chocolate Chunk Cookies

My sister Judy has made these every Halloween and Thanksgiving for so many years she's known for them. The butterscotch chips are ground into the dough and give the cookies a subtle butterscotch flavor without the cloying experience of biting into a bite full of butterscotch.

MAKES 2 DOZEN 3-INCH COOKIES

- 2 cups all-purpose flour
- 1 teaspoon baking soda
- 1 cup butterscotch chips
- 12 tablespoons (1^1/2 sticks) unsalted butter, softened
- ^{2}/3 cup granulated sugar
- ^{2}/3 cup packed light brown sugar
- 1 large egg
- ^{2}/3 cup cooked canned pumpkin puree or fresh mashed pumpkin
- 1 cup old-fashioned rolled oats
- 8 ounces white chocolate, cut into ^{1}/4-inch chunks, or 1^1/2 cups white chocolate chips
- 1 cup chopped walnuts

1. Preheat the oven to 350°F. Line two baking sheets with parchment paper or grease lightly.

2. Put the flour and baking soda in the bowl of a food processor fitted with a metal blade and pulse to distribute the baking soda evenly. Add the butterscotch chips and process until the chips are ground, with some slightly larger bits remaining. Turn the flour and butterscotch chips out into a large bowl.

3. In a separate large bowl, cream the butter, granulated sugar, and brown sugar together for 2 to 3 minutes, scraping down the bowl from time to time, until fluffy. Add the egg and pumpkin puree and stir to combine.

4. Pour the butter-pumpkin mixture into the flour mixture and stir to combine. Add the oats, white chocolate chunks, and walnuts and stir until the ingredients are combined and no flour is visible. Cover the bowl and refrigerate for at least 10 minutes or overnight.

5. Use a ^{1}/4-cup measure or ice cream scoop to drop the cookie dough onto the prepared cookie sheet, leaving 2 inches between the cookies.

6. Bake the cookies on a center rack in the oven for 13 to 15 minutes, rotating the cookie sheets halfway through for even baking, until they're light golden brown and no longer doughy looking. Cool the cookies on the cookie sheets for 10 to 15 minutes before transferring them to a wire rack or clean surface to cool completely.

Peanut Butter Chocolate Chip Cookies

Two American classics rolled into one, these fly out the door at the Market.

MAKES ABOUT 2 DOZEN 3-INCH COOKIES

- 8 tablespoons (1 stick) unsalted butter, softened
- ^{3}/4 cup creamy peanut butter
- 1 cup packed light brown sugar
- 1 large egg
- 1 teaspoon pure vanilla extract
- 1^1/2 cups all-purpose flour
- 1 teaspoon baking soda
- ^{1}/4 teaspoon salt
- 1 cup semisweet chocolate chips

1. Preheat the oven to 350°F. Line two baking sheets with parchment paper or grease lightly.

2. Cream the butter, peanut butter, and brown sugar together in a large bowl with an electric mixer on high speed until fluffy. Add the egg and vanilla and mix until all the ingredients are combined.

3. In a separate large bowl, stir the flour, baking soda, and salt together. Stir the flour mixture into the peanut butter mixture until the flour is no longer visible. Stir in the chocolate chips until evenly distributed.

4. Scoop the dough with a ^{1}/4-cup measure or ice cream scoop and drop it onto the prepared cookie sheet, leaving 3 inches between the cookies. Use the tines of a fork to flatten the tops of the cookies to ^{1}/2- to ^{1}/4-inch thickness with a crosshatch pattern.

5. Bake the cookies on a center rack for 15 to 17 minutes, rotating the pans halfway through for even baking, until the cookies are golden brown. Let the cookies cool on the baking sheet for 5 to 10 minutes before transferring them to a wire rack or clean surface to cool completely.

Chocolate Chip Oatmeal Cookies

The cooks and bakers at the Market all have their own variations on drop cookies, which include oatmeal, chocolate chip, and peanut butter cookies. I let them do what they want because our customers seem to like any variations we put out.

MAKES ABOUT 3 DOZEN 3-INCH COOKIES

1/2 pound (2 sticks) unsalted butter, softened
1 cup packed light brown sugar
1 cup granulated sugar
3 large eggs
2 teaspoons pure vanilla extract
3 cups old-fashioned rolled oats
2 cups all-purpose flour
1 teaspoon baking soda
1 teaspoon ground cinnamon
1/4 teaspoon salt
2 cups semisweet chocolate chips or 12 ounces semisweet chocolate, cut into 1/2-inch chunks

1. Preheat the oven to 350°F. Line two baking sheets with parchment paper or grease lightly.

2. Cream the butter, brown sugar, and granulated sugar together in a large bowl with an electric mixer on high speed until fluffy. Add the eggs, one at a time, scraping down the sides of the bowl and blending thoroughly after each addition. Stir in the vanilla.

3. In a separate large bowl, combine the oats, flour, baking soda, cinnamon, and salt and stir to mix. Add to the creamed butter–sugar mixture and stir just until the dry ingredients are moist and blended in. Stir in the chocolate chips.

4. Scoop the dough out with a 1/4-cup measure or ice cream scoop and drop it onto the prepared baking sheet, leaving about 3 inches between the cookies. Press the cookies to 1/2- to 1/4-inch thickness with the palm of your hand or the back of a spatula.

5. Bake the cookies on a center rack for 12 to 14 minutes for soft, chewy cookies or 15 to 17 minutes for crunchy cookies, rotating the pans halfway through so the cookies bake evenly. Allow the cookies to cool on the baking sheet for about 5 minutes before transferring them to a cooling rack or clean surface to cool completely.

White Chocolate Chunk Hazelnut Cookies

These are a nice, sophisticated alternative to chocolate chip walnut cookies, but just as familiar and comforting.

MAKES ABOUT 3 DOZEN 3-INCH COOKIES

1/2 pound (2 sticks) unsalted butter, softened
1 cup granulated sugar
1 cup packed light brown sugar
3 large eggs
2 teaspoons pure vanilla extract
3 cups all-purpose flour
1 teaspoon baking soda
1 teaspoon ground cinnamon
1/4 teaspoon salt
12 ounces white chocolate, cut into 1/2-inch chunks, or 2 cups white chocolate chips
1 1/2 cups hazelnuts, toasted, skins removed, and chopped

1. Preheat the oven to 350°F. Line two baking sheets with parchment paper or grease lightly.

2. Cream the butter, granulated sugar, and brown sugar together in a large bowl with an electric mixer on high speed until fluffy. Add the eggs, one at a time, scraping down the sides of the bowl and beating thoroughly between each addition. Stir in the vanilla.

3. Combine the flour, baking soda, cinnamon, and salt in a separate large bowl and stir to mix. Add the flour mixture to the butter mixture and stir just until the flour is no longer visible. Stir in the white chocolate chips and hazelnuts.

4. Scoop the dough with a 1/4-cup measure or ice cream scoop and drop it onto the prepared baking sheet, leaving about 2 inches between the cookies. Press the cookies to 1/2- to 1/4-inch thickness with the palm of your hand or the back of a spatula.

5. Bake the cookies on a center rack for 12 to 14 minutes for soft, chewy cookies or 15 to 17 minutes for crunchy cookies, rotating the pans halfway through for even baking. Allow the cookies to cool about 5 minutes on the baking sheet before transferring them to a cooling rack or clean surface to cool completely.

Mexican Wedding Cookies

These are crunchy little melt-in-your-mouth cookies. They keep for a week so they make wonderful gifts. You can substitute bourbon or rum for the Kahlúa.

MAKES ABOUT 2 DOZEN COOKIES

  1 cup slivered almonds
  2 cups all-purpose flour, plus more to flour your hands
½ teaspoon salt
  1 teaspoon ground cinnamon
½ teaspoon freshly grated nutmeg
½ pound (2 sticks) unsalted butter
  1 cup confectioners' sugar, sifted
  2 teaspoons pure vanilla extract
½ teaspoon pure almond extract
  2 teaspoons Kahlúa (or other coffee-flavored liquor)
    Grated zest of 1 lemon

1. Preheat the oven to 350°F.

2. Spray 2 baking sheets with vegetable oil spray or grease them lightly with oil.

3. Scatter the slivered almonds in one layer on a baking sheet with sides and toast them in the oven for 8 to 10 minutes until golden brown. Set them aside to cool to room temperature.

4. Place the almonds, flour, salt, cinnamon, and nutmeg in the bowl of a food processor fitted with a metal blade and process until the nuts are finely ground, about 30 seconds.

5. Cream the butter and ½ cup of the confectioners' sugar together in a large bowl with an electric mixer on high speed for about 3 minutes, scraping down the sides of the bowl occasionally, until fluffy. Add the vanilla, almond extract, Kahlúa, and lemon zest and beat until incorporated.

6. Add the flour mixture to the creamed butter-sugar mixture and stir until just combined with no flour visible, being careful not to mix any more than necessary.

7. Dust your hands lightly with flour. Pinch off a piece of dough and roll it between your hands into a 1½-inch ball. Place the balls about 2 inches apart on the prepared baking sheet.

8. Place the cookies in the oven to bake for 20 to 22 minutes, rotating the pans halfway through, until the cookies are golden brown around the edges. Remove the cookies from the oven and let them rest for about five minutes on the baking sheet until they are cool enough to handle.

9. Meanwhile sift the remaining confectioners' sugar onto a plate. While the cookies are still warm, roll them in the confectioners' sugar to coat. Place the coated cookies on a baking rack to cool completely. These cookies will keep, stored in an airtight container, for up to 1 week.

Ice Cream Sandwiches Your Way

Making ice cream sandwiches—soft ice cream bound by two 3-inch cookies—is more construction than cooking. You can make them in any combination of cookies, ice cream, and sprinkles to decorate the sides.

Some combinations I like are:

○ Chocolate cookies with coffee ice cream

○ Chocolate chip cookies with rocky road ice cream

○ Pecan Sandies with peach ice cream

○ Oatmeal raisin cookies with rum raisin ice cream

○ Gingerbread or spice cookies with coffee Heath bar crunch ice cream

○ Pumpkin White Chocolate Chunk Cookies (page 271) with vanilla ice cream

○ Peanut butter cookies with caramel swirl or dulce de leche ice cream

MAKES 6 ICE CREAM SANDWICHES

1 pint ice cream or sorbet, softened
12 3-inch cookies
½ cup sprinkles (optional)

1. Place 6 cookies on a baking sheet or in two baking pans that will fit in the freezer.

2. Scoop the ice cream with a ¼-cup measure or ice cream scoop and place one heaping scoop of ice cream on each of the cookies. Top each with another cookie, so the top of the cookie is facing up, and gently press down on the top cookie to squish the ice cream until it reaches the edge of the sandwich.

3. Pour the sprinkles, if using, onto a plate. Roll the sides of the sandwich in the sprinkles or hold the sandwich over the plate and pour the sprinkles over the sides of the sandwich to coat the edges of the ice cream sandwich. Return it to the baking sheet and repeat with the remaining sandwiches.

4. Cover the baking sheet tightly with plastic and freeze until the ice cream is firm, about 2 hours, or wrap the sandwiches individually and keep them frozen for up to 1 month.

Ice Cream

Use any good-quality ice cream, frozen yogurt, or sorbet, softened to room temperature or microwaved for 10 to 15 seconds so it's soft enough to squish between the cookies.

Cookies

Homemade cookies and ice cream are great, but the point of this dessert is that it is something fast and fun to make, so I encourage you to seek out good store-bought cookies, such as Pepperidge Farm. You want them to be 2 to 3 inches in diameter. Anything smaller becomes difficult to make—and too small to satisfy. Anything bigger is unwieldy to eat.

Sprinkles

These are part decoration, party whimsy, and definitely optional. Use what you like: chocolate sprinkles, finely chopped peanuts, pecans, almonds, or walnuts, Oreo cookie crumbs, crushed peppermint or butterscotch hard candies, colored decorating sugars, demerara or turbinado sugars, or candy bar pieces.

Shortbread Hearts with Fresh Strawberries and Crème Fraîche

Simple and straightforward, this is the kind of dessert that relies on the flavor of the strawberries. Use raspberries, blackberries, or blueberries in place of the strawberries if you like. It is also very pretty and ideal for serving to your sweetheart.

MAKES 12 COOKIES

For the shortbread hearts

8 tablespoons (1 stick) unsalted butter, softened
¼ cup sugar
1 cup all-purpose flour, plus more for dusting
⅛ teaspoon salt
Grated zest of 1 lemon

For the topping

1 cup **Crème Fraîche** (recipe follows) or sour cream
¼ cup sugar
1 pint fresh strawberries, stems removed and thinly sliced
Confectioners' sugar, for dusting

1. Preheat the oven to 350°F.

2. Cream the butter and ¼ cup sugar together in a large bowl with an electric mixer on high speed for about 3 minutes, scraping down the sides of the bowl from time to time, until light and fluffy.

3. In a separate large bowl, stir the flour, salt, and lemon zest together to combine. Add to the creamed butter and sugar and stir with a wooden spoon or the paddle attachment of an electric mixer until the dough comes together. Gather the dough together and pat it into a flat disk. Wrap tightly in plastic and place the disk in the refrigerator to chill for at least 20 minutes or overnight.

4. Lightly flour a rolling pin and work surface and place the dough in the center. Roll the dough to ¼ inch thick and cut with a 2-inch heart-shaped cookie cutter (or any shaped cutter of similar size). Carefully transfer the cut dough to a cookie or baking sheet. Bake the shortbreads for 8 to 10 minutes, or until they are pale golden around the edges. Allow them to cool completely on the cookie sheet.

5. Whip the Crème Fraîche with the ¼ cup sugar until slightly stiff.

6. Place two shortbreads on each plate and dollop 1 heaping tablespoon of the crème fraîche on each. Top with several slices of fresh strawberries and dust with confectioners' sugar passed through a mesh sieve. Serve immediately.

Crème Fraîche

Crème fraîche is a rich, tangy matured cream from France. It is very easy to make, and worth the effort; the tangy, complex flavor adds so much to soup.

MAKES ABOUT 1¼ CUPS

1 cup heavy cream
¼ cup well-shaken buttermilk

Stir the cream and buttermilk together in a glass jar or bowl. Cover tightly with a lid or plastic wrap and place it in a cool (not refrigerated) place out of direct sunlight for at least 8 hours and up to 24 hours, until it thickens to the consistency of sour cream. After it has thickened, stir and refrigerate in an airtight container up to 3 weeks.

Pecan Sandies

These rich butter cookies containing ground nuts are a traditional Southern cookie, probably because pecans are grown in the south. These keep for up to a week, so they make a nice gift. WHAT TO SERVE WHEN I like to serve these crunchy cookies alongside ice cream. They make a delicious exterior for Ice Cream Sandwiches (page 274).

MAKES ABOUT 2 DOZEN 2½-INCH COOKIES

    1 cup chopped pecans (about 4 ounces)
2¼ cups plus 2 tablespoons all-purpose flour
 ½ teaspoon salt
 ½ teaspoon freshly grated nutmeg
 ½ pound (2 sticks) unsalted butter, softened, at room
    temperature
 ¾ cup granulated sugar
 ¼ cup packed light brown sugar
    1 large egg, lightly beaten
    2 teaspoons pure vanilla extract
 ½ cup pecan halves (about 2 ounces)

1. Preheat the oven to 375°F.

2. Lightly spray 2 baking sheets with vegetable oil spray or grease lightly with butter.

3. Scatter ½ cup of the chopped pecans on a baking sheet with sides and toast them in the oven for 8 to 10 minutes, until golden brown and fragrant. Set aside to cool to room temperature.

4. Put the remaining ½ cup of the chopped pecans in the bowl of a food processor fitted with a metal blade. Add 2 tablespoons of the flour and process until the pecans are finely ground. Turn the ground nuts into a large bowl. Add the remaining flour, the toasted pecans, salt, and nutmeg and stir to mix.

5. Cream the butter and granulated sugar together in a large bowl with an electric mixer on high speed until light and creamy, about 2 minutes, stopping to scrape down the sides of the bowl from time to time. Add the brown sugar and beat to incorporate it. Beat in the egg and vanilla. Add the flour mixture and stir with a wooden spoon or the paddle attachment of the mixer until the dough just comes together.

6. Scoop the dough with a heaping tablespoon and drop on the prepared baking sheet, leaving about 2 inches between each cookie. Flatten the cookies with a spatula or the heel of your hand and press a pecan half into the center of each cookie.

7. Bake until golden brown, 12 to 15 minutes, rotating the baking sheets halfway through the baking time so the cookies brown evenly. Allow the cookies to cool on the baking sheet for about 5 minutes before transferring to a baking rack to cool completely. Store in an airtight container for up to a week.

Hot and Creamy Cocoa with Gooey Toasted Marshmallows

Grown-ups might want a shot of espresso, Kahlúa, or brandy in theirs. This version is so thick and rich, a small portion is enough; it is meant to be served in a demitasse cup.

SERVES 4

    1 cup heavy cream
    1 teaspoon sugar
    2 ounces good-quality semisweet chocolate
      (such as Valrhôna, El Rey, or Scharffenberger),
      shaved or chopped
    4 large marshmallows

1. Place the cream in a heavy-bottomed saucepan and bring to a boil over medium-high heat. Reduce the heat slightly so the cream remains at a low boil, and boil for 3 to 4 minutes, until it begins to thicken.

2. Stir in the sugar and chocolate and continue to simmer, stirring constantly, until the sugar dissolves and the chocolate melts. Remove the saucepan from the heat and set aside to keep warm.

3. Place the marshmallows on a metal skewer and hold them over the open flame of the stove, turning, until all sides of the marshmallow are toasted and the center is soft. If the marshmallow starts to flame, blow it out and continue to toast the marshmallow; the charred flavor, as we all know from campfires, is ideal.

4. If necessary, reheat the hot chocolate over low heat, stirring constantly. Pour the hot chocolate into four demitasse cups. Top each with a toasted gooey marshmallow and serve immediately with spoons.

Acknowledgments

A project of this size is a group effort. I am forever grateful to each and every one of the people who, knowingly or not, contributed their talent and time to the creation of this book. A special thanks to:

Our customers, who keep us going on a daily basis and who, through their patronage and enthusiasm, make Foster's Market the warm and wonderful place that it is. The purveyors and farmers who supply us with such rich resources, without which we could not do what we do. My husband, Peter Sellers, for his endless support and gusto for tasting and for his patience in talking about all things food, book, or Market. Patrick Edwards, my business partner and nephew, for holding down the fort while I devoted so much time to this project, and for the many nights spent testing, tasting, and telling me when something tasted just right.

The behind-the-scenes team that helped put these books together, new and old friendships that I will cherish forever: Carolynn Carreño, my coauthor; her creative input, knowledge, humor, and dedication made this project better each day. Quentin Bacon, for his keen, original eye, and for truly capturing my recipes with beautiful and stylish photographs. Pam Krauss, our editor, for the guidance she gave us to help us organize and refine this book, distilling it to its truest essence. All those at Clarkson Potter who worked so hard to make this book come together: Jennifer DeFilippi for always being available to guide us through our crises, Jane Treuhaft and Marysarah Quinn in the design department for producing a beautiful book, Joan Denman for making sure it got done and printed, Trisha Howell for her attention to detail, and Wayne Wolf and his team at Blue Cup Design for creating a book that far surpassed my most optimistic visions. Wendy Goldstein and Sheri Castle for testing recipes in a relentless pursuit of perfection and deliciousness. Francis Boswell, Wendy Goldstein, and Alison Attenborough for the creativity they brought to styling the photographs. Jonathan Waxman, for being a great friend and for staying so cool in the kitchen—in so doing, he lead the way for many cooks like myself. Janis Donnaud, for her tough love in keeping us focused and for always demanding the best of us. Martha Stewart, for clearing the path for me and a generation of cooks and homemakers.

To the entire staff at Foster's Market for making our business special and for contributing to and supporting this book, each in his or her unique way: Laura Cyr for her simple creative approach to food, Meg deLuca for her devoted attention to detail, Eric Muhl for his creative, tasty brunch specials, Randy Bolick, Nick Whaley, Rick Straubel, Flavia Alves, Monica Jeada, Kevin Rutledge, Susan Hutchinson and many more who bring so much of themselves to the Market every moment they are there.

To all my family and friends who contributed recipes, props, and, most important, who have given encouragement and inspiration not just during the creation of this book, but during my continued journey as a cook. Especially Judy Edwards, my sister, for her honesty, enthusiasm, and creativity. Katie Kilburg, Maggie Radzwiller, Jennifer Maxwell, Phyllis Doby, and Charlene Blount, for always finding time to share their time, their recipes, and their honest opinions. My dad, Aunt June, Aunt Ginny, and all my family for their guidance, love, and all of those memorable family gatherings that were, in a sense, the true beginning of this book.

It is all of you who made this happen, so thanks again.

Index

Conversion Chart
EQUIVALENT IMPERIAL AND METRIC MEASUREMENTS

American cooks use standard containers, the 8-ounce cup and a tablespoon that takes exactly 16 level fillings to fill that cup level. Measuring by cup makes it very difficult to give weight equivalents, as a cup of densely packed butter will weigh considerably more than a cup of flour. The easiest way therefore to deal with cup measurements in recipes is to take the amount by volume rather than by weight. Thus the equation reads:

1 cup = 240 ml = 8 fl. oz.   ½ cup = 120 ml = 4 fl. oz.

It is possible to buy a set of American cup measures in major stores around the world.

In the States, butter is often measured in sticks. One stick is the equivalent of 8 tablespoons. One tablespoon of butter is therefore the equivalent to ½ ounce/15 grams.

Liquid Measures

fluid ounces	u.s.	imperial	milliliters
	1 teaspoon	1 teaspoon	5
¼	2 teaspoons	1 dessertspoon	10
½	1 tablespoon	1 tablespoon	14
1	2 tablespoons	2 tablespoons	28
2	¼ cup	4 tablespoons	56
4	½ cup		110
5		¼ pint or 1 gill	140
6	¾ cup		170
8	1 cup		225
9			250, ¼ liter
10	1¼ cups	½ pint	280
12	1½ cups		340
15		¾ pint	420
16	2 cups		450
18	2¼ cups		500, ½ liter
20	2½ cups	1 pint	560
24	3 cups		675
25		1¼ pints	700
27	3½ cups		750
30	3¾ cups	1½ pints	840
32	4 cups or 1 quart		900
35		1¾ pints	980
36	4½ cups		1000, 1 liter
40	5 cups	2 pints or 1 quart	1120

Solid Measures

U.S. and Imperial Measures		Metric Measures	
ounces	pounds	grams	kilos
1		28	
2		56	
3½		100	
4	¼	112	
5		140	
6		168	
8	½	225	
9		250	¼
12	¾	340	
16	1	450	
18		500	½
20	1¼	560	
24	1½	675	
27		750	¾
28	1¾	780	
32	2	900	
36	2¼	1000	1
40	2½	1100	
48	3	1350	
54		1500	1½

Oven Temperature Equivalents

fahrenheit	celsius	gas mark	description
225	110	¼	cool
250	130	½	
275	140	1	very slow
300	150	2	
325	170	3	slow
350	180	4	moderate
375	190	5	
400	200	6	moderately hot
425	220	7	fairly hot
450	230	8	hot
475	240	9	very hot
500	250	10	extremely hot

Any broiling recipes can be used with the grill of the oven, but beware of high-temperature grills.

Equivalents for Ingredients

all-purpose flour - plain flour
coarse salt - kitchen salt
cornstarch - cornflour
eggplant - aubergine

half and half - 12% fat milk
heavy cream - double cream
light cream - single cream
lima beans - broad beans

scallion - spring onion
unbleached flour - strong, white flour
zest - rind
zucchini - courgettes or marrow